Our Family
DREAMS

THE FLETCHERS' ADVENTURES IN NINETEENTH-CENTURY AMERICA

DANIEL BLAKE SMITH

St. Martin's Press
New York

www.stmartins.com

Design by Letra Libre, Inc.

Library of Congress Cataloging-in-Publication Data

Names: Smith, Daniel Blake.

Title: Our family dreams : the Fletchers' adventures in nineteenth-century America / Daniel B. Smith.

Description: New York City : St. Martin's Press, 2016.

Identifiers: LCCN 2015028245 | ISBN 9781137279811 (hardback) | ISBN 9781466879386 (e-book)

Subjects: LCSH: Fletcher family. | Fletcher, Jesse, 1762–1831—Family. | Fletcher family—Correspondence. | Fletcher family—Diaries. | Pioneers—United States—Biography. | United States—History—1783–1865—Biography. | BISAC: HISTORY / United States / 19th Century.

Classification: LCC CT274.F593 S65 2016 | DDC 973.5092/2—dc23

LC record available at http://lccn.loc.gov/2015028245

Our books may be purchased in bulk for promotional, educational, or business use. Please contact your local bookseller or the Macmillan Corporate and Premium Sales Department at 1-800-221-7945, extension 5442, or by e-mail at MacmillanSpecialMarkets@macmillan.com.

First Edition: August 2016

10 9 8 7 6 5 4 3 2 1

To my parents

Contents

	Illustration Credits	ix
	Introduction	1
One	Beginnings	5
Two	Heading West	29
Three	Settling In	57
Four	"The Best Fortune We Can Give Our Children"	89
Five	Public Life	125
Six	Calamities	159
Seven	War and Loyalty	193
Eight	Legacies	231
	Fletcher Family Genealogy	253
	Acknowledgments	255
	Notes	257
	Index	271

Illustration Credits

Frontispiece photograph, Calvin Fletcher family reunion, 1858. Courtesy of the Indiana Historical Society.

Elijah Fletcher, ca. 1815. © 19__ Sweet Briar College. All rights reserved. Image used with permission of Sweet Briar College.

Calvin Fletcher, ca. 1832. Courtesy of the Indiana Historical Society.

Sarah Hill Fletcher (Calvin's first wife), ca. 1832. Courtesy of the Indiana Historical Society.

Indiana Fletcher. © 19__ Sweet Briar College. All rights reserved. Image used with permission of Sweet Briar College.

Sarah Fletcher with daughters Lucy and Maria. Courtesy of the Indiana Historical Society.

Tusculum, Elijah Fletcher's Lynchburg home. © 19__ Sweet Briar College. All rights reserved. Image used with permission of Sweet Briar College.

Calvin and Sarah Fletcher, 1844. Courtesy of the Indiana Historical Society.

Calvin and Keziah Fletcher, 1856. Courtesy of the Indiana Historical Society.

Elijah Fletcher, ca. 1855. From a daguerreotype in Portraits and Memoirs of Eminent Americans, by John Livingston (this book and all its contents are in the public domain).

Miles Fletcher. Courtesy of the Indiana Historical Society.

Dr. William "Billy" Fletcher. Courtesy of the Indiana Historical Society.

Brothers James Cooley and Stoughton Fletcher. Courtesy of the Indiana Historical Society.

INTRODUCTION

On a "bad cloudy day" over the Christmas holidays in 1858, Calvin Fletcher, a sixty-year-old self-made lawyer, banker, and farmer in Indianapolis, welcomed his eleven children home for a family reunion. To commemorate the event, he gathered everyone at Orr's Daguerreotype in Indianapolis to take a family picture. As the patriarch of one of the city's wealthiest and most prominent families, Calvin attracted attention. The editors of several newspapers stopped by and complimented him on his large and mostly successful family. "Such a family is rarely known anywhere," the editor of the *Daily Journal* observed. "Of eleven children none have died, all are well educated, well trained, honest, industrious, and well esteemed. Some of them are filling posts of high honor and great responsibility, not in politics but in walks more honorable. Not one has fallen into dissipation, or below the high level on which their father's character has placed them."[1]

While he was suitably flattered, Calvin was unwilling to take much comfort in such praise. As the ever-careful, self-appraising father saw it, "no one can justly & properly be pronounced good or great till a final winding up of mortal life."

The picture itself showcases a well-dressed and solid, if humorless, middle-class family, noteworthy more for an apparent sense of mourning for their lost mother of four years past (seen in the framed daguerreotype at the bottom of the picture) than for any discernible joy at being together.

Calvin's relatively new wife of three years, Keziah, did not appear in the daguerreotype. Gathered in one small space were several troublesome Fletcher sons—one who had run off from home at precisely the age Calvin had departed his own family as a teenager; another who had struggled mightily with Calvin over management of the family farms; a sickly older son, who at one point had abandoned his studies to take off for Mexico; and Calvin's eldest son, whose ongoing financial dependence prompted his father to think of him as a failure. As with most family reunions, one can only imagine the uncomfortable mixture of pride and tension that must have filled the room.

Calvin called it a "truly happy day to me." "It is no small blessing, no ordinary blessing," he confided in his diary, "to have such a privilege as I now enjoy of assembling my children that they are all alive, none missing, that all have their faculties & none extremely dissipated or wicked in the sense the world views such matters." He took pride as well that all were to one degree or another Christians, but as he looked around the room he tellingly concluded, "I know they are not without their faults & have given me great trouble, great care, great anxiety."[2]

Calvin and his family had come a long way from the meager origins of the Fletcher family, which the patriarch, Jesse Sr., settled in rural Vermont in the years after the American Revolution. As time passed, one branch of the Fletchers, led by Jesse's eldest son Elijah, a teacher-turned-plantation owner, made its way to southwestern Virginia, while another branch, led by the younger Calvin, pioneered the way west, finally ending up in Indianapolis. From the beginning, the Fletchers' story opens up a remarkable window on what it meant to be an American in the early days of the nation. And because Calvin and his brother Elijah left a rich and revealing collection of family letters and diaries, we can witness the family's often-fierce struggle to define itself through an unyielding commitment to personal and educational advancement. As the visiting newspapermen doubtless observed, the Fletchers, like most of their fellow middle-class Americans, focused their minds and hearts on the relentless pursuit of respectability and success.

They were in many ways an ordinary family, but their experiences, especially those of Elijah and Calvin, provide an astonishingly candid look into the American dream as it was unfolding across the nineteenth century. The Fletcher story offers nothing less than an emotional X-ray into the heart and soul of a middle-class American family trying to survive and advance in the American nation.

Their story is our own.

One

BEGINNINGS

T he Fletcher family's American experience stretches back to the very beginning of the European presence in New England. The family descends from Robert Fletcher, who settled in Concord, Massachusetts, in 1630. Jesse Fletcher, the patriarch of our story, was among the sixth generation of Fletchers in America. That generation made its mark not as founders, but as patriots, for it was the American Revolution that shaped and gave meaning to Jesse and his family. Born to Timothy and Bridget Fletcher in 1762 in Westford, Massachusetts, a small farming and cattle-raising village about twenty miles west of Boston, Jesse was the youngest of four children. His eldest brother, Elijah, became an ordained Congregationalist minister in nearby Hopkinton, Massachusetts, in 1773. But it was his brother Josiah to whom Jesse remained most attached, especially with the outbreak of hostilities at Lexington and Concord in 1775. Josiah was among the Minutemen who answered the call at Bunker Hill. Although he was only thirteen at the time, Jesse acted as an aide to Josiah during the very battle at which blood was first spilled in the American Revolution. Josiah went on to serve as a private in the Massachusetts militia at Ticonderoga, White Plains, and Saratoga.[1]

After the war dozens of Revolutionary soldiers from the Boston area—many of them men who had served in the same militia company—made their way northwest into Vermont for fresh land. Some nineteen war veterans from Westford alone migrated with their families to Cavendish and Ludlow, Vermont, in the mid-1780s. They chose the rolling alluvial hills and valleys at the foot of the Green Mountains in part because the area had been well known to soldiers as far back as the end of the French and Indian War in the 1760s, when British general Lord Jeffrey Amherst carved out the Crown Point Road through the northeast corner of Ludlow. The road opened a flow of intelligence, arms, and men between Massachusetts to the east and New York to the west that helped counter French and Indian raiding parties coming out of Canada. So the northwest migration into southeast Vermont was itself an artifact of war, and Josiah and his friend Simeon Read were the very first settlers who moved into the area and began clearing virgin soil on the flats bordering the Black River, on the east side of the present-day town of Ludlow.[2]

With Josiah's example before him, Jesse was a good candidate for a migrant out of Westford. Growing up in a humble family on a small farm with little access to any sort of advanced education, Jesse matured quickly, especially in wartime. He courted a local Westford girl, Lucy Keyes, and on August 8, 1782, they were married. He was nineteen; she was sixteen. The next year, now with an infant girl, Jesse and Lucy ventured up to Ludlow to visit Josiah and his family. They liked what they saw. Jesse found an especially alluring fresh spring along the banks of the Black River and, with the help of his brother—who, as town clerk, was able to cheaply snatch up various properties in Ludlow that were being auctioned off for delinquent taxes—decided to make the move to Ludlow too. In 1784 Jesse built his log cabin along the little stream that ran near the base of the Green Mountains. It was a very simple move for a young family with few skills and almost no resources. "They came in an ox cart to the place over the most rugged road," his son Calvin recalled.[3]

Early settlers like the Fletchers built log houses with roofs made from tree bark, which meant felling a lot of trees to make clearings. Fellow settlers came together as neighbors for "logging bees" to do the clearing, rolling all the logs into huge piles and burning them. One old resident in the mid-nineteenth century recalled standing at his father's house as a small boy and counting the fires of some seventy-five different chopping areas where land had been cleared.[4]

Like many other young men and women of the Revolutionary generation, Jesse and Lucy began their life together as migrants "quite young & inexperienced," as one of their children later remembered. A short, stout, sandy-complexioned man, Jesse had to make the best of things as he struggled to till the unforgiving soil, rugged rocks, and unimproved forestland of his one hundred acres in Ludlow. "My father had no money," one of Jesse's sons recalled, and "had to rely on his own energy" rather than any skills as a trader or experienced farmer. He and Lucy labored hard and lived poor. Grass and hay were cut by hand using thick, clumsy scythes fastened to large, heavy iron bands—not a task for old men or weak boys. As parents, Jesse and Lucy had to endure their share of personal tragedies. Their eldest daughter, Charlotte, died at age twelve; their son Stephen was run over by a horse and killed when he was only six. Given their large and growing family—fifteen children over the years—Jesse built a larger frame house in 1805 to accommodate their growing household.[5]

Despite their relatively primitive rural setting—or perhaps *because* of it—both Jesse and Lucy worked hard to instill the importance of education in their children. A small, shrewd woman, Lucy reportedly had unbounded confidence in her children, provided they were willing, if need be, to leave home and go out and compete for their own independent fortune and place of honor. Family lore claims that when Lucy stamped her foot like a rabbit, all arguments ended and she got her way. It was a trait that only grew stronger with time. Many years later, in 1831, when Elijah, one of her older sons, ordered the youngest, twenty-two-year-old Stoughton, to "go cut that field of rye," Lucy reportedly stamped her foot. "No, you will never touch that scythe again," she told Stoughton. "You are going out into the world to make your way." She gave the boy a horse—just a nag—and a few dollars and sent him off. What she lacked in literacy and education—she could write her name and read a bit, but could do no more—Lucy made up with faith and hard work. A Baptist her entire adult life, she held fast to the word of God and busied herself sewing clothes and laboring on the farm both for her family and for the poor. She carded, spun, and wove the woolen cloth for the winter clothes of some fifteen children. When her son Calvin became wealthy later in life, he wrote his mother asking her to make him a suit, since her cloth, he insisted, was better than any he could buy, and she was clearly the best tailor he'd ever known.[6]

But both Jesse and Lucy fully grasped that hard work was not nearly enough to guarantee a happy and successful future, especially for their children. Becoming educated—or at least acquiring basic schooling—was a central tenet not only in their childrearing but also in their view of what made a person truly useful in the world. So despite their meager circumstances and the pioneer world of rural Vermont into which they had moved, they were determined to find schooling for their children. And here they relied again on Jesse's brother Josiah. Besides being a working farmer with a thriving real estate business, Josiah Fletcher also taught school, initially out of his own home. In the village, Jesse followed his brother's lead, taking on the responsibility of arranging schooling for the settlers' children. But progress came slowly. The settlers were thinly spread out over the township, and many of them were very poor, resulting in too few students and too little personal capital available to support a local school. As one of the town's selectmen, Jesse urged the raising of money from individual families. On April 10, 1801—some eighteen years after initial settlement—the town voted to raise $66 from contributing families to build a modest, one-story frame schoolhouse, twenty by twenty-four feet. Each student had to furnish two feet of wood for the school. In its first year some fifty-seven students were enrolled, most likely including Jesse's youngest children: Stephen, seven; Lucy, nine; Timothy, ten; and Elijah, twelve.[7]

In such a primitive setting only the basics were taught—reading, spelling, writing, and elementary math. Penmanship was difficult to teach, as it required making and mending the quill pens that the students used—steel pens didn't come into use until the 1830s. Girls were taught the art of needlework, which, once completed, created a "sampler," a square of canvas on which the alphabet was displayed in various colors and forms. The girls' parents often proudly framed and hung these samplers up in the best room of the house.[8]

What mattered most to Jesse was that his children work hard and become "useful" adults with strong moral and religious principles. Although he never formally joined a church, Jesse attended Congregationalist services and was deeply imbued with religious feeling. According to his son Calvin, Jesse drew his whole worldview from the Bible, believing in "a direct superintending Providence, punishments & rewards." He never went anywhere without his Bible and a newspaper and regularly read aloud from the Scriptures with his family. Despite this strong moral grounding, Jesse led a somewhat timid and fearful life—always struggling to stay out of debt and, with such a large family, often worrying that he was failing at his responsibility of taking the best possible care of them. Indeed, he suffered frequent bouts of "depression of spirits," as one son called it, a condition that may well have prompted him to indulge in excessive drinking in his middle age. Despite these financial worries, he made himself a very "useful" figure in Ludlow politics. In addition to serving as a town selectman, Jesse was elected the first town clerk and recorder of all deeds and birth, marriage, and death records. From 1798 to 1799, he followed in the footsteps of his brother Josiah, representing Ludlow in the Vermont legislature and also serving as justice of the peace for nearly thirty years.[9]

Given their relatively impoverished agrarian circumstances, Jesse and Lucy understandably wanted to make sure their own children could imagine a future beyond becoming poor plowboys in rural New England. This desire underscored for Jesse the necessity of providing his children a serious education beyond the simple elementary training available after 1801 in Ludlow. In fact, according to his sons, he didn't think much of people who had not pursued a liberal education. His brother Elijah had attended college, and Josiah had begun college, though he was unable to finish. At minimum, Jesse wanted to make sure that all of his own children had at least a rudimentary formal schooling. And, as in many farm families with limited resources, he privileged the eldest children (especially sons) with the most elaborate educational plans. "The first children received more personal attention in their education from my father than the middle & last," one of his youngest sons, Calvin, remembered.[10]

So it was not surprising that when Elijah, one of Jesse's older sons, showed promise in his studies, he became the focal point for his family's hopes for a college education and a future that would send him away from home, a home he loved but that offered mostly poor and hopeless prospects. Clearly a young man with scholarly potential, Elijah was sent out as a boy of fifteen to live with his grandmother in Westford and attend the Westford Academy to prepare for college. The cost of going to college in the early nineteenth century—paying for tuition, room and board, and tutors, and suffering the loss of able-bodied labor back home—proved prohibitively expensive for most families. Only the truly gifted, the well-to-do, and the most determined made the choice of pursuing a college education. Elijah was one such young man. He attended college at Dartmouth and Middlebury, and then, in the spring of 1810, he transferred to the University of Vermont, where he finished his liberal arts degree.[11]

He was about to embark on what would become a signature theme among the Fletchers, especially its young men: leaving home at an early age to find a better future. It was a departure fueled by equal parts hope and desperation.

$$\text{✻} \quad \bullet \quad \bullet \quad \text{✻}$$

At eight in the morning of July 4, 1810, a slender, twenty-year-old Elijah Fletcher mounted his bay mare outside his family's modest frame house in Ludlow, Vermont. Fresh from his college education at Middlebury and the University of Vermont, and wearing clothes spun and woven by his mother and sisters, Elijah bade farewell to his impoverished farm family. He had a teaching offer at an academy in Raleigh, North Carolina, that paid well and so was an alluring prospect. A few months before he left, Elijah admitted that "the thoughts of six hundred dollars per year has such influence upon

Elijah Fletcher, ca. 1815

my mind that I am employed in contriving a plan for affecting the object."[12] Teaching school in the "distant country" of the American South offered a powerful alternative to the drudgery and dead-end farmwork that lay before him if he stayed behind to help his father and brothers. In fact, life in Ludlow working Jesse's farm conjured up thoughts of nothing but hardship and debt. "My inability and dependence made me miserable while with you," Elijah later confessed to his father. "Such was my determination when I left home that nothing but death or a total deprivation of corporeal strength would prohibit me paying my distrusted and at best fast-bound debt of gratitude. I would rather [have] labored in the field with the negro slave and so earned a recompense for your kindness than have involved you in difficulty." Leaving behind his often-depressed and struggling father—even with several other sons and daughters to help out on the farm—Elijah rode off that day under a cloud of presumed self-centered motives, a suspicion that continued to gnaw at him months later. Even his friends in Ludlow, he confessed, "doubted my affection for the family and said my motives were all selfish, I had a care for nothing but to aggrandize myself."[13]

Part of Elijah's "selfish" agenda surfaced in his effort to coax the University of Vermont into granting him his diploma "without I tarried till Commencement." When that was granted, all he needed was $50 to cover the diploma and a means of travel: "Trust me for a horse," he wrote his father from college, "[and] I shall be ready for the expedition." A final task was to secure some key letters of recommendation to take with him. The first day of his journey was a thirty-two-mile ride to Manchester, Vermont, followed by eight more miles to Arlington, where he had to wait on a letter from Governor Isaac Tichenor. He was told to go to Bennington, where the governor, out fishing, prompted "another disappointment." Instead, two hours later, he managed to obtain a letter from Vermont U.S. senator Jonathan Robinson.[14]

Armed with a diploma, a letter of introduction, and a few dollars, Elijah finally grasped how daunting his "long and strange journey" would be. Calculating that he could ride forty miles per day, he figured he would arrive in Virginia in a little over two weeks. Confident that his "expedition" was necessary, Elijah nonetheless keenly felt the potential danger and uncertainty of the path before him. As he was about to head south from Albany, New York, he admitted to his older brother, twenty-three-year-old Jesse Jr., that he had fallen into a "hypochondriacal or melancholy reflection when I consider I have seven hundred miles to travel, with nineteen or twenty dollars to bear my expenses. However, I will do the best I can. I am in no fear of starving, although I must live prudently."[15]

Living prudently meant finding cheap taverns for meals and lodging along the way. To conserve his meager funds, Elijah subsisted on bread and cheese and, when "the gnawings of hunger compelled me," a cup of milk. When he stayed at a Dutch tavern in New York, he asked the female proprietor for a little milk. Her response was prophetic in terms of the cultural shift he was in for as he moved south: "The good woman wanted to know if I chose sweet milk? No, I told her, I did not want my milk sweetened. She says: you don't understand me, do you want sweet milk or sour? I laughed at my mistake, and told her I was a Yankee; I preferred sweet milk." During his journey he mostly tried to appear "a liberal gentleman" among strangers, when in fact he "was as poor as Job's Cats . . . thus did pride struggle against poverty." Sometimes, though, meeting and staying with suspicious strangers prompted fear and anxiety. At one tavern in New Jersey, Elijah noted, "I went to bed, and slept but very little, for the house was full of swearing, drinking, Irish gamblers. They tried to get me into their company before I went to bed. I told them mildly I was unacquainted with their game and thus excused myself." The landlord worried him nearly as much as the dubious lodgers. Before going to bed, he asked the owner for his luggage, "telling him I should want to change my clothes, when in fact I was afraid to trust them with him. I spent a restless night, with many fears, and apprehensions of robbery, murder, and the like, but was so fortunate as to find myself alive the next morning."[16]

Nearly every place he rode through revealed a surprising landscape. And he clearly found the differences from his ancestral home in Vermont fascinating and worthy of ethnographic reportage. Fletcher witnessed "truly excellent Land and some fine plantations" along the banks of the Hudson but thought the people looked "indigent despite being wealthy Dutchmen." He caught sight of log homes in New Jersey, but in Pennsylvania, he reported, nearly all the buildings were stone houses and barns, mainly inhabited by Germans, "an inhospitable, ignorant, uncouth set."[17] After leaving Philadelphia, he took a back road to avoid the more heavily taxed turnpike, but in doing so, he temporarily became lost. As he headed south of Philadelphia, Elijah reported his first signs of slavery: "I saw herds of negroes in fields—men, women and children, some dressed in rags, and others without any clothes." Traveling the final leg (forty-six miles by his calculation) from Baltimore to "Washington City," he found "scarcely an inhabitant" along the way. There were very few taverns, he lamented—mostly just poor people scattered far from the main road. After nearly drowning while trying to ford a creek in Maryland and soaking his clothes, Fletcher looked in vain for a place to dry out. Finally he saw a "little hut" with a little girl standing by the door. She told him the humble little structure was an "*ordinary* for such they call taverns." Elijah got off his horse and went inside. "I thought it was an ordinary indeed," he recounted. "No body at home, but the girl and another little bare-assed child. I told her my misfortune and desired her to make a fire that I might dry my clothes. I felt hungry, anxious and much provoked to think I must stay two or three hours to dry my clothes, but I had endeavored to make the best of all misfortune, and not despond at trifles." He asked the girl for some milk and bread. She gave him "a dirty pint tin cup full" of milk and baked "a *jonny* cake" in the fireplace. "I ate a little of it," Elijah wrote, "dryed myself and travelled on my way, rejoicing that I had escaped being drowned."[18] Elijah clearly could be judgmental, yet, given his youth and the strain he was under, he also possessed a powerful streak of optimism and resolve.

Soon after his arrival in Alexandria, Virginia, Elijah made the fateful decision not to push on to Raleigh for the teaching appointment he had originally agreed to take. His long and laborious journey from Ludlow had left him with an ailing horse ("very poor, sorebacked and shabbed"), and, once in Alexandria, he made the acquaintance of another young teacher in the area who happened to have friends in Raleigh and "solicited an exchange of situation." Elijah eagerly agreed to the switch: his friend would take the Raleigh job, and Elijah would take the other's position teaching at the Alexandria academy. Although he had never been to Raleigh, Elijah felt immediately confident about his change of plans: "I think I have made a good exchange. I know it is equally profitable and I doubt not it will be equally pleasant."[19]

Alexandria, "one of the largest, handsomest, and most commercial cities in Virginia," struck Elijah as a very pleasant place with a brisk trading business along the Potomac River. His academy was situated away from the center of the city. There he taught some fifteen "scholars" ranging in age from thirteen to twenty, instructing them in math and English grammar, and boarded with a "nice genteel family" of the well-to-do planter General Thomas Mason, "a man of note and respectability" who was son of the prominent Virginia Founding Father George Mason. As Elijah soon realized, he was now ensconced in a place where great wealth and slavery were on full display, a point he was unafraid to convey to his antislavery "Yankee" father back home. "Our living is rich," he wrote his father, "and what in Vermont would be called extravagant. . . . I also feel independent, have two negroes at my service and live considerably at my ease." He was practically giddy over how clever and comfortable he felt living in the "distant country" of Virginia. "I am so satisfied with my employment, so pleased with the people, and so agreeably situated every other way that I would not exchange my situation for any I ever held in Vermont," he wrote.[20]

As if he could sense his father shaking his head in doubt, Elijah was at pains to acknowledge the quite visible social and cultural differences he saw all around him. "To be sure," he wrote, "I find the manners and customs of the Virginians different from the people in the North, but the difference I think habit will soon make a pleasing one." First, there was the Virginians' well-known fondness for sports and socializing, especially "Barbecues and private parties," which Elijah claimed to find "novel and amusing." But he was clearly also taken by his new planter friends' "open-hearted liberal sentiments, a certain noble spirit and social feeling, which distinguish them from the Yankee or selfish, narrow, earthborn-souled Vermonter."[21]

To his older brother Jesse Jr., charged with helping run the family farm back home in Ludlow, young Elijah offered a more critical perspective on his new southern surroundings. While he remained serenely confident about his academy—"I have found no difficulty as yet in governing my scholars. They appear to be very studious and tractable . . . much better than I expected"—he was clearly shocked by the master–slave interactions he observed every day on Mason's plantation. "The planters and their sons," he told Jesse Jr., "appear and dress with rich and neat apparel. They live in idleness and some in dissipation." The rich planters owned from fifty to one hundred slaves, he noted, and "they buy, and sell them, as we do our cattle. . . . Some men make it their principal business to buy droves of them, and drive off, as our drivers do cattle." Most slaves were dressed in rags, except the children, "who [go most]ly naked." Overall, "they have but very little to eat and are under the constant eye of an overseer, who makes them work from sunrise, till sunset."[22]

But what really troubled Elijah was the harsh and often-inhumane treatment he witnessed masters inflicting on their slaves. "They whip them for every little offence most cruelly," he observed shortly after arriving in Alexandria. He told his father the story of General Mason who, upon discovering that one of his slaves had borrowed Elijah's horse for a brief joyride, "tied up the boy and whipt him about a quarter of an hour, and he was begging and praying, yelling to a terrible rate. They then took the man, and I will assure you, they show him no mercy. The more he cried and begged pardon, the more they whipt and in fact I thought they would have killed the poor creature." When Elijah explained to Mason that he didn't really mind the slave borrowing his mare, he was quickly rebuked: "They said it would not do to indulge them. They must whip them till they were humble and obedient."[23]

Elijah's depiction of slavery veered between sympathy for the ill-treated slaves and disdain for how "the negroes" lived. While he noted that slaves looked down on their white overseers ("the negroes think as meanly of the poor white people, as the rich white people do themselves"), he was contemptuous of the primitive and promiscuous existence he perceived them as living. Slave marriages, he pointed out to his brother Jesse, amounted to little more than casual, informal agreements. "They have but little more ceremony about such things than the cattle do," he wrote. "They lay all together on the floor like hogs, have no beds. The negro women have a great many children," which they began to conceive in their early teens. "There is such promiscuous intercourse between the sexes," Elijah concluded, and, with "no regard to decency or chastity, they will have as many children as a bitch will puppies."[24] Left out of this harsh commentary was not only any sense of moral judgment about the institution of slavery itself, but also any recognition that slave marriages were not legally recognized in the South.

Such a scathing assessment of slave morality prompted concern from Elijah's father. An antislavery man with Puritan roots, Jesse Fletcher Sr. not only took a dim view of white masters in the South but strenuously pressed his son to do his part to right the many wrongs of chattel slavery. Caught between respecting the New England antislavery precepts his father had taught him and needing to justify the dramatically different necessities of his new plantation surroundings, Elijah did his best to explain himself to his concerned father. "You wish to have me relieve and assist the slave in distress," Elijah wrote. "I assure you it is a task I would do with pleasure, if I could with profit." What he meant by "profit" was his rising place in the Virginia ruling class, something he was becoming reluctant to endanger. Thus he believed that honoring his father's request that he assist the poor slaves would only harm his own status: "To vindicate the rights of that degraded class of human creatures here would render me quite unpopular. There are none the Virginians despise so much as Quakers and those who disapprove of slavery." Still, Elijah insisted, he cautioned slaves to behave with "obedience and resignation," and he treated his house servants "kindly," even attempting "once in a while to save their black backs from the lash." Unlike General Mason, Elijah protested, he didn't engage in scoldings, threats, or "cruel whipping"; instead, he tried to encourage them as best he could. In the end, though, there was little hope for the slaves. Because they were illiterate, possessed no political rights, and had no ambition and "no chance to rise and become eminent," black slaves existed at a level far below that of even the poorest whites Elijah had seen all around him in Vermont. "Happy, thrice happy are the poor people of New England when compared to that class here," he told his father.[25]

Given such a dark picture of southern culture, it was scarcely surprising that many young men from the North who moved south in the early nineteenth century to take advantage of teaching positions simply couldn't adapt to a world of harsh slavery and white dissipation and extravagance. Yale graduate–turned–plantation tutor Henry Barnard regarded the residents of Chapel Hill, North Carolina, as "indolent" people who, "like most southerners[,] . . . like very much to lounge about and let the slaves do the work." Repelled by the alien and often-distasteful customs of the southern ruling class, many of these young "Yankee" instructors fled back to the more familiar world of the North.[26]

But Elijah stayed, in large part because he saw real opportunity—both financial and personal—in the "respectable" plantation world into which he quickly ingratiated himself. In fact, less than a year after arriving in Alexandria, Elijah chose to deepen his commitment to becoming a southern man. In March 1811, he responded to an invitation from a prominent lawyer and large planter, David Garland, to take over an academy in New Glasgow (now Clifford), Virginia, over 200 miles to the south. In explaining to his father why he was moving, especially since his position with General Mason was "agreeable," his "salary decent," and the general wanted him to stay, Elijah made it clear that it was his "ambition" for profit that propelled him. "I should have a larger salary (which is my first object)," he observed.[27] Moving himself away from debt and closer to the world of genteel planters formed the core of Fletcher's game plan as he began his new adventure in Virginia.

He traveled first to Charlottesville, where Garland provided him with a horse and servant to take him the remaining forty miles. During his stay in Charlottesville, Garland also arranged for Elijah to get "an interview with the Philosopher of Monticello." When the young man arrived at the top of the mountain, "Mr. Jefferson appeared at the door." They repaired to the drawing room, where "wines and liquors were soon handed us by the servant." Elijah's recounting of his visit with Thomas Jefferson revealed his largely disrespectful, disapproving impression of the former president. Retired from the presidency, Jefferson had been the subject of nine years of scandalous gossip over his rumored relationship with his slave Sally Hemings. "I confess I never had a very exalted opinion of his moral conduct," Elijah told his father, "but from the information I gained of his neighbors who must best know him, I have a much poorer one. The story of black Sal[ly Hemings] is no farce. That he cohabits with her and has a number of children by her is a sacred truth, and the worst of it is, he keeps the same children slaves, an unnatural crime" that to Elijah was "so common that they cease here to be disgraceful."[28]

If his journey to Monticello suggested that Elijah hadn't yet made complete peace with Virginia's slave culture, his relocation to the hills of New Glasgow soon brought him much closer to a position of acceptance. A small village of about 200 people, located twenty miles northeast of Lynchburg, Elijah's new home at the New Glasgow Academy gave him a "handsome dwelling house for myself," complete with a classical library and surrounded by a few acres of land.[29] Even more appealing was the opportunity to meet eligible, well-to-do young women. "I am quite the favorite of the ladies about here," Elijah boasted to his sister Laura. The teenage "ladies" he instructed in French out of his home sent him gifts (four pounds of cheese, a prayer book, and cotton stockings from one girl "which she had knit with her own hands") and, when they came to recite their French lessons, would sometimes bring him fruit "with the first letters of their names marked upon them."[30] Elijah could well have used the gifts of food: he reported that he weighed only 129 pounds at the time.

Most significantly, teaching at the academy offered Elijah the chance to meet nineteen-year-old Maria Antoinette Crawford, one of his students and, just as important, the daughter of William Crawford, a distinguished lawyer and wealthy plantation owner in New Glasgow. At Christmas of 1811, he confessed to being swept away by Maria's charms. He had "become acquainted," he told his father, "with a young Lady . . . of amiable manners and disposition for whom I have more than common [regard] & with whom I am on terms of intimacy." At first, he was determined not to let the allure of romance impede his economic success. "Giving away to the softer passions & feelings in too great a degree is detrimental to my worldly interest," he wrote. But nearly a year later, his courtship had grown into "a subject of serious thought," and it was time to make a full case to his father regarding Maria's—and her family's—reputation and importance. Referring to Maria as "a most amiable, accomplished, sensible Lady," the daughter of "one [of] the most rich, extensive, respectable families in the State," Elijah wanted his parents to know that in Maria "I have a bosom friend and connections about who will feel an interest in my fate." Deflecting the appearance that economic security rather than genuine affection was fueling the match, Elijah told his sister Lucy (who was herself contemplating marriage), "Property is desirable. It adds to the comforts and conveniences of life. But property alone cannot make us happy."[31] But he was just as concerned to reassure Jesse Sr. and "Ma'am" (as Elijah referred to his mother Lucy) that they would remain "my first best human friends." "If I have chosen a companion recently," he carefully pointed out, "my highest esteem, dear to me as life itself, my filial regard for you is unaltered."[32]

One can scarcely imagine the worry and concern that must have seized the Crawfords as they watched this courtship unfold. On the positive side, Maria must have been truly drawn to Elijah by romantic love, since he brought almost nothing by way of property or status to the relationship—a problem that doubtless the genteel Crawfords fully grasped. Wealthy planters like the Crawfords routinely guarded their families from intrusions, especially those involving "Yankee" outsiders like this Vermont tutor. But they may also have sensed that Elijah Fletcher, unlike most visiting teachers from the North, was fast becoming something of a convert to the southern way of life. For his part, Elijah happily reported that the Crawfords lived "in the genteelest style" in a carpeted, two-story home called Tusculum. "Mr. C" was a man in his fifties, "quite grey headed, educated at Princeton, formerly a distinguished lawyer." Maria's mother, Elijah noted, "is a most amiable woman."[33]

On April 15, 1813, Elijah and Maria were married and soon began to live "in the Virginia style," with a comfortable home, plenty of whisky or wine for visitors to drink, and "black servants enough." "Tell Ma'am," he wrote his father, "we have good Imperial tea and coffee." Married life clearly agreed with Elijah, and he marveled at how his life had changed in so many unexpected, if welcome, ways. "Little did I expect three years ago to be in such a situation as I am," he told his father two months after his wedding. "How little do we know what a day will bring forth."[34]

One thing he felt certain the day would not "bring forth" was children. "We have no children," he told his father, "and hope and pray we never shall have any." While Elijah understood that children often proved a source of comfort and consolation to parents, he felt that offspring "more frequently prove a vexation. Hardly any family where they all do well." In what was no doubt a commentary on the inconsistent, uncertain outcomes he had witnessed in his own family, Elijah adopted the cynical position that whatever parents' most fervent hopes for their children might be, "they are too frequently blasted."[35]

If the newly wed Elijah was renouncing parenthood, he was most certainly not condemning his newfound wealth, not to mention his much more public embrace of southern slaveholding culture. Linked by marriage to one of the leading planters in Amherst County, Elijah now possessed a kind of financial security never experienced by anyone thus far in the Fletcher family. He even suggested that his father brag about his financial success in Virginia to his friends back in Vermont: "You may tell our good friends in Ludlow that I have become President of an Academy here with a salary of a thousand dollars per year which will do for their envious spirits to gnaw upon."[36] But Elijah was also a man of generosity: he quickly and effectively assumed the mantle of moneylender and family advisor to all his kin, especially his impoverished and unhappy father.

Jesse Sr. was now over fifty, in poor health, and unable to scratch out much of a living from his small farm in Ludlow—even with several sons and daughters around to help out—and Elijah fully grasped his father's precarious plight. Before he married Maria and securely settled into his position in New Glasgow, Elijah tried to sympathize with his father, claiming that early on he also felt "poor and dependent," but, as he told his father, "I know your wants are so urgent . . . I frequently ask myself when I shall be independent and not dogged about and troubled for want of money."[37] And so, from the beginning of his time in Virginia, Elijah began sending his father and siblings money, almost every month—usually $50 to $100 in hopes the money would lessen "your fears & ease you a little from your embarrassments."[38] Nearly every letter Elijah received from his father contained not only another request for money but a melancholy lament about his poverty. "I am sorry, daddy," Elijah wrote in 1813, "you are so poor in *spirit*." When Elijah directed him on how exactly he should distribute one particular batch of money he had sent them, Jesse complained about his over-controlling son. "You say the rich cannot sympathize with the poor and intimate as tho I wanted feeling," Elijah shot back. "After reading the first page of your letter I stopped, I laid down the letter and cried. It made me so melancholy to think my good Father was not happier. Oh, thought I, were the mines of Mexico mine, how gladly would I share them with you."[39]

As much as he loved his father and seemed almost desperate to be thought of as a respectful and dutiful son, Elijah also wondered why a man who had worked so hard and was surrounded by such a loving family could become so dispirited. After getting yet another letter that "breathes the accustomed melancholy, doubt, and difficulty," Elijah confronted Jesse Sr. about the meaning of his life, past, present, and future:

> I presume you think your lot is a hard one. I am sensible from your first setting out in life you have encountered many a hardship, trial and trouble. You first penetrated into a wilderness country, had few neighbors but the wild beast of the forest and encountered all the inconveniences necessarily attending such a situation. You have supported a very numerous and expensive family by the mere earnings of honest industry, always too noble-hearted, upright, and honorable to descend to the arts of cunning speculation to take advantage of the weakness and necessities of your fellow creatures. It melts my heart quicker than anything else to think, after so many troubles, you cannot enjoy a happy old age, and go down to the tomb in peace, plenty and quietness. I hope this will be the case. I hope a brighter sun will shine upon your prospects.[40]

Nothing brightened one's prospects, according to Elijah, like a good education. If only Jesse Sr. in his youth had had the opportunities for learning that were made possible for Elijah and several of his brothers and sisters, things would have been different. "Omit no opportunity in learning," Elijah reminded his seventeen-year-old brother Stephen as the younger Fletcher prepared to go off to college. Strategizing with his father about whether to give young Stephen property or an education, Elijah contended that "a little advantage for an education is the best portion you can give him." He went on to advise that "if you can keep him at school two years and he makes good advancement in study, I can get him into business here," in Virginia, where Elijah predicted his brother could earn $300 to $400 a year. Jesse eventually agreed, and when Stephen went off to Middlebury College, Elijah rejoiced, hoping that such a commitment to his brother's education could be made without selling the family farm, as so many gossiping neighbors in Ludlow had predicted would happen ever since Elijah had gone off to college. "Let the envious grind and gnash their teeth as much as they please," Elijah advised his impoverished father. "The only way of revenging ourselves upon them is by doing well."[41]

And education, Elijah insisted, was just as important for women. As his younger sister Lucy reached eighteen years of age, Elijah emphasized how critical it was for her to follow the educational path that had led to his own success. "A girl will be more respected with an education than with wealth," Elijah wrote after sending Lucy $100 to help defray the cost of her schooling. "I think female education is too much neglected. They are the ones who have the first education of children and ought to be qualified to instruct them correctly."[42] While it was increasingly common in the early Republic for ambitious young men to focus on the necessity of an education, Elijah's conviction about the equal value to be placed on schooling young women represented a uniquely progressive position in his day, one that would lead to an unexpected but revealing personal legacy.[43]

❦ • • ❦

Still in his early twenties, Elijah Fletcher was fast developing a durable—and, for him, successful—personal credo. Personal ambition rather than faith or entitlement fueled the young Fletcher's life. "I am one of those 'wicked ones,'" he told his father early in his Virginia adventure, "who put great dependence upon works; and verily believe my future success will depend rather upon my own exertion, perseverance, prudence, and economy than on the Fates, Fortunes, Destinies, that can be mentioned." And, unlike today, there was no help, no cushion, and no safety net from society for those whose efforts came up short or ended in failure. The fate of a young man like Elijah truly rested on his skills, determination, and luck—and little else. Understandably, then, the culture placed a huge premium on hard work and self-sufficiency. Like increasing numbers of young men in the early Republic, especially those who had uprooted themselves from their ancestral homes in the East for new prospects in the South and West, Elijah fully embraced the ethos of self-reliance and self-advancement. "I have an ambition to make myself respectable," he wrote. "I am sensible I possess no extraordinary gift or talent, and to gratify my ambition nothing will do but industry, labor and the practice of virtue."[44]

But it was the "practice of virtue" that was the rub for young men like Elijah Fletcher. Receiving an education, moving away from family and friends, and making a new life in a very different, even alien, place like the slave South—all of this self-improvement, risk taking, and adventuring in "a distant country" sometimes caused some very difficult moments with family back home.

Nowhere was Fletcher's "virtue" more contested than in his growing embrace of Virginia slave culture. From the beginning, Elijah's father had pressed him about the unfamiliar world of these wealthy southern planters and the chattel slaves they controlled. Finally, three years into his time in Virginia, Elijah reached the breaking point. In response to more of his father's "questions about our people here," Elijah wrote, "I rather think you have too bad an idea of them. There are a great many good men here as well as many bad." Furthermore, he argued, his father's idea of emancipating the slaves "would be the height of folly and danger." Now married into plantation society, Elijah had become a partial defender of slavery, seeing it as "rather a misfortune than a crime." The present generation of slaveholders, he argued, could not be condemned for something their fathers had done, namely, introducing slavery in the first place: "They are only censurable for not treating those they possess well." To Elijah, those slaves with enlightened, humane masters "are in a better situation" than they would be otherwise, a common rationalization among southern slaveholders. Elijah tried to pass off his conveniently changing perspective on slavery as simply what happens when ideology—such as his father's anti-slavery notions—confronts daily reality: "I know what horrid ideas I formerly had of slavery," he wrote, "and how I despised the man who would traffic in human flesh. My feelings may be a little softened by living in a country where such things are common, but they never will be perfectly reconciled to them." But then came the real blow: "You must not think too badly of slave holders," he cautioned his father, "for your *son* is one."[45]

Although he struggled with his father over slavery and Jesse Sr.'s chronic financial needs and "melancholy spirit," Elijah loved him deeply, sometimes even desperately. The physical distance between them only heightened his yearning for his father and the family he had left behind. One summer Sunday morning, Elijah decided to reveal his feelings. "My thoughts are with you," he wrote Jesse Sr. "I have sat me down before meeting-time to communicate a few of them." Elijah had been thinking of home and his "dear father and mother, brothers and sisters" and was looking for "some way to speak and converse with you." He hoped Jesse Sr. would not find it "burthensome" to pay the twenty-five cents—in that era the recipients paid the postage—"for a good long letter from me for I know you are my father, and that your children are more precious to you than money."[46]

Much had changed for Elijah Fletcher since riding off from home—some of it surprising, the unexpected effects of living in a plantation setting. But much of that change grew out of the fading memories that came with such distance and time apart. He held firmly and fondly to the memory of his leave taking: "I mounted that little bay mare and left the house of my Father. I cannot reflect on that time but with mingled emotions."[47] And those reflections left him at least occasionally homesick. "I long to behold the sacred spot of my nativity and its inhabitants," he wrote. "I frequently think of the changes that has probably taken place since I left you."[48] But without portraits or photos, and with no visits home yet, Elijah could cling only to his quickly diminishing memories as a way of visualizing his family. He told his sister Laura that "I can't think of you as you *are,* but think of you as you were when I left you. I suppose you look quite different from what you did then, and that all other things are much changed."[49] Upon reading in one of the Vermont newspapers that his father was now fifty, Elijah immediately requested information on every family member's age. "I set down your age and ma'am's in my pocket book before I left home," he told Jesse Sr. "I wish I had the age of all my brothers & sisters. If it be not too much trouble, I wish you would send them to me."[50]

The easy solution to these frayed memories and yearnings for family would have been a trip back to Ludlow. The day he left Vermont, Elijah had promised his mother that he would be back to visit within two years. It was a promise he did not keep, and soon after arriving in Virginia he seemed aware that his departure might be permanent. After being gone only a year, Elijah advised his father to prepare "Ma'am" to accept that she might never see her son again. "I earnestly hope I shall return home and see you all again in life, health and prosperity," he said, "but my return is enveloped in the darkness of futurity. It does no good to trouble ourselves about it. All we can do is to wish and pray for the best and leave the residue with God."[51]

But in time Elijah began to feel the pain of separation from his family, living so far away. Once that pain was produced by a vivid homecoming vision: "I dreamt last night that I was at home, that I saw you all, that you were much altered. Even the vision was exquisitely pleasing—how much more will be the reality!"[52] But that reality did not happen anytime soon. On July 2, 1814, Elijah Fletcher stopped to contemplate his fourth anniversary of leaving Vermont for Virginia. "Little did I imagine then that four years would revolve ere I had the pleasure of seeing you all again," he conceded to his father. "Tho' I live in hopes that two years more will not pass away before I revisit the Green Hills of the North."[53]

🜍 • • • 🜍

Elijah did not return home just yet, but he did get an inspiring and un-expected glimpse of it: his cousin John Patten arrived in late June 1815 from Boston. An aspiring businessman looking to make his way in the mercantile world of New Glasgow, Patten hoped to settle "somewhere in this southern world" and, as Elijah noted, "is the first relation I have seen since leaving New England."[54] The visit with Cousin Patten no doubt set Elijah to thinking even more about his ancestral home: "My thoughts have been more particularly roving to the north for a few days past," he wrote, and he once again announced that, barring any "unforeseen accident," he would visit his parents "sometime next season." Elijah's focus on Vermont fell just as keenly on his siblings and the uncertain future that awaited them. Seeing Patten in Virginia only deepened those concerns. "What is Calvin doing in Windsor? And where does Jesse live?" Elijah asked his father. He was especially concerned that his older sister, now twenty-nine years old, should resist the impulse to supplement their father's meager farm income. "Tell Fanny she must not go from home to live. She must stay at home and assist Ma'am and work for herself," Elijah insisted. "I will give her more money than she can make by going out."[55]

Making money may not have seemed an appropriate goal for a young woman in the Fletcher family, but, as it turned out, it had become the guiding force in Elijah's life, largely as a result of his marriage. When his father-in-law, William Sidney Crawford, was struck by a severe illness in the spring of 1815, Elijah watched with concern mingled with admiration: "He was sick seven weeks," Elijah wrote, "bore his illness with the fortitude of a Philosopher and died with the composure and resignation of a Christian." Upon Crawford's death, Elijah was named executor of the sprawling Crawford estate. That responsibility not only consumed his time, but prompted a major change in his lifestyle: "The management of all Mr. Crawford's affairs devolving upon me makes my task arduous. He was a man of extensive concerns and great estate. He left his affairs much deranged and unsettled, which renders the settlement of his concerns doubly troublesome." Elijah first had to sell off the crops, especially the tobacco and wheat, which alone were worth $5,000. Then, he had "to manage all the Plantations, or at least visit them now and then to see if the overseers are going well." One of the plantations was fifteen miles away; another, nine miles. From his perch closing up all of Crawford's business, Elijah witnessed the human tendency toward grasping exploitation; there were so many people trying "to take all possible advantage. I have a very good opportunity to discover the rascality of my Fellow Creatures. My little experience would present a gloomy picture of human depravity."[56]

Amid the "rascality" and "depravity," though, lay a good opportunity to keep his own affairs "straight and correct," and a profitable life as a plantation manager. Watching his father-in-law die and knowing he would be asked to supervise the far-flung plantations, Elijah made a big decision: he permanently set aside his entire reason for journeying to Virginia: the aim of working as a schoolteacher. Having already married into the slaveholding class, he would now become a gentleman farmer himself, complete with slaves and plantations of his own.

It was a transition that few, if any, of his Vermont kinsmen could have imagined, let alone applauded. But as Elijah's younger teenage brother Calvin would also discover, leaving home was but the first of many surprises for young men on the make in the early Republic.

Two

HEADING WEST

When Elijah Fletcher asked his father what his teenage brother Calvin was doing working away from home in Windsor, Connecticut, in late summer of 1815, Elijah was inquiring out of mounting concern. Four months earlier, on April 11, 1815, to be exact, Calvin had informed his father that he did not get along with his brother Jesse Jr. and could no longer work with him on the family farm. Strapped for money and already driven into poverty from debts incurred by Jesse Jr., his father seized on Calvin's predicament and, at 7:30 a.m. "in a rather pettish moode," Calvin remembered, "[my father] gave me permission to leave him at 17 yrs, 2 months and 7 days old." Ninety minutes later, Calvin had borrowed $2.50 from his sister Lucy and set out "with a small bundle of clothes."[1] This act of youthful leave-taking—though it would involve a brief return to his family's neighborhood, but not to his father's household—would become the most emotionally charged and formative event in Calvin Fletcher's life. Like Elijah, he was leaving his ancestral home for good, but unlike his brother's triumphant and hopeful departure, Calvin's was born out of frustration and failure.

In part, Calvin's abrupt departure grew out of his unfortunate place in the family birth order: being one of the youngest of fifteen children, he, like his younger brothers and sisters, was expected to sacrifice for the good of the oldest children. So it was Elijah and Stephen—not Calvin—who received the lion's share of the family's meager resources and hopes for a different, more successful, future. That meant that when it came to Calvin, everything from formal schooling to any sort of planning for a job happened in a hit-or-miss fashion, with no greater expectation than that he would scratch out a poor, depressing existence as a plowboy on a small New England farm.[2]

Despite his father's emphasis on educating his children, Calvin's early schooling was decidedly haphazard and incomplete. As a young boy he was sent to school for a few days under the uncertain tutelage of a nearby farmer. Then he attended an informal school kept by a woman on a barn floor. Between the ages of eleven and thirteen, he received no formal education at all, because the schoolhouse burned down and the district was unable or unwilling to rebuild it. "This intermission of schools," Calvin later noted bitterly, "was of great injury to me." As a teenager, his schooling took place in the winter or summer months only; he attended summer schools until he was thirteen and winter schools thereafter until he was sixteen. The winter schools were kept by men "of not much education." He was taught to read, write, and "cipher to the Golden Rule," but the instructors "were usually tyrannical & knew very little about the philosophy of teaching." At least by then there was an actual schoolhouse within a half mile of the Fletcher house, but each student had to furnish his own wood. Even with all the interruptions and halfhearted educational plans, Calvin insisted that he developed "a great thirst for knowledge & treasured up all I heard before I could read. Yet [it] was extremely hard to learn to read or attain figures with ease and I had labored so hard at 10 that my hand was as stiff & hard as an old man's hand. Indeed, I had no mechanical ingenuity which makes a writer."[3]

Poverty then, as it does now, led to great sacrifices, even on matters of significance such as education. Calvin watched his mother and sisters spin and weave and make clothes—all to benefit Elijah as he went on to a proper school in Westford, Massachusetts; then to Hanover, New Hampshire; and to Middlebury College and the University of Vermont. Everything was done "to give him a college education." In the meantime, Calvin's older siblings, Lucy and Stephen, were sent from home to afford them a "better education." Calvin's much-older brother Michael was likewise sent off to Massachusetts to work for several years in order to help out their father. He was followed by his then-twenty-year-old brother Timothy, who in 1810–1811 removed to Albany, New York, to live. Thus, Stephen, Elijah, Timothy, and Michael had by 1811 all departed the family farm in Ludlow, leaving only Jesse Jr., Calvin, and the sixteen-year-old Miles "to help [their] father."[4]

Working with his twenty-eight-year-old brother Jesse Jr. proved to be disastrous for Calvin, in part because of Jesse's irresponsible spending habits and his apparently grasping new wife. "Jesse was speculative proude & destitute of much calculation and forsight," Calvin noted, which got worse after his "long courtship" and marriage to "a woman more vain & proude than himself." Jesse's "profligate" tendencies deepened the family's financial problems. "He bo't things on credit without Judgment & involved my father so that the annual income did not meet the outgoes," Calvin noted, and as a result, "my father suffered pecuniarily thereby."[5]

The War of 1812 added even greater hardships to the already-marginal existence of Jesse Fletcher Sr. and his children. The split with England and the non-intercourse embargo led to limited currency and credit and depressed the commercial potential of the New England farm economy, creating by the time of Calvin's departure in 1815 "truly . . . hard times." His father's diminished physical and mental abilities only worsened matters. By the time Calvin left home, his father had reached fifty, which was commonly viewed as old age in the early nineteenth century, and Jesse Sr. had become overweight and "not able to perform much labor." His "corpulence" (which proved to be a lifelong issue that Calvin monitored in himself) had developed from his habit of "drinking regular drams."[6] Thus, by the spring of 1815, the time was indeed ripe for Calvin to rethink trying to remain a plowboy on his father's meager farm.

His journey out of Ludlow, though, was anything but planned and effective. Initially, he went to Windsor, where he was hired to do work on the cattle farm of Squire Jabez Delano. That job lasted only a few days, as the man Delano had originally hired for the job returned to work, but Delano found work for Calvin at Esquire Cummins's farm near the West Windsor meetinghouse. But that job too only lasted a few days, as Cummins "was looking out for a full-grown man that could hop & do field work," and Calvin "was not able to perform such work quite equal to a man." Eventually, Delano connected Calvin with Phineas Hemenway in Windsor. Here he worked for six months at $10 per month. Calvin never lost a day of work during this period, he liked to brag, staying with Hemenway until October 24. Hemenway said goodbye to Calvin "with great regret"; Calvin recorded that Hemenway urged him "to continue my services another year & flattered me with being one of the *best laborers* they ever had." Calvin walked away having earned close to $70 in wages.[7]

Realizing he needed to continue his schooling, Calvin left in November for Royalton, Vermont, a small town on the White River, sixty miles from home, where he attended an academy run by "one Chamberlain, a man of no great ability, a sort of dandy." He boarded with a man over the winter, but it was an unhappy, painful experience. Everything he was taught at Royalton was "superficial & a blunder." After a few months Calvin "became disgusted with my teacher & place of boarding, & left for Randolph some 20 miles North West." There he encountered a more reputable school whose teacher, Rufus Nutting, taught him English grammar and Latin. Unfortunately, Nutting initially made a spectacle of Calvin, exhibiting him to the other students "as a specimen of a poorly taught boy at a rival school." Calvin himself wrote, "I was excessively dull & much discouraged & came near leaving but Nutting thro another pupil gave me to understand that I should no longer be made a subject of exhibition on account of want of knowledge in what I had supposed I had learned at Royalton." At Randolph Calvin spent half his time attending school and the other half working. In December 1816 he made a brief return to Ludlow to study with a distant kinsman, Horace Fletcher, before leaving again in February for Westford, Massachusetts, to board with his "uncle" Joseph Fletcher (they were not related, but Joseph was referred to by that title) while going to school there.[8]

Calvin Fletcher, ca. 1832

Now nineteen, two years out from his fateful departure from Ludlow, Calvin realized that his seemingly random odyssey of cobbling together various jobs and studies at school thus far suggested no discernible direction or meaning. Indeed, for the first time, two years to the day of his initial leave-taking, he sat down in Westford and unburdened himself to his parents back home: "I have no particular place of destination determined as yet," he conceded, "but think I then shall go to the Southward." By "Southward" he meant in the direction of Boston. Beyond that simple geographical direction, his plans were foggy; furthermore, he was distressingly short on funds: "I shall be under the necessity to start with but very little money; the thought of it gives me a very disagreeable sensation and it pictures much hardship to me in the journey I have proposed to myself." Such a near-penniless condition, he sensed, rendered his meager plans even less appealing. "This undertaking I am feared will not meet your approbation," he told his parents. Then, in a poignant closing, Calvin, clearly looking for help and guidance, revealed he had become a bit desperate: "I should be happy to consult your opinion about it; I feel to want a Father's advise."[9]

We don't know if Jesse Fletcher Sr. responded to Calvin's thinly disguised plea for help, but if he did, it did not materially affect Calvin's plan, such as it was. Calvin left Westford "destitute of money and in debt three dollars." Before taking off, he managed to borrow $7.50 from his uncle Isaac Patten, giving him a total of $14.50, which he wisely predicted "would not carry me through" to Albany, New York, where he intended to stay with his brother Michael. So he sold his trunk and dictionary for another $5 and bought some bread and milk in exchange for "a skein of silk and four needles." On April 30 he left his uncle Joseph Fletcher's house, where he had stayed the previous eight weeks, but he "did not part with Shagrin" and proceeded to "Uncle Deacon's" to stay overnight.[10]

By this point, Calvin had settled on pursuing "a seaman's life," and in April 1817 he headed to Boston, "a total stranger, and tried my best to obtain a berth on board an East-Indiaman, but failed." Two weeks later he was trading his mittens for a knapsack to use as luggage for carrying his clothes. The children of Samuel Fletcher carried him via buggy six miles to Harvard, then on to Worcester—thirty-five miles farther. There, on May 2, Calvin wrote, "I fell in company with a young man from Maine." They walked to Connecticut, eventually arriving in Hartford. "I calculated to go from there across to Staatsburgh which was 80 miles; but my feet were very much swollen and blistered so that I was not able to walk," Calvin told his parents.[11]

Weary from walking, he decided to travel by water. He took a sloop to New York at a cost of $1.25 (leaving him $7.25). He journeyed through Meriden and Wallingford, arriving at 5:00 p.m. in New Haven, where he paid $2.50 to take a packet scheduled to sail for New York at 10:00 p.m. "I underwent a great fear that I should be seasick," he noted. When he awoke the next morning he discovered to his surprise that the boat hadn't left the harbor but that he could see the town in full view. As they sailed away with a good wind, they passed Long Island, where he witnessed "the most butiful farms that ever I beheld." Once they anchored in New York, Calvin walked around the city with a young man from Connecticut. In what was a common bit of serendipitous planning, he and his newfound friend "calculated to go to Philadelphia together." They left New York late the next morning and traveled to New Jersey, where his friend "was taken unwell and could not travel." So Calvin moved on without him, traveling twenty-eight miles and eventually putting up at a "Dutch Tavern." The next day he went to New Brunswick (a distance of fourteen miles), "a very flourishing place and a handsome Colledge." There he got on a stage, traveling with two French "gentlemen" who were also headed south. For the next six miles, "they asked many questions which I answered," he wrote his parents. "They wanted to know what I would drink. I refused to take anything, told them I did not drink any liquor. They went [and] got a mug of Cider. I drank as much as I could of it." They arrived the next day in Philadelphia with only a few pennies left.[12]

Where was Calvin headed? To the southwest region of Pennsylvania. "Here you will perhaps wonder what should induce me to go there," he noted in his diary. Ironically, or perhaps predictably, he was following his brother Elijah's strategy, mingled with his own random connections. As he recounted, he had met two young men in Connecticut returning from southwestern Pennsylvania who "had been teaching schools there and gave me great encouragements to go there, together with some recommendations to a gentleman." So Calvin stopped at a tavern, changed clothes, and set out after the two men. They were a Mr. Hall and his cousin, John Patten, who had moved to New Glasgow, Virginia, and then to Lynchburg, marrying into the same Crawford family as Calvin's brother Elijah. Patten promised to return, quite possibly with Elijah himself, who, he told Calvin, would be arriving in Philadelphia in four to five days. Excited and encouraged by the prospect of seeing his brother soon, Calvin returned to the tavern, where another chance meeting, this time with a "Quaker gentleman," led to an act of welcome generosity. The unnamed Quaker, "whom nothing but the loss of reason will ever obliterate from my mind," spent the day seeing the city with Calvin and directed him to a much better, safer place to stay. Where Calvin was boarding, his Quaker friend informed him, "was a very bad Tavern . . . very dear and did not keep good company . . . He sayd 'If thou will go with me to a Tavern (and the Landlord of which is a friend of mine) thou shall be welcome to stay one or two weeks and rest thy self and if thou are in want of any thing, ask me."[13]

Having found safe lodgings and helpful guidance about teaching prospects from his entirely random connections in Philadelphia, Calvin finagled the final piece of his game plan. Stephen Steward, a "gentleman" who was a fellow New Englander from Walpole, New Hampshire, and an acquaintance of the Fletcher family, gave Calvin a letter of recommendation signed by a local doctor, Gilbert Flagler, and another well-to-do person, John Moulson. Recommendations were the ticket to respectability and connections for young men like Calvin Fletcher, on the make in a strange place without family or close friends. Steward's note suggests that Calvin had successfully dropped the names of his brother's prominent Virginia connections and his own father's status back in Vermont: Steward refers to Calvin as "a young man with whom I am acquainted and particularly with his parents and near connections" and states that "from such acquaintances [I] have no hesitation in recommending him to the public as a moral, industrious worthy young man, and deserving the patronage and encouragement of his countrymen. His business is teaching the various branches of literature, and from his untarnished Reputation [I] believe him well qualified to give the utmost satisfaction as a Teacher."[14]

Calvin's hoped-for rendezvous with his brother Elijah, as it turned out, never happened: Elijah did not arrive in Philadelphia until early July, a full six weeks later than he had predicted. While searching for Calvin, Elijah voiced concern that he "could get no particular information on Calvin's situation." But he ran into Steward, who told him that Calvin had been in the company of a Quaker "who seemed to be particularly attached to him" and had even offered him a small teaching job, which Calvin had declined as "not an object sufficient for him to stay for" in the city. Elijah took special comfort, though, in his friend's assessment that Calvin had seemed "in good heart and good spirits" and "seemed to have money and not be in any want." Particularly hopeful was Steward's report of Calvin's "happy faculty of forming acquaintances and making friends," which ensured that almost everyone "seemed to take an interest in his welfare."[15]

With Steward's letter in hand, Calvin now possessed what he needed to enlist the support of prospective employers in his current "business" of teaching. On May 22, the very next day after getting the recommendation, he headed southwest, hoping to find some kind of gainful employment. The first day he made it to Abbottstown, one hundred miles from Philadelphia, where he stayed a week or two working in a brickyard. "I was drove to this by Poverty," he acknowledged. Yet another chance meeting with a young man from Connecticut who was himself headed to Ohio gave Calvin a traveling companion and other prospects. "He was anxious for me to go and I was glad to get away from high Dutch," Calvin wrote his parents. "They could not talk a word of English where I worked and lived worse than Canibals of New Zealand." Foot, Calvin's new friend, was planning on buying land and had "considerable money and was afraid of being robbed," a common problem for unsuspecting young men crossing the Allegheny Mountains. So on June 2, 1817, Calvin and Foot took off on a most uncertain trek across the mountains. "There . . . I could picture a Catelogue of Disagreeable scenes we went through in traveling 250 miles among a most inhumane set of beings," Calvin reported to his parents. By the time they crossed the mountains, Calvin had run out of money and explained to Foot he couldn't go any farther. Foot replied that if Calvin would continue on with him, "he would let me have what I wanted by paying him when I could earn it."[16]

Seizing on a good deal when he saw one, Calvin went with him to Wheeling, West Virginia, and from there by boat to Cincinnati, arriving on June 10. From Cincinnati, Calvin intended to journey with Foot as far as Dayton, "but Providentially he [Foot] was taken to Urbana, Ohio." So there, providentially, Calvin settled. Urbana was a recently settled frontier town of perhaps five to six hundred people at the time. Founded in 1805, it became the county seat and, thanks to the War of 1812, prospered when it was turned into a military camp during the conflict. Calvin began boarding with a Mr. Hunter on June 25, reporting to his parents that he was "living at a little dirty tavern" in Urbana. Ten days later he began teaching school. He had thirty scholars, about half of them "men grown," and was paid $2.50 per quarter. For a while he boarded with the Joseph Hill family, who lived five miles out of town. One of his first pupils was Joseph Hill's oldest child, Sarah, who was fifteen at the time. A small, slender girl, very modest by nature, Sarah caught his eye and a mutual flirtation began.[17]

From his newly settled perch in Urbana, Calvin allowed himself to look back at his peripatetic journeying: "I have been Traveling ever since I wrote you at Westford," he told his father, "at which you may be astonished for it exceeds all premeditated calculations of my own; and I look with amazement on the distance I have conveyed myself from my Parents and Friends."[18]

Finally in possession of something more secure than an uncertain day job, Calvin dove into his teaching responsibilities the only way he knew how: with total devotion and perhaps an excessive degree of seriousness. At first, he was not at all sure he was cut out to be a teacher. He told his father in January 1818 that "school-keeping" might well be "an honorable employment . . . but it is the most fatiguing and wearing to the constitution of those who dislike it of any employment whatever. I have not met with any difficulty as yet nor fear none, except they complain I am too rigid and strict."[19]

It didn't help matters that the previous teacher at Urbana had been a very successful, popular Methodist, which left Calvin feeling "timid" about trying to follow in his footsteps. So he paid a visit to his personable predecessor, made friends with him, and determined never to speak ill of him, "though the scholars who have left him & come to me would frequently tell me of his partiality, negligence, &c. But to them I have always turned a Deaf Ear." Apparently, Calvin's non-provocative, get-along spirit aided him in acquiring a respectable reputation among the students. "It is not my disposition to have unprofitable controversies & people must try some more noble means to hurt my feelings, than to report a thing about me that I am not guilty of," he wrote his father. Soon he was teaching a full school of forty-three scholars, and most everyone seemed "cordial" to him: "They meet me with smiles in their faces & appear to be happy in my company."[20]

By November 1817, he had begun using his time away from teaching to read law with the prominent Urbana attorney James Cooley. Cooley clearly served as a role model, even a father figure, for Fletcher as he informally tutored him in not only matters of the law but also how to get along in the world. "He uses me like [a] friend and confident," Calvin fondly remembered. "He uses no bad Language nor descends to no small intreagues." Working with Cooley—and eventually boarding with him—soon became his main focus and hope for the future, especially in his ongoing effort to fully and permanently separate from his family and life back in Ludlow. "I have no desire to return to Vt.," Calvin claimed. "Though I frequently draw involuntary sighs when I think of home!"[21]

He probably had little time to think of home, given the time-consuming regimen he applied to his studies and his teaching. Calvin kept school for six hours a day and studied an hour at noon, plus another four hours each evening, going to bed at 11:00 p.m. every night and rising no later than 5:00 a.m. All this discipline, he insisted, grew out of feelings of inadequacy and the need to advance himself quickly. "I feel very avaritious of my time," he wrote his father in November 1818. And then, in a passage that had to have felt painfully honest—both about his own weakness and about his father's failure to guide him—he confessed: "I find myself extremely ignorant. I shudder at recollecting how I left home. I was but a mere helpless infant! I mourn that it was not my fortune to have got a liberal education. I think it would have made me a man."[22]

Though he was clearly struggling to stay afloat, Calvin nevertheless felt sufficiently confident to offer employment advice to his older brother Stephen. Like Calvin, Stephen was considering leaving home to make a go of things in the west. At twenty-four, Stephen was contemplating a move to New Orleans by way of Cincinnati. To Calvin, this was an unpromising game plan. Better to follow his younger brother to Urbana. "I fear you will not get business in Cincinnati and to start for New Orleans at this time of year looks despicable," he wrote Stephen in January 1818. "I again intreat you to come to Urbana if nothing more favourable offers. I have made some inquiries relative to getting business here as a clerk. I think you would succeed but wages are small and cash is call'd scarce."[23] Stephen never received his younger brother's advice: the letter, addressed to him in Cincinnati, was returned to Calvin undeliverable. As it turned out, Stephen unfortunately followed his own advice and made his way to New Orleans, where he died from a fever in August of that year.

Calvin's highly disciplined path toward success and achievement did include occasional diversions. He continued an intermittent courtship with Sarah Hill, even as he moved about boarding in various homes. And frontier life in Urbana offered a picturesque—and sometimes violent—reprieve from his focus on teaching and reading law. He attended community harvests where he witnessed farmers consuming "a great deal of whiskey" and often getting into fights. "The Kentuckyans & Virginians frequently have a piched Battle between each other. Dueling is strictly prohibited in this state," he noted, referring to a statutory penalty of seven years in prison, "but this does not entirely prevent it."[24] Urbana's crude political discourse likewise prompted angry outbursts that made a powerful and lasting impression on the young man. "Political animosity" reached such intensity in the local elections that "some hot headed fellows dispute all night. Men of the most unexceptionable characters were not exempt from slander." Calvin witnessed several mobs that had to be taken down by local authorities. In one such group, "one man got his thumb bit off and another his eye much damaged." Calvin couldn't resist reporting on the odd—and, to his eyes, degrading—rituals of frontier masculinity: "When two men fight as ever they clinch they fall to biting and gougeing. I have witness'd several of these scenes of human depravity which at first made my blood freeze in my veins." Religion didn't provide much relief from the crude, violent world all around him. Despite being brought up in a highly moral Congregational family, Calvin did not seem drawn at this point to religious life, mostly because he found the same scandalous frontier behavior in church that was on daily display in society and politics. "I do not hardly ever [at]tend church, for which I feel justified, as the ministers are uncouth, low bread Methodists whom I despise," he wrote his father. "I generally retire to the office where I spend the day in solitude."[25]

That solitude sparked the desire for a more professional life than he had found in teaching. After eighteen months at the academy, Calvin decided to move on to more substantial prospects by trying to become a lawyer. When he took leave of his Urbana school in March 1819, he did so believing he had acquitted himself quite well and, having earned $125, clear of all expenses. He was offered $575 a year to continue teaching, but he turned it down: "Money is no temptation," he told his father, "tho I never spent a cent, as I know of, needlessly. I do not value it in comparison with my Time no more than the sods I walk on." He left the academy with a sense of pride in having taught all the "widows, sons and Daughters—orphans" who couldn't afford the tuition but whom he had tutored for free.[26]

After settling his accounts in Urbana, Calvin traveled to Cincinnati, a growing city that impressed him greatly. It was April and the trees were in bloom. The Ohio River was "lined with Steam boats, flatt Bottoms &c." No longer impoverished or a wanderer, he already detected a difference in his new stature. "When I enterd Cincinnati I felt very different from the time I left it in 1817, at which time I was pennyless and without friends or acquaintance," he told his father. "I attended the auction—bought myself $30.00 worth of books that I have since had brought on." A week later he rode his horse to London, Ohio, where he settled into the home of Thomas Gwynne. A thirty-three-year-old former sea captain who had moved from Maryland to Ohio, Gwynne owned a store in Urbana as well as one in London. Over the next couple of months, Calvin shared the house with Gwynne and his six children, "five of them . . . confin'd with me six hours in a day"; the rest of the time he devoted to his ongoing study of the law. He had a horse at his disposal and would return to nearby Urbana to recite his legal lessons to Cooley. For his part, Cooley applauded Calvin for his "conduct" and progress, offering him the use of his books and "all other privileges" for a $1 fee.[27] With Cooley and Sarah Hill in Urbana, Calvin expected to return to the small frontier town before long, but by late spring he had become ill and was confined to the Gwynne house. According to those who saw him in this period, Calvin "had become a mere skeleton" from overwork, and "his physicians thought a ride would help him."[28]

Calvin's frailty and the uncertainty of his life in Ohio prompted concern in Elijah, who understood all too well that a young man like Calvin needed a guiding hand to find a respectable place in the world. Elijah begged Calvin to come to Virginia to complete his legal studies. "I thought he was sacrificing precious time and that he ought to have an opportunity better than he could get in Ohio," Elijah wrote his father. In corresponding with Calvin and Cooley, Elijah determined that his brother "was very promising and only wanted an opportunity to make a distinguished man." So Elijah advised him to "buy himself a horse, settle up his affairs . . . and leave the wild woods & uncultivated society" of Ohio to establish himself in the more civilized world of plantation Virginia, where "he should have every opportunity of Books & Instruction." In Elijah's view, Calvin was living in a cultural wasteland where "his opportunities for Books was so bad that Calvin told him he had read thro one Book eighteen times." In Virginia, Elijah argued, Calvin "would have an opportunity of seeing more of men & manners, and when he completes his education he may return to any part of the western country he prefers to settle in."[29]

In June 1820, Calvin took Elijah's advice, bought a horse, left behind his mentor James Cooley and the Hill family, most notably Sarah, and moved to the slave South. When he arrived in Lynchburg that summer, he was almost unrecognizable. "I have the pleasure of informing you," Elijah wrote his father, "that Calvin is now with us . . . He introduced himself to me, for I should have no more known him than the greatest stranger in the world." Brother Timothy, who was also living in Lynchburg, likewise didn't recognize him. As if assessing a newly discovered brother, Elijah speculated on who Calvin resembled in the family: no one, he concluded, except their brother Michael, of whom he was "the very picture": "Low, stout-built, broad-shouldered, but rather thin at present, tho he has perfectly restored his health." As to his mind and heart, there was no question: "He has disciplined his mind to a good code of morality. He has the most tender and delicate feelings . . . He is like a sensitive plant. Take Calvin all in all I think him a son you may be proud of."[30]

While Calvin's health improved during his stay in Virginia—Elijah noted that he "eats a good allowance, rather inclined to be fat"—he clearly found the culture inhospitable, especially the pervasive presence of chattel slavery. Elijah was by now an established, well-to-do plantation owner with numerous slaves, both house servants and field slaves, on various farms. Raised in a strong antislavery tradition in New England, Calvin doubtless felt no small degree of revulsion witnessing his brother's new domineering attitude toward an entire race of people. Before the summer's end, then, he was already plotting another leave-taking, this time back to Ohio. Elijah offered Jesse Sr. a benevolent, detached account of his brother's unhappiness in the slave South: "He thinks of returning to the Western Country some time first of Nov. next. He will get a License to practice Law first. I shall be sorry to part from him."[31]

Elijah was only half right: Calvin never received a license to practice law in Virginia, but he did return to Urbana in November 1820. Immediately upon arrival, Calvin proposed a law partnership with his former mentor, James Cooley, who accepted the arrangement. Right away, he discovered he was "extremely ignorant in the practice" of the law, despite the "confidence in me" Cooley projected. "I therefore feel extremely anxious not to disappoint him," Calvin recorded in his diary. Early on, he recognized that he would be facing "many combats with my ignorance" of legal matters. "The lawyers do not appear to manifest the least degree of friendship towards the young and rising."[32]

Calvin's first case involved a dog. "I was not prepared to say any thing of consequence. I was not so very much affrighted as vacant—yet I felt a little intimidated with fear," he wrote. And now that he was beginning a professional life as a lawyer, he had to ride the circuit, which in the sparsely populated American West meant that he had to travel at least once a month to county courts throughout central Indiana. Traveling by horse over roads rendered impassable in winter and choked with dust in the summer, Calvin and other circuit riders carried their law libraries in their saddlebags and re-hearsed their anecdotes and speeches on each other as they bounced along from one court to another. Circuit riding proved a primitive experience— "the inhabitants extremely rough," Calvin noted in his diary—and the temporary quarters unexpectedly intimate. Lodged in one of the four log cabins in the county seat of Bellefontaine, for example, Calvin ended up sleeping in the same bed as a leading barrister, O. Parish, while two other lawyers played cards. At midnight, Parish asked for something to eat, and the men "had bread and cheese."[33] The next morning Calvin rode his horse across frozen snow back home to Urbana, but was overtaken by Parish, who talked him into swapping horses. At first, Calvin agreed to the swap, but by the time he got home he concluded that he "had got cheated."[34]

Calvin continued to be plagued by feelings of inferiority and ill-preparedness in the courtroom, which he attributed to his incomplete for-mal education growing up. "I found myself very incapable in my profession as a Lawyer," he admitted. "I find myself very ignorant of the world and destitute of that fund of book knowledge that is necessary for to acquit my-self with honor and eclat at the bar."[35]

Even as he blamed much of his early failure on his crude upbringing, Calvin began to look upon his Vermont origins a bit more charitably and promised himself a visit back to his "native state in two years." "I now be-gin to look with a more philosophic eye on my past misfortunes," he re-flected. "I can't but desire once more to clasp the hand of my aged parents who will both soon yield to the rude and corroding movements of time. I then with them can see the improvements made on my younger Brother and sister and I hope many new affections would arise I feel not."[36]

In the meantime, Calvin tried to reach out and make friends in the little community of rising young men of Urbana. He joined a local debating society, in which he "enjoyed [him]self very well," but, as would often be the case during his life, his unyielding obsession with self-improvement and hard work left him intolerant of free-spirited youth. "I saw in it much talk and but very little reason," he noted. "In this society I cannot expect to make great improvements as there requires but a very trifling exertion." But he was becoming "intimate" with several prominent families in Urbana—the Gwynnes, with whom he boarded, among others—despite what would become a near-lifelong struggle with self-doubt: "I am yet under some apprehensions that I shall not do right and shall neglect to do my duty," he acknowledged.[37]

Amid his expanding connections and personal growth, Calvin Fletcher felt like something was missing. Though he now had a purpose—he had fully embarked on a legal career that clearly focused his energies, he was sufficiently sociable to connect with other like-minded folks in the community, and he was beginning to acquire a good reputation as a young man on the make—he still experienced an inner sadness, an incompleteness that demanded attention. Calvin needed a partner, a "helpmeet" in life. And he approached the resolution of that need with consummate conviction, just as he had done with his limited education and legal training. After returning from church one Sunday in December 1820, he announced his strategy: "I returned home with a resolution to prosecute a certain project which I am *determined to commence as soon as possible and shall do it with as much dexterity as I possibly can*," he recorded in his diary. His object was Sarah Hill, his former student at the academy. His "project" was to win her hand in matrimony, even if defeat loomed as large as success. "*I may be defeated yet I know I am in truth able to bear such a defeat*," he wrote. "*I do not know the time I shall ever be more able to effect this or a like project. I shall commence next Sunday. I will see what progress I make in one month from this. I may say I was foolish—but I can say I have done greater feats within one year than what this would be if accomplished*."[38]

And he did. Four days later, Calvin admitted to feeling "very much depressed," confessing, "I am rather uneasy—cannot but believe that if I were married I should be contented." Though worried that he was "perhaps reaching forward for a scorpean instead of a lamb," he focused on his strategy: "I this night found another theory—that is to educate [Sarah Hill] and then * * * * * * * * * * By this plan I have thought I should be able [to] keep alive ambition, cherish virtue and make myself known." He realized he could spend "one or two years preparing" for this event, but confessed, "I shall like to be precipitate."[39]

So on Christmas Day, Calvin went to Mr. Hill's to visit Sarah and lay out his plan. "I had some talk with her on the road upon the subject" of marriage, he wrote in his diary. Restless but energized, Calvin went to a concert and a party (where, he noted, he "was persuaded to dance") and spent the rest of the week "walking up and down the streets."[40]

A few days later, after attending church in the evening, he went to a friend's house with Sarah, where he once again sat up until late in the evening and talked with her "on the former subject" of matrimony. Although he attended a New Year's Day party where he again "danced several times" and met "two ladies," his focus remained on Sarah and their hopeful future: "I am now about to make a decision on what I shall do—yet Pride has a very great influence, Poverty some considerable, and other objections I shall not mention," he reflected.[41]

Pronouncing himself "rather discontented" out of a "fear that I shall not perform the functions prescribed for me to fulfill," Calvin attended a friend's wedding one late winter evening that galvanized his feelings about marriage into action. "The Nuptials were celebrated . . . in a very solemn and grave style. I never till then was impressed with the solemnity of the marriage contract," he wrote in his diary. Perhaps more to the point, "Miss Hill was present at the celebration of these marriage rights," and "for her," wrote Calvin, "I have a very great esteem." Furthermore, he had "good and sufficient proofs" that this "esteem" was reciprocated. Trouble was, he feared, she might not be the right person for such a "rising" man to marry. "She is poor and without Education," Calvin bluntly conceded. But was she not "amiable notwithstanding all those defects"? Besides, wouldn't it do him and his reputation good "to rescue the victim" from life's two "maladies, ignorance and poverty"?[42]

Unlike Calvin's perception of the courtship as an agonizing odyssey, Sarah viewed her relationship with Calvin as a natural and mutually affectionate path from first contact to marriage. From the moment she became his fifteen-year-old pupil, there was a clear attraction between them based, perhaps oddly, on his serious demeanor and bouts of depression: "I had a strong attachment for him which originated mutch from the melancholy & studious habits he then possess'd and I am pleased to state that our affection for each other was mutual and continued so till it was consummated in marriage," she later wrote her sister-in-law Louisa.[43]

Clearly struggling over Sarah's perceived liabilities and his own uncertainties, Calvin gave thought to looking elsewhere for a "helpmeet" in life. His nights partying and dancing with other, more attractive, young ladies influenced his thinking and introduced the idea of "abandoning" Sarah. He had to acknowledge that Sarah "perhaps was not the most beautiful" woman he had met, but he praised her for being "the most modest." After some "new reflections on the proceedings," he finally concluded, "I would make and fix my choice on *her* permanently." A few days later, on February 2, he put his plan into action: "I mounted my horse and without much excitement I rode with careless steps and slow across the river thro' mud to be the herald of my own intentions. I arrived about dark. A room was prepared. I there had an interview with the object of my desire—and to her I disclosed my intentions I presume to her surprise." The next morning he revealed his intentions to her parents as well and received their approval "without hesitation."[44]

On Calvin Fletcher's twenty-third birthday, February 4, 1821, he composed an "essay on my agreement to be married," a deliberate self-assessment aimed at proving (both to himself and to anyone who he imagined would eventually read his diary) that he was entering into marriage fully sensible of all its attractions and all the "disadvantages under which [he] labor[ed]." Waxing philosophical, Calvin insisted that affection and friendship were the foundation of "respectable, useful, and happy" men. And no one was better suited to "bind" men to that "spot" of friendship and esteem than "a *wife,* a helpmeet for man." But once again, he stumbled over the issue of poverty—his own and Sarah's: "I am poor—can I take a person into poverty? Can I find one that is willing to enter into poverty and run the risk of being delivered therefrom by my exertion?"[45]

Calvin continued to fret. What was worse, he was obviously confronting two personal issues at once: whom he should marry and how that choice would affect his evolving professional and reputational future. As he frequently noted, "I am poor and ignorant of my profession, which are both obstacles to my marrying." Adding urgency and worry to his decision was the nagging concern that an unwise or "precipitate" marriage might hinder his professional ambitions. "It is said by my friends that I cannot obtain any eminence in my profession if I now marry," he noted, an observation that he stated, "I cannot dispute." But he decided to let the chips fall where they may. Even though, he acknowledged, he had "much to do to attain any eminence in my profession," and the very idea of "droop[ing] in the grades of mediocrity is painful to me," Calvin decided to take this apparently controversial marital choice and turn it into a personal virtue: by helping lift Sarah out of her own weaknesses through marriage, he would in the end rise in the world's opinion. "I think I shall applaude myself hereafter should I bear one who is destitute thro' the ocean of troubles which beset us in this world," he reflected. Life was all about struggle, perseverance, and virtue, so perhaps marrying this poorly educated, impoverished woman offered just the right virtuous challenge. "I am sensible that if I ever wish to attain any worthy honors in my profession they must come thro' the medium of application, integrity and virtue," Calvin noted. "Let me pursue. Let me reach forward."[46]

But he had one final obstacle—convincing his mentor and father figure, James Cooley, that he was making the right choice. It clearly bothered him to know that Cooley, whom he described as "one that I do not like to thwart in opinion," was "rather opposed" to his "project of marriage." On March 28, 1821, Calvin noted in his diary, "I laid my intentions before Mr.

C[ooley] as to my getting married. He at first rather disapproved of it but I got his consent by rather insisting upon the necessity than otherwise of the case. He intimated to me the disadvantages that would arise from my marrying a poor girl and one of low parentage. But this I am determined shall not be an obstacle."[47]

Much of Fletcher's hand-wringing and self-justifications were nothing more than a young man's commonplace eleventh-hour worry over taking such a big step as marriage presented. But for Calvin, marrying Sarah represented a huge challenge and threat to his emotional stability in the midst of palpable financial need and youthful incompetence in his career. "I sleep without dreaming," he acknowledged, which struck him as a worrisome indication of an excessively "tranquil mind"—proof that maybe he was headed toward "negligence and inattention to the most important events" all around him. So he tried bucking himself up: "Awake, arise," he wrote. "Now is the time for mental exertions and acquisitions . . . I feel ambitious to acquit myself at least with decency in my first sally into the world as a public character."[48]

Having agonized and doubted long enough, he began making final preparations for the wedding he had set for May 1. On his wedding eve, he approached the coming event with "some degree of solemnity": "I know it is one of the most momentous events in my life," he wrote in his diary. "I hope it is the only one of the kind that I shall pass thro'. I am now twenty three years old—commencing a life which requires the performance of all the functions of a real citizen." As he would do for the rest of his life, Calvin merged his leave-taking from Ludlow as a seventeen-year-old with his wedding day in a fictively single anniversary date of May 1 (he had actually left Ludlow on April 11). "This night and tomorrow are two memorable days in my life," he wrote. "Four years from tomorrow I left my friends in New England. I started I think into the world then as I am now starting into the marriage state."[49]

It was a start fueled equally by hope and doubt. "I hope as a married man that I shall pursue the paths of rectitude and virtue," he claimed, "that nothing shall be said of me that will be a reproach to my former life which I now declare has been upright in my intentions. I have chosen the companion of my heart. May it be my happy lot to sustain her through the mazes of a terestial world. May it be my fortune to bring to light hidden excellence of personal goodness."⁵⁰ But his doubts about his own professional standing as well as about Sarah's ignorance and their poverty persisted well into the early years of their marriage.

For the wedding ceremony he had previously arranged with his new bride that outside of her immediate family neither her friends and relatives nor his own would be invited. So when Calvin rode up to Mr. Hill's home at 1:00 p.m. on May 1 he was taken aback when he found "a few country chaps collected for the purpose of being forward at the celebration of the marriage." But he relented and let go of his concerns. "I was received by smiles by the family," he recorded. At 3:00 p.m. the minister arrived and "had a conference" with Calvin, and then they went into the "chamber" to wait on Sarah. When she entered and walked to the makeshift altar, Calvin sensed that she was "rather disconcerted and affrighted." But he took her by the hand and the ceremony went off without incident. Later that evening, though, he noted that things did not go so well, suggesting some sexual problems: "I spent the evening not very pleasantly but I was uneasy." The couple left the next day and moved into James Gwynne's home, where there was a belated reception with "a few choice friends."⁵¹

Given Calvin's condescending view of Sarah's intellect and social status, it is perhaps unsurprising that he treated her as a work in progress. For himself, he planned high-minded pursuits: he employed a young boy to live with them that summer so that, he wrote, "I need not make a slave of myself and family for I know now is the time I ought to devote my hours to literary pursuits."⁵² When it came to Sarah, he watched over her like a kindly schoolteacher, "feeling desireous to improve a person in whose welfare I take as great an interest as I do in my own."⁵³ Upon finding Sarah alone one day, Calvin sat down with her for a few minutes and listened to her go through her grammar lesson. "She complains of a bad memory which I think has never been cultivated & how can the prairie bring forth any thing but wild flowers till it [is] cultivated by the careful hand of man?" he wrote in his diary. In a more benevolent spirit, he acknowledged that Sarah possessed considerable potential: "For a mind in a state of nature I never have seen one that I thought bid fairer for a fertile garden than hers." But initially Sarah rebelled at all the self-improving watchfulness that Calvin created. She was clearly discouraged, he noted, "and wishes to drag out the remainder of her too precious life to me in ignorance & obscurity which thought is a piercing goard to me."[54] But lifting his new bride out of her presumed ignorance remained critical to Calvin, and he persevered.

If Calvin's courtship of Sarah Hill played out like a methodical, well-conceived plan, less than a month into his marriage his world nearly collapsed in disarray when a dangerous, emotionally wrenching allegation surfaced. On May 26, 1821, he confided in his diary that "a circumstance . . . has occurred, one more painful than any in my life." A young black servant girl who had lived at his friend Gwynne's house during the time Calvin boarded there announced that she was pregnant by Calvin. The truth, according to Calvin, was that this claim had been made as early as late April, when he was still living at Gwynne's. "I let the report pass without saying much," Calvin wrote in his diary. "After I got married the report still continued to be current and was suggested as being the cause of my precipitate marriage. * * * * * I let it pass till this morning—when to my surprise L.G. [Llewellyn Gwynne] told me that the girl had told his mother that I had been the instrument of her pregnancy!!!!!" Acknowledging the obvious, Calvin conceded, "I feel something agitated at present—I think the declaration of the girl will tend to injure me very much in the estimation of the family."[55]

And so he leapt into action, calling on his friend Tom Gwynne to look into the girl's accusation. "I hardly thought he credited it in as much as what she had stated respecting the time of her conception did not correspond with her looks on Sunday," he wrote. "I kept still—my friends as well as myself were a little agitated." The next day Calvin visited Mrs. Gwynne and, he recorded, "I there saw the girl. She kept at a distance." That evening he spoke with Tom Gwynne, who conveyed the belief that their mutual acquaintance, Sam McCord, was "an instrument for the propagation of the diabolical charge." Tom, Calvin wrote, "also told me I might make an experiment by fright to elicit the truth from her." Before he could formulate his plan of intimidation, Calvin learned that "Cresy"—the only reference to the servant girl's name—had just packed up her clothes and cleared out of the Gwynne household. So, upon the advice of Tom Gwynne, Calvin followed the girl but couldn't find her. He then rounded up two other friends, and, he noted, "we scoured every negro house in town. I broke into one where I was refused admittance. I at length found her at Simon's. She utterly refused charging me with it but refused being with any person whatever." Calvin grabbed the whip from his friends and, as he wrote in his diary,

> I chastised her in a very severe manner without any compassion for which, considering her forward state of pregnancy I may perhaps feel a degree of remorse and I already cannot but shed a tear of regret at the frailty of her own sex and am now of an opinion that but a very few women are the fit companion of a Philosopher. She at length confessed that Col. Flourny of Columbus had been the villain who had put her up to make this report about me. I left her then.[56]

Calvin's vengeful mission was not over. The next morning, after hearing reports "about what had happened as coming from McCord," he resolved "to have some satisfaction." He demanded McCord come to his office. When he did, Calvin "charged him with the baseness of his conduct," triggering a violent response: "He gave me some insulting language. Accordingly, I attacked him and have full faith to believe that I should have whipped him if I had not been prevented." Calvin came away from the confrontation feeling vindicated and empowered, claiming, "I will fight whenever I am insulted."[57]

Unsurprisingly, there is no evidence that Calvin ever revealed to Sarah (or anyone in his family) anything about this allegation involving "Cresy." As to his guilt or innocence in the matter, there is no way to know for sure. But to be fair, it seems out of character, given his normally careful personal behavior and his otherwise high regard for African Americans (unusually high for this era in American history), that he would have been the father. While it may well be true that it was another man who was responsible for the pregnancy, Calvin's violent conduct toward "Cresy" showcases a regrettably arrogant attitude, not only in his physical act of intimidation but also in his smug conclusion that the whole episode proved that "very few women are the fit companion of a Philosopher."[58]

Ironically—or perhaps in direct consequence of this misadventure—Calvin made a point in a July court case of standing up for black defendants. While the state's supreme court judges were in town, Calvin took the opportunity of speaking out for the often-neglected people: "I made a speech in favor of bringing Black & mulatto persons to Justice . . . by which I done myself perhaps a little credit," he recorded in his diary. His performance, though, left him wondering about his youthful, uncertain status: "I cannot yet reason as I should like. I have not a sufficient acquaintance with mankind in general to possess a reasonable degree of confidence [in as much as I am] conscious of my own ignorance."[59]

Now a married man and "a real citizen" with a legal career to nurture, Calvin Fletcher searched in earnest for a place to launch his new life with Sarah. Urbana had been his home away from home, a critical training ground for teaching school, studying the law, and making connections, but he needed a bigger stage to establish his reputation, to make his mark. And again, he looked west. In early August he made a trip to Indianapolis, which had just been settled and was in the early 1820s a town of about five hundred people. After viewing this "new seat of government," he returned "well satisfied" with its prospects. On September 19, 1821, Calvin and Sarah left Urbana for Indianapolis.

It was not an easy trip, especially for Sarah, who was leaving behind her family. Parting from her young sisters, she told an Urbana friend, "was the most grievous trial I ever met with."[60] The wagon loaded with their belongings took off in the morning, and Sarah followed later on horseback. Such a journey through central Indiana in the early 1820s was difficult at best. Indiana's so-called roads were in very poor condition, as they were little more than blazed trails through the forests. Settlers wielding axes cut away and removed enough of the trees and logs so sturdy wagons could slowly make their way over roads that usually followed old Indian and animal trails; most personal travel was limited to foot or horse. Frequently, even on "cleared" roads, tree stumps projected twelve inches above the ground. Travelers, bumping along the roads in wagons with no springs in their seats, had to dodge miles of mud holes and stumps. Mosquitoes, bad water, and infrequent and poorly provisioned public houses (taverns) along the way only worsened the traveling experience. Sarah's account, via letters to her father and friends back in Urbana, of the agonizing eleven-day journey to Indianapolis give voice to the struggles of the trip. "We proceeded with much difficulty to this place," she wrote. "The fatigues were much greater than I could have imagined, therefore would advise every body who have a good situation in Ohio, to be contented . . . We were travelling two days while it rained thro' the wilderness." Having to rough it camping out in the woods several nights, she noted, "prepared me excellently well to be contented with the modest cabin" the pair could afford in Indianapolis.[61]

When they arrived in Indianapolis on October 1, the weather was raw and cold with a high wind. The town was crowded with strangers from all over who had come to settle in Indianapolis or to secure property. The town's three taverns overflowed with settlers, prompting residents to share their homes with the newcomers until the latter could erect cabins. Like many of the new settlers, the Fletchers initially stayed at one of the taverns. Some 314 lots were sold in their first week in Indianapolis. Sarah tried to focus on the positive in their otherwise-primitive, uncertain new prospects: "There are many very genteel families in this place," she wrote her friend Maria Britten. "Some of them I have become acquainted with . . . they are very polite and attentive to each other. Mr. Fletcher says there are many fine young men settled here from Kentucky who are somewhat more attentive to the ladies than those at Urbana."[62] Indiana had become a crossroads for those in search of new lands, with an infusion of settlers from the upland South (Kentucky and Virginia) as well as from western Pennsylvania and the Carolinas. And consequently, it became far more southern in character than its neighbors, Ohio and Illinois, which attracted far more New England transplants and immigrants from Europe. Indiana became a place for "town-making," with plenty of boosterism and men on the make who were eager to engage in commerce and anxious to not get "lost in the woods." As one state historian has noted, new settlers like Calvin and Sarah "wanted to be noticed. They wanted people to come to them. They wanted to be linked together with the rest of the United States."[63]

Amid the scramble for a spot in this New West frontier was the desperate search for any kind of housing. Calvin and Sarah managed to locate a vacant cabin that had been deserted by its builder "because of the prevailing sickness." It was rough frontier living by anyone's standards: the cabin had no floor; only a door and a place for a chimney had been cut out of its walls.

All around them were fellow adventurers, gritty settlers looking for something better in this new territory, forced to contend with primitive conditions and dangerous illness that threatened to dash the hope that hung in the air. "The people [were] all sick and distressed," Sarah observed. "Many were moving into the old settlements from whence they came which caused me to wish myself back again, yet I have courage and hope that we may escape sickness."

And, as Sarah tellingly ended her note: "Mr. Fletcher is not discouraged."[64]

Three

SETTLING IN

As a young, ambitious attorney, Calvin made his presence felt early on in the settling of Indianapolis. At a meeting at the Hawkins Tavern on November 1, 1821, he was chosen as secretary of a committee that was lobbying to organize a new county, Marion County. The leadership role he took on was clearly flattering to him ("this mark of distinction I very much appreciate," he noted), and he hoped it would lead to other public positions. But stepping into the public arena, he realized, carried the potential not only for accomplishment and notoriety, but also for conflict and ridicule. "I find there is much strife and contention brewing among the citizens of this place," he observed, "yet I sincerely hope to escape all censure by asking no favors myself."[1]

Calvin began his first winter in the newly settled town of Indianapolis feeling hopeful yet uncertain. "I perhaps enjoy myself as well as ever I did in my life," he wrote in his diary on December 31, 1821, in what would become a traditional end-of-the-year self-appraisal. "I know not what I am to do next summer for a living and indeed I am totally ignorant of my future situation and have learned from the precipitant and unpremeditated movements of my life that it is not best to be too anxious about the future events which may happen—but think it the best thing I can do is to prepare myself to meet any events that occur in the world." As always, the event he most prepared for and worried about was poverty. "Of all the fears, that of poverty I most dread, yet it has been a companion thus far thro' life," he reflected. He and "Mrs. F." would be attending a party on New Year's Day, but, he acknowledged, "I am not able to tell the aggregate of the happiness we shall enjoy."[2]

What continued to worry him was the nagging concern that he was perhaps not cut out to be a lawyer. "I often get vexed in my professional concerns and almost swear I will become one [a farmer] myself or at least I imagine I should be happy if I were digging my mother earth," he wrote in a letter to his brother Michael. "A lawyer here must become a good advocate or speaker in public . . . I was diffident to the extreme when I first began to speak. I have got over this much and am said to be abundant in irony & sarcasm when I aim therefore." Even his best friends tended to agree about Calvin's oratorical abilities. Simon Yandes remembered him as a very careful speaker: "On the trial he was not what is called oratorical, but had a fine clear voice and was a shrewd and effective speaker. His most prominent talent was an insight in the motives of parties and witnesses; and he was especially strong in cross examining witnesses."[3]

As Calvin and Sarah looked around them, they witnessed a world "vastly different" from what Calvin had known growing up in New England. Early on, Calvin adopted a positive, progressive tone in speaking about Indianapolis and the "West" in general. "The people here are vastly different from N.Y. or N.E.," he observed. "Most of them are emigrants— all have traveled more or less." And, most important, "they are bold & independent" in their politics. Unlike the New Englander, he noted, who lives in an "aristocratical" world of deference, even "the most ignorant man here knows who governs him & who administers justice."[4]

Calvin's heavy caseload and determination to make his mark as a young lawyer required frequent trips out of town riding the Fifth Judicial Circuit, which, besides Marion County, included Lawrence, Monroe, Morgan, Greene, Owen, Decatur, Bartholomew, Shelby, and Jennings counties.

For example, he left on March 1, 1822, for two weeks of attending court throughout a large part of central Indiana. Calvin departed, Sarah wrote, on "a very muddy & disagreeable day and I fear he will be very sick of his trip." While he was gone, her neighbor, Mrs. Paxton, stayed with Sarah for four nights; during that time, her husband, "Mr. P.," returned from Ohio bearing newspapers and letters from Sarah's father. For Sarah, reading such family letters, especially when living alone, clearly conveyed a powerful sense of connectedness and helped relieve the solitary feeling of an absent loved one.[5]

As a result of her husband's frequent absence, Sarah spent a good deal of time at home alone, carrying out a nearly endless stream of household work: her diary recounts a routine of washing, husking corn, spinning, baking, and making bonnets ("I was spinning at Mr. Noldins"; "I was bakeing Pumpkin pys"; "I spun some candlewick"; "I washed").[6] She also participated in—and benefited from—a good deal of neighborly visitation and help with chores. Frequently, neighbor women came by and shared in the work of ironing, mending, scrubbing, or altering dresses, or else simply visited.[7] Sarah also made time for church, regularly attending services at the Eagle Tavern, where she "heard a very good sermind delivered by a Newlight minister. The text was thus see then that ye walk circumspectly not as fools but as wise Redeeming the time because the days are evel."[8] She attended a neighbor's quilting but became annoyed at the coarse language of some of the newly settled Kentucky women present: "There were several ladys who were formaly from Kentucky & I think in there descorse among the Females they use a gradual of vulgarity."[9] Sarah frequently took a dim view of Kentucky women, noting on another social occasion that "a young Lady Jest from Kentucky . . . at a distance . . . looked very flashy & carried a very high head." "I did not have the pleasure of getting acquainted with her," Sarah observed with her own brand of self-effacing wit. "Perhaps if I had I would of found the lady as empty as myself."[10]

Despite an abundance of neighborly contact, Sarah clearly preferred quieter, more private forms of entertainment. She read romance and horror novels, which she most likely found via traveling libraries. She especially

Sarah Hill Fletcher, Calvin's first wife, ca. 1832

enjoyed the gothic tale *The Horrors of Oakendale Abby,* published in 1797 by a Mrs. Carver, which told the story of a young woman and her attempted seduction by Lord Oakendale in a haunted abbey where she stumbles upon body snatchers. More commonly, though, Sarah loved reading letters, since they offered closeness and information without the unhappiness that sometimes accompanied face-to-face encounters in the neighborhood.

For example, her friend from Urbana, Maria Britten, sent her a letter on December 16, 1821, that contained a dress pattern. This pleased Sarah, although it reminded her of how little she was hearing from her own family: "When I read it," she wrote, "I began to reflect to think how much more esteem an acquaintance expressed by writing to me & not one of my relatives evin sent a compliment." A few days later her sister-in-law Louisa Button, who had married a Newark doctor, sent her a letter, and Calvin received seven letters; this, she noted, "give us both great Satisfaction in peruseing them." Occasionally, Sarah allowed herself more conventional, public entertainment. When the noted fiddler Alexander Russell came to Indianapolis from Kentucky, he was in great demand, and Calvin went to hear him. Clearly entertained by this performance, he convinced Sarah to go as well, though even on this occasion her attendance depended on her completion of letter writing for the day: only after she composed "a few more lines" in the letters she owed would she attend, "though," she reflected, "I feel very much fatigued for it has been so long since I have heard the fiddle plaid that I think it would sound very melodious & I am jest going to start to hear it."[11]

Even when Calvin was at home, Sarah seemed content cultivating a shy, private life. When they were invited to a party on Valentine's Day in 1822 at a neighbor's, Calvin attended but Sarah stayed home. "I had no anxiety to go therefore I staid at home," she wrote in her diary. "Mr. F., I suppose by this time, is there but whether he will enjoy himself or not I cannot tell tho he appeard to anticipate a grateal of pleasure. I am all alone at this time & injoy myself very well. I use to think that I should be very lonesome when Mr. F. was abscent but it is quite to the reverse if he dose not stay out till a late hour, for as soon as he starts & I get my domestic afares in order then I get my penn ink & paper & feel quiet Happy." Her plans for that very evening, in fact, included writing. She put her papers in order and meditated on how well she had spent her time since getting married the past year. As usual, she fretted that she had indulged in "trifling" matters, but noted that "if I had the same time to live over again I would Spende it quiet different tho I am confident that I have done my duty this night." Her "duty" consisted of satisfying what "Mr. F" would have wanted her to accomplish in daily writing. "I have wrote as much tonight as I have wrote within 2 weaks," she boasted, "& I hope he will not be displeased with my Composition."[12]

Sometimes her more conservative relatives in "backwoods" Ohio took issue with the more cosmopolitan, "frivolous" world of Indianapolis in which Sarah and Calvin lived. Malinda Hill, Sarah's younger sister and a recent, ardent convert to Methodism, even with all that denomination's reverence for physical displays of religious zeal, reproached Sarah and Calvin for attending and dancing at an Indianapolis ball: "You must know that bodily exercise of that kind has no tendency to qualify . . . for the important duties of religion . . . neither is it very praiseworthy or honorable," she admonished her. "I was secondly astonished that you could not discriminate between the atrocity of the crimes as you called them of dancing all night or shouting & jumping at a camp-meeting &c . . . O My Bro. & Sister Fletcher 'seek the Lord while he may be found . . .'" Sarah pronounced her sister's condemnations unsatisfying.[13]

But criticism from her husband was an entirely different matter. "Mr. F.'s" displeasure was often a palpable reality. In one diary entry, Sarah recounted how she spent a particularly anguished evening with Calvin visiting another couple. Her version of the visit revealed Sarah's aching lack of self-esteem as well as Calvin's omnipresent condescension: Sarah allowed that their host was "a very sociable woman, though I did not injoy myself in the least altho I might appeared to do so. Mr. F. was present a great part of the Eve which rendered me quiet unhappy & imbarast thinking he was mortified at my actions. I made no convercesion and trembleing, fearing there mite be some question asked that would expose my ignernce." But instead of resenting being judged for any inadequacies, Sarah internalized her apparent weaknesses while trying to display a wife's dutiful and positive spirit. "He's taken a greateal of pains with me," she observed about Calvin. "It seames as if my eyes are just opened and I view evry thing in its darkest dyes and some times make myself miserable again. I reflect I know it is my duty to be cheerful and make everything appear in the best light."[14]

Her wifely duties found their fullest expression, at least in the eyes of the prevailing culture, when she delivered her and Calvin's first child. On April 15, 1823, Sarah gave birth to a son. Attending Sarah was the usual female-centered company: six married women from the neighborhood who had seen and experienced childbirth many times. One woman stayed in the Fletcher home, attending to Sarah for two weeks after the delivery; another lived with them the following two weeks.[15] The boy was called James Cooley Fletcher, notably named *not* after Calvin's father, Jesse, but after his father figure and legal mentor, James Cooley.

This rejection of his father's legacy, especially as a parent, clearly weighed heavily on Calvin's mind even before his son was delivered. In a letter to his brother Michael two months before little James's arrival, Calvin offered confident advice on how Michael should properly educate his son, Timothy, who had just turned six: Six years old, Calvin insisted, was "an age at which you ought to consider as essential to his education. I most fervently hope my brothers and sisters will not neglect the Education of their children . . . I feel anxious that the family of Fletchers from which we sprang tho' now obscure should one day or other be able to trace a respectable lineage. In bestowing an education on our children, let us not break down the noblest traits nor subdue that natural boldness which every one possesses." By invoking "boldness," Calvin was not only showcasing the defining trait of his enterprising life in the American West, but also making a deliberately hurtful stab at their father for how he had sadly failed the Fletcher children. "It always was a victory in our father ever to enslave the mind & hamper the spirit of his children," Calvin observed bitterly. "Damned be that policy. Let it forever be blotted out of my tablet & forsaken as a guide."[16]

But, as Calvin painfully learned, such "boldness" might give a man ambition, but it could also push him into unwelcome conflict. As someone who tended to openly voice his emotions, Calvin struggled throughout his life, especially in these early years, with controlling his temper. More than once it got the better of him. In May 1823—just a few weeks after the birth of James Cooley Fletcher—Calvin, provoked by a fellow attorney, Obadiah

Foote, assaulted him "in a rude insolent angry and unlawful manner," striking and wounding him, "to the great damage of the said Foote . . . and against the peace and dignity of the State of Indiana."[17] Calvin was indicted, pled guilty to assault and battery, and was fined $2.

Two years later, in 1825, Calvin became embroiled in another scuffle, this time with a prominent politician, James Ray, who would soon be elected governor of Indiana. Both were practicing law when Calvin, as others had done, accused Ray of corruption. Ray told Fletcher "that if he repeated the offensive remark he would thrash him." The politician apparently didn't realize that such threats, far from dampening Calvin's anger, served only to provoke more animosity. So when Calvin repeated the accusation, Ray slugged him in the nose. At this, Calvin struck Ray in the face, and the two men were in the middle of a full-out brawl before bystanders finally separated them.[18]

Small wonder episodes like this left Calvin worrying about his intemperate conduct and need for self-improvement. "I always have had an aversion to look back upon my most recent transactions—arising, I suppose, yea, I well know it, from a dissatisfaction of the manner in which I perform—I am half a misanthrope thro' fear," he noted in his diary. So he occasionally returned to church—Baptist meetings, mostly—feeling "some remorse" and looking for guidance. Attending church, he decided, offered him an opportunity to become more comfortable with different sorts of people and to find ways to make himself a better person. "I find by attending meetings I familiarize myself with the countenances of people—it wears off that affrighted misanthropy which I feel more or less," he reflected. "I certainly feel a thirst for improvement."[19]

As was frequently the case throughout his life, for Calvin, taking a trip seemed like the best medicine for the gloom of self-doubt. Despite his many quarrels with his father, he nonetheless felt the need to return home to Vermont, to "once more set my foot upon the soil of my native land."[20] Even though Sarah was again pregnant and expected to deliver in August, Calvin decided to make the trip. So, on May 19, 1824, seven years after his unhappy leave-taking from his parents, Calvin began the long trek back to his roots. The journey started with a piece of bad luck. As he left his house on Washington Street he was stopped by his neighbor, who, Calvin later recorded, "hailed me & told me I had left my pocket book behind me which he brought to me." More specifically, his friend insisted that Calvin wait on him to bring the pocketbook, reminding him "that it was ominous ill luck to turn back after any thing forgotten when a person had started a journey."[21]

Calvin started the 860-mile journey with several local men who had business of their own along part of the route he was taking. Among them were Austin Bishop, an Indianapolis merchant; James M. Ray (no relation to the James Ray with whom Calvin had fought), the highly regarded Marion County clerk whom Calvin described as "quiet, unobtrusive, vigilant, never idle, never careless"; James Blake, who would become one of Calvin's great friends and who was traveling with Ray to Fort Wayne, Indiana, to lay out the county seat and a state road to Indianapolis; Samuel D. Woodworth, a Hamilton County surveyor; and William Conner, an Indian trader, scout, guide, and interpreter. They camped the first day at sundown near the banks of the White River. It had been a good first day, Calvin thought. "The country we came thro this day," he noted in his journal, "will all admit of a good settlement. We prepared our camp & made some of the best coffee I ever drank." And he couldn't help adding a bit of humor: "Our camping ground we named Smell Shot camp ground in honor of a very facetious expression of Mr. Conner." He was also amused and "rather charmed by the shrill voice of a Whipowill a little distance from our camp. This bird is rather scarce in this country."[22]

Early on, traveling through the Indiana wilderness, Calvin's company wandered into Indian country. While searching for a tree to make a bark canoe for a river crossing, he recorded in his diary, "we herd an Indian yelp which was answered by Mr. Conner and we made towards the voice. Found 2 Indians who knew him." The Indians advised them to follow them farther downriver instead of attempting a river crossing at their present location. Later that same day, Calvin learned that "in consequence of the whites selling them whisky," several Indians in the area had gotten into a drunken fight and killed several of their own.[23]

Like his brother Elijah, Calvin had a penchant for ethnographic description, and he was especially intrigued by the look and customs of the native peoples he and his companions encountered. As they traveled through one of the Miami Indian towns burnt to the ground in the War of 1812, they found fifty Indians "worshiping or performing some ceremonies rather of a festive kind." As Calvin marveled, "They were certainly superbly dressed surpassing any thing in splendor that I ever beheld among them," especially the young Indians, who were decked out "in scarlet with large silver bands 'bout the head. When we came up they were seated on barks in a circular row smoking. We camped 'bout 200 yards from them under the hill by a spring. We soon heard them singing and dancing after the hollow sound of a large drum . . . A number knew Mr. Conner & appeared to be friendly." Later the party encountered "a great number of Indians & squaws who were drunk, tolerably well dressed," in the company of French Indian traders returning from the woods with their furs.[24]

At Fort Wayne, Calvin, Ray and Blake took a canoe downriver with French guides, "keeping time with their paddles with a number of French songs they sung which were very pleasing and delightful," although, Calvin lamented, "I could not understand much of the language." That night, after seventy-five miles of travel descending the river, they stopped above Fort Defiance at a little cabin on the north side of the river. "The man of the house," Calvin noted, "treated us very hospitably, furnished us with blankets & permitted us to sleep on the floor without any compensation."[25] Two days later the men arrived at Fort Meigs. After touring an 1812 battlefield, Calvin made a visit to the family of an old acquaintance, a Mr. Patterson. "I found his lady at home I once knew while she was a blooming romantic coquettish girl," he wrote. "I now found her the mother of one little girl, living poor and disconsolate. She did not know me at first." Calvin concluded by visiting the battlefield at Fort Meigs, where in 1813 the British had attacked, ambushing and killing many American soldiers. Here Calvin stumbled upon numerous "human bones" among the bushes. "This caused a most sad reflection," he observed. "I thanked my stars that the shrill trump of war had ceased to blow, that gentle peace was now waving her olive branch over the same place that but a few years past was a scene of carnage."[26]

By June 6 Calvin had reached Buffalo, New York, where he sampled two church services, finding neither of them worthy of his time. First, he walked in on a Presbyterian service and asked "a gent who stood at the door if there was seats for strangers; he answered in the negative. I turned on my heel & went directly to a . . . house where was preaching a Mr. E [. . .], a Universalist who had advanced some ways in his sermons . . . His congregation were mostly young men—clerks, merchants, doctors & lawyers." Calvin found the man's doctrine calculated "to be subversive of morality, religion & education. He ridiculed most the idea of giving young men a classical education in order to prepare them for the ministry."[27] Deeply interested in religion and morality, Calvin nonetheless struggled to find comfort in any particular faith.

Later that evening, Calvin left Buffalo on a stage for New York City, accompanied by his friend Austin Bishop and a few other unidentifiable travelers—"it was so dark that I could not discover whom" they were, he wrote in his diary, although one of them, he was certain, "was a pick pocket." Traveling along a "smooth road by the light of lamps for it was dismal & dark," he recorded that "we saw a light in almost every house which I told our company was caused by loving couples who were setting [off] sparks" with their amorous activities. When they arrived in Geneva, New York, they met "a young lady" who regaled everyone with "a history of the fashions. The fashions now in use as to bonnets are golashes & Hoods," which, Calvin observed, "I never have seen in Indiana." The biggest thrill came when they crossed from the Genesee River into Albany via the Erie Canal that had just opened to traffic in 1823. "I was tired," Calvin noted, "yet I felt a peculiar sensation to think I was riding on the great, the famous Western Canal."[28]

Originally spanning about 363 miles from Albany, New York, on the Hudson River to Buffalo, New York, at Lake Erie, the Erie Canal was the first transportation route between New York City and the western interior of the Great Lakes that didn't require pack animals. Because it was so much faster than carts pulled by draft animals, it reduced transportation costs by close to 95 percent. Proposed in 1807 and built beginning in 1817, the canal opened on October 26, 1825. But its middle section, stretching from Utica to Syracuse, a portion of which Calvin experienced, was completed in 1820 and prompted immediate popular interest. The Erie Canal not only greatly contributed to the wealth and significance of New York City and Buffalo, but fostered growing trade in the nation overall by opening eastern and foreign markets to Midwestern farm products and promoting settlement in the West. With the influx of thousands of settlers using the canal to travel to upstate New York and points west, new markets opened up for New York City businesses. Furthermore, European businesses could now access an all-water route into the Midwest. But it was New York City that profited the most from the Erie Canal, as it quickly became the main international gateway and financial capital of the nation.[29]

After crossing the river via the Erie Canal, Calvin stayed at the Newark home of his sister Laura, who had married a local doctor, Calvin Button. His two other sisters, Lucy and Louisa, both married and living in Newark, came to the Buttons to spend the evening with Calvin. Clearly moved by the meeting, he remarked, "Almost eight years had passed without my seeing them." From New York, he wrote his brother Elijah, hoping to convince him at the last minute to come to Ludlow for a mini-reunion. Elijah, who had once famously vowed that his life as a gentleman planter in Virginia would not be burdened with children, now had two young boys underfoot and reluctantly decided not to attend. Over the next ten days Calvin visited his sisters, his other New York relatives, and his brothers Michael in Staatsburgh and Miles in Marlboro. There was so much to talk about with these family members whom he rarely saw but with whom he had remained close. He took a steamboat carrying some poor Irish passengers from Montreal, which prompted a derisive comment: "They were a mottle mess—men, women & children from Ireland some horses & dogs. The Irish looked poor and distressed. I could not but contrast the difference in the appearance between the passengers of this boat."[30] A stagecoach carried him finally through Vermont and on into Ludlow, arriving early on the morning of July 4.

His journey from Indianapolis had taken forty days, thirty of them traveling by horse, stage, or steamboat. As the stagecoach stopped for breakfast at an inn just six miles from his father's place, Calvin's anxiety at the rendezvous mounted: "I began to feel an unbounded solicitude to enter the old domicil. We at length proceeded. The distance seemed short . . . At length we reached the old place which had so long occupied my thoughts. The stage drove up." Not unlike when his brother Elijah first set eyes on Calvin during his visit to Virginia in 1820, Jesse and Lucy Fletcher responded with surprise and shock to the sight of their son after so long an absence. Their surprise quickly turned to deep emotion. "He & mother both wept at being informed I was *Calvin*," Calvin wrote in his journal. "I was pleased to find them in good health & spirits and in much better circumstances than I had anticipated. After gratifying them in my answers to their many questions we took dinner." Later that evening, at a Baptist service, Calvin was struck by how things had changed. "There I beheld many new faces," he recorded. "All the young people were to me strangers," even though the older folks looked mostly the same.[31]

Perhaps weakened by all the travel and anxiety, the next day Calvin became very sick—in part, homesick for his little family back in Indiana. "I felt tremendously ill out of my head & crazy to see my wife whom I tho't was the only person fit to wait upon me while sick," he wrote. He recovered sufficiently to visit with kin and friends in the area and took a walk with his father after church, during which they had a conversation on "religious subjects." "I was supprised to find he and I tho't much alike, bothe restorationers," Calvin commented, alluding to a strand of belief built on a desire to return the church to a purer, more primitive form.[32]

But soon he was ready to go home. He tried to focus on his parents and life in Ludlow, but as the days wore on, he found himself increasingly obsessed with thinking about his new life out West. Within a week after arriving at his ancestral home, he determined to return home to Indiana, where, he noted, "I have attractions that nothing but Death can prevent its force. I have endeavored whilst with my father & mother to banish all tho'ts of wife & child however I can't help devoting some thots on them."[33]

On July 12, he took leave of his parents and his sister Fanny, though, he reflected, "[I] did not flatter myself with ever seeing them again." Brother Stoughton traveled with him as far as Schenectady, and then he found the leave-taking too much to bear: "Stoughton appeared to be very much affected at parting with me [and] could not eat nor drink. This made me as unpleasant as every thing that has occurred since my leaving home."[34]

A week later Calvin was heading for Geneva, New York, where he parted company with his sisters, leaving early in the morning in an open wagon. "I felt in some measure a mixed sensation of grief & sorrow," he remembered. "I had just parted with kind sisters whom I never expect much to see again yet I was consoled to think I had accomplished all my visits and had started for Indiana where I hoped to arrive soon."[35]

The trip home, if relatively quick, was hardly easy or comfortable. On the way back from Warren, Ohio, he proceeded down the river thirteen miles and "staid with a dirty Irish man only four miles from Thompsons." Calvin finished his journey in a very humble and exhausting fashion. During the final stages of his return home to Indianapolis, he traveled with a young man, Joseph Moore, via pirogues. They rowed until sundown, until they were eight miles from Franklin, Indiana, but at that point "the young lad" gave out, unable to paddle any farther. "I made him lay down and I managed the boat alone and arrived at 11 tired & weary at Franklin," Calvin recorded in his diary. After some trouble locating a place to stay, Calvin found "a poor dirty cabin," which, he commented, was "the worst calculated to entertain of any one I ever met with." From the Ohio River to Indianapolis Calvin and Joseph struggled home on a single horse, arriving on August 8.[36]

Now eight months pregnant, Sarah had been expecting her husband's return for a week with growing concern. When he arrived exhausted around midnight, she was profoundly relieved. "I need not tell you I was surprised as well as rejoiced to see him after the absence of Eighty-two days," she later wrote Calvin's sisters. But even with Calvin's arrival and her own looming delivery, Sarah didn't fully command Calvin's attention. "We had so much company for a week after Mr. Fletcher returned that I scarce had an opportunity to pass a leisure moment with him," she wrote in the same letter.[37]

Less than two weeks after Calvin's return, the baby came, a boy, the Fletchers' second son. And predictably, given his busy work schedule, Calvin missed the birth, as he was away attending a trial, which, he noted, netted him $5 in fees.[38] Early on the baby struggled with feeding. "It was very unhealthy at first," Sarah noted, "and I had but little hopes of raising it but it has grown of late and appears to be very healthy." Strangely, neither she nor Calvin could settle on a name for a few months. "I wished Mr. F. to name him after his father or some one of his brothers," Sarah wrote her sisters. The boy would be named not after his father, but instead after his beloved brother: "We have concluded to call him Elijah Timothy F. When we use only the first letter of the middle name, it sounds very well." When little "Elijah T" was only three months old, though, Sarah grew worried about his safety at home because, she noted, "two of our nearest neighbors lately whilst playing round the fire have had children about his [Elijah's] age burnt so they died. They both had on cotton dresses. One was burnt in October and the other in November. This I consider is an awful warning to parents to guard against clothing children with cotton the fall & winter."[39] In colonial America such tragic accidents would have been viewed as God's will; by this time, they were viewed as a matter of preventable safety measures in the home.

❧ • • ❧

Elijah Fletcher was no doubt honored by Calvin naming his second son Elijah. By the time his young namesake was born, Elijah had begun his own family. By 1824, Elijah and Maria also had two boys: Sidney, three, and Lucian, eight months. With such young children in hand, it was not surprising that Elijah declined to make the trip that summer to visit his parents in Ludlow. After missing the family reunion, though, he regretted the lost opportunity. "I was much pleased at Calvin's making you a visit last summer," Elijah told his father. "I intended to have done so myself but I found it [impossible]." He emphasized how important it was for "relations to live near each other. I would give anything if it were my happy lot to be situated close by you."[40]

Elijah frequently voiced such a longing for a closer connection to his larger family up north and out west, but left unspoken in that sad sentiment was his quite deliberate choice to stake out his own individual claim to a family in the "distant country" of the South. Besides, ever since putting down roots with Maria and his growing family, he had become busy acquiring land, managing plantations and slaves, and beginning to make a name for himself in Lynchburg and beyond. By the summer of 1824 Elijah had bought nearly 1,300 acres in Amherst County, much of it used as summer pastureland for his increasing stock of cattle.

It was this strange plantation world that eluded understanding among many members of his family, especially his parents. While Calvin had comparatively little trouble explaining his efforts to make a living as a young and ambitious attorney in the Midwest, to which growing numbers of New Englanders were migrating, Elijah struggled to justify his life as a slave-owning planter in the peculiar world of the South. "You say you want to know what I am about," Elijah began a reply to his father in the summer of 1825. "Like the way of the world, as I grow older and perhaps richer, my business, my cares and concerns, and of course, troubles, increase. I have a plantation settled with negroes and overseer and cultivate Tobacco, wheat &c. This Plantation is more than 20 miles off. I have five other tracts of Land which I rent out. I got this property cheap, had to take some of it in payments of debts, as this country has been very much embarrassed and money has been very scarce."[41] Within Amherst County, Elijah Fletcher would soon become one of the largest landowners and one of the ten largest slave-owners. While his slaveholdings in the 1820s were probably more modest—numbering fewer than 50—by the mid-1840s he and his oldest son, Sidney, owned 115 slaves.[42]

And there was more. He had also become a printer. "I own another species of property at which you will be somewhat surprised. I own a *printing establishment* called the *Virginian*," he informed his father. In this venture, Elijah was joining the paper's previous sole owner and publisher, Richard H. Toler, known as one of the godfathers of the Virginia Whig Party. "This was the first paper that advocated Mr. [John Quincy] Adams in this State," Elijah noted, "and had such influence as to make Adams very popular in this part of the State." Originally established in 1823, the *Virginian* quickly became a prominent political publication that had some 1,500 subscribers and favored the Whig position of John Quincy Adams that—in Virginia, at least—was then in the minority. Since the late eighteenth century, newspapers like the *Virginian* had functioned as central players in an often-acrimonious party system in which editors frequently served as chief party spokesmen and newspaper offices served as party headquarters. Focused more on the printer/owner aspect of the newspaper while leaving his partner, Toler, to handle the thornier partisan politics, Elijah initially took considerable pride in his role as publisher. He offered to send his father, as well as his brother Calvin, a paper, "if," he told Jesse Sr., "you will take any pleasure in reading it."[43]

Calvin enjoyed reading the *Virginian,* for he had become very politically active in Indianapolis. In 1826 he ran successfully for the state senate seat for his four-county region in Indiana, campaigning on a distinctly Whig platform that favored *ad valorem* taxes and a total commitment to internal improvements—roads, canals—of every kind. Two years later he ran unopposed and won reelection.[44] Like Elijah, Calvin found politics a compelling but dangerous temptation. A democratic republic depended upon the participation of a responsible, informed citizenry, but public life often seduced men into a world of conflict and turbulent displays of emotion. Calvin insisted he was never going to become a "violent partisan," observing, "I have thus far got along without making but few enemies . . . I have taken great pains to quell all jealousies among my brother lawyers at this place and I have now the apparent friendship of every one. They sometimes accuse me of being a peoples man—that I have ambitious views— that I want to go to Congress at the next apportionment &c&c. All this I take good naturedly." His ongoing search for self-control and an even temperament, he insisted, had led him to a much better emotional place. "I was a little captious when I lived with you," he told Elijah, "but I now have compleat controle of myself compared with some others."[45] But only a year into his work as state senator, Calvin grew concerned about the energy and time required to serve the public. Elijah, sensing that Calvin had a good instinct for the political world, remained encouraging, writing to him, "You speak again of being tired of the political life and your views upon the subject are prudent and correct, but you cannot back out at present. You will see perhaps before long a favorable opportunity to retire."[46]

Torn between his own clear ambition and a fear that the political world could corrode a man's highly valued sense of independence, Calvin tried to explain his difficult choices to his father. "Political life," he wrote him in 1828, is "calculated to bring upon a man cares and troubles for which he never receives anything like an adequate compensation. It makes him less independent; but in order to keep up the public tone and good will in his favor, he must often sacrifise his own private interest."[47] Calvin conceded that he had been receiving "warm solicitations" from his friends to run again for the Indiana state senate, entreaties he wanted to resist but clearly could not:

> I have not fully determined against it. It would be against my pecuniary interest should I even suceede—but pride and I may say the honor of being the choice of a majority of the freeman of 4 counties to represent them in the Senate & likewise a desire to ascertain whether my past services meet their approbation so far as to reelect me, are almost inducements sufficient to suffer myself to become a candidate once more under the conviction above stated.

Two months later, Calvin decided to run again and won.[48]

Like his brother, Calvin worried greatly about national politics, especially fearing the outcome of the upcoming 1828 presidential election between John Quincy Adams and Andrew Jackson. "If I should measure the . . . feelings of your subscribers or the people of your town, by your paper," he told Elijah, "I should conclude you all felt a very considerable interest in the event of the coming Presidential election and that there must be a corresponding heat & violence opposed to your sentiments." Like his brother, Calvin felt "very anxious for Jackson's success." Even though he respected Jackson as a man, he could not tolerate Jackson's policies, insisting, "As long as I regard the interest & welfare of my country and as long as I regard the honor and integrity of a partisan who intends not to desert his friends I cannot support any man for president who goes heart and hand with the friends of Gen. Jackson."[49] Particularly offensive to Calvin was Jackson's opposition to a system of internal improvements.

Elijah shared his brother's disdain for Jackson and anyone who supported him, including some of his fellow New Englanders. "I am sorry to see any of the New England States worshipping Jackson—New Hampshire &c.," he wrote Calvin. "Such people are fit for nothing but slaves. If the northern states have not sense to stick together and protect their own interest, they ought to suffer and they will."[50] Elijah likewise read the Indianapolis papers and offered equally stinging critiques of Indiana's political leaders. "I think your Governor Ray has heretofore deceived you all," he told Calvin, referring to the very man with whom Calvin had gotten into a fistfight a few years earlier. "He must be a desperate poltroon, and I think his late conduct has sealed his fate for life or at least it ought to damn him everlastingly." What was worse, Elijah noted, was the division in the Whig ranks. "We ought to unite all our strength to insure success," he insisted. "By dividing we may be conquered." Nevertheless, Governor Ray, who had been elected in 1825, was reelected in 1828.[51]

Despite the brothers' sharp political instincts and daily consumption of various political papers, Elijah remained far more detached from public life, viewing its often-volatile tone as always distinct from his own, more carefree, private world. He may have been deeply anxious about the prospect of Andrew Jackson winning the presidency, but he remained on pleasant personal terms with his political opponents. "We have all been pretty animated and warm in politics in this place but it has not entered into our social circles," he told Calvin. "I am as intimate and friendly with those differing from me as those agreeing with me. I do not know but few personal differences here on account of politics."[52]

Steering clear of consuming passions of all kinds—political and personal—seems to have been Elijah's unspoken strategy for living. Even as he became more engaged in raising his children in the mid-1820s, he adopted a singularly detached tone in describing them. With two small boys—Sidney and Lucian—already in hand, Elijah did take some pride in announcing to his father in November 1825 that "we have now a little daughter about 2 months old. So you may expect that I shall have a large Family yet and extend and perpetuate your name in this distant country from you."[53] Yet this note announcing Laura was sent some two months after her birth. Perhaps unsurprisingly, when there was tragedy to report, it too came after considerable delay and with only the slightest hint of emotion. Five months after Laura's birth, she died unexpectedly. Oddly, in reporting the death, Elijah couldn't remember if his father knew about the loss. "I do not remember whether I have written to you since we had the misfortune to lose our youngest child," he wrote Jesse Sr. "She was about five months old at the time of her death. Our two boys are hearty fine fellows." Not only did he wait two months after Laura's death to disclose it to his father, but he referred to the loss with notable brevity and detached language ("misfortune").[54]

A full five months after Maria gave birth to twins—one male, one female—Elijah informed Calvin of the news, casually noting that neither had yet been named. "Our little babies . . . they are both very hearty and well children," he reported. "We have not yet decided upon any names for them. Sometimes Maria talks of calling one Elijah and the other Maria Antoinette but then again she will call them something else. Names are a matter of little consequence, a short name suits me best."[55] The boy, it turned out, died weeks later unnamed. The girl, Indiana, named in honor of the new home state of Elijah's favorite brother, thrived and would become his favorite child.

Calvin was fortunate in never experiencing the early death of a child— thanks to cholera, dysentery, and malaria, infant mortality in this era of pioneer regions was around 25 percent—but he had a scare shortly after Sarah delivered their third son, Calvin Jr., on September 30, 1826. Twelve days after the birth, when Calvin was away at court in Noblesville, about ten miles from Indianapolis, the apprentice of a local doctor, Kenneth Scudder, rode up to Noblesville in the middle of the night and delivered Calvin a note describing an unfolding emergency: "The situation of your wife is such that it is absolutely necessary that you should come home immediately. She has had one of those cold spells which are always dangerous. This is her first day's sickness and should the disease increase she must inevitably die."[56] Calvin had been awakened by the news, and he took off immediately: "I left at Midnight had to follow a[n Indian] trace thro the dark woods," he wrote in his diary. "Got lost & did not get home till next morn at sunrise. As I entered the door poor old Mr. Ralsten, a good neighbor, had been in & was just coming out of the house. I learned from him Mrs. F. was alive and better. She recovered after a severe spell." Apparently Sarah had eaten some watermelon, which, according to Calvin, "bro't on a chill & she came near dying."[57] Two years later, the Fletchers had another child, their fourth son, Miles, named after one of Calvin's brothers.

The depth of paternal emotion Calvin invested in his young boys, especially compared to the more detached observations offered by his brother Elijah, was plainly evident early on, especially when it came to their education. In January 1829, Calvin and Sarah decided to send their two oldest boys, James Cooley and Elijah, off to the Indianapolis equivalent of an informal live-in kindergarten, run by Curtis Mallery. In an era before common public schools were established in the 1840s, both in the East and out West, small children were often informally taught out of private homes in which the teacher would sometimes board; fuel was provided by the students' families. James Cooley and Elijah's departure for school that winter morning was a big event for Calvin and Sarah. Calvin got up early. "The wagon arrived at ½ past 8 o'clock," he recorded. "At 9 we put our babes our boys, one 5½ years old, the other 4½. It caused no very extraordinary sensations to part with these children. However, I soon found that I should miss them very much & in the P.M. I felt much concerned for them as it grew cold. I felt glad I had sent their uncle James Hill along with them to see them safe along." After they left, Calvin reflected on their absence and distinctive temperaments: "We felt very much lossed by the absence of James C. & Elijah. They when at home very active & sportive about the house when not at school. Elijah only 4½ of age I found was more a favorite that I was sensible of until I had parted with him." Sickly since birth, Elijah had not been able to develop as much aptitude for learning as had James Cooley, but Calvin and Sarah still found him to be "a sterling independent fellow—talks much—and asks many questions." "Cooley," as he was called, had "more art and a little more brilliancy than E," Calvin noted, "but I do not think a better mind."[58]

With the regular arrival of so many boys, Calvin and Sarah found themselves the object of admiration in the family, especially from Calvin's brother Elijah. "I congratulate you on your prospect of raising so fine a regiment of soldiers," Elijah told Calvin just after the birth of Miles in the summer of 1828. He was particularly taken with Calvin's comments on his rambunctious four-year-old son, his namesake, Elijah. "From the description you give of your second Boy, he must be like our Lucian—a headstrong, unmanageable fellow."[59] Also four years of age, Lucian was a noisy, willful child: "Lucian," Elijah told his father, "is now constantly talking to me and interrupting me. He is very fond of my telling him about Grandpa and what I used to do when I was a little boy. I have to tell him long stories about my youthful exploits."[60] Elijah's early insight into his willful son proved prophetic: what seemed like the amusing qualities of an energetic, inquisitive little boy would later develop into major concerns for the young man's viability as a successful person.

✼   •   •   •   ✼

Now that he had become the father of a large and expanding family, Calvin began to turn his restless, ambitious spirit inward, clearly worrying about the larger issues of life. As he approached his thirty-first birthday on February 4, 1829, drawing closer to what he called "the meridian of life in this country (thirty-five)," he announced that he was now more "strongly impressed with the importance of religion and . . . sensible of the vanity and great uncertainty of the things of the world." He confessed that religion was a "subject of which at first I had some serious doubts—yes, I even found myself to be almost an infidel." But he had looked around him and realized there was a peace and calm missing in his life: "I applied to a number of my friends who had professed religion . . . I found on inquiry that they were injoying treasurs of which I was intirely ignorant."[61]

So Calvin began attending class meetings at the Methodist Church, in which, he observed, "I found further evidences of the good things which religious & pious people enjoy." He further resolved to attend the Indianapolis Methodist Church and to devote himself to prayer and preaching all year. "It would take volumes to tell the doubts and fears I had in coming into a conclusion on this gr[e]at undertaking," he noted in his journal. "I had for a long time clung close to the world and my affections [were] strongly rooted therein." But on January 1, 1829, he declared, "I tremblingly advanced this morning and gave my hand there openly to the world more strongly confirmed on my part the covenant I had made to serve God as far as in me lay during the year 1829." The very next morning he got up before sunrise, "determined to set my house in better order than before," and, following the example of his brother-in-law James Hill, who was also a Methodist, Calvin "performed a duty which before I had always neglected [family prayer] to have performed in my family."[62]

As part of his spiritual renewal, Calvin even decided to make amends with his old enemy, James Ray, the politician with whom he had literally fought in public. When Calvin told Ray about his spiritual transformation, Ray "very affectionately expressed his Joy" and, as Calvin recorded in his diary, sat down with him to "review our whole life & proceedings since we had been residents of this place at its first settlement. We covenanted with each other to watch, pray for, and admonish each other—to suppress all heart burnings in and against the respective churches to which we belonged." (Ray belonged to the Presbyterian Church.) While together at the Presbyterian meetinghouse, Calvin noted, "Ray at my request made a most pathetic and feeling prayer which to me was as the refreshing dews to the parched earth. We parted, pledging to be each others friends not only in the world but in the cause of Christ."[63]

Calvin's emotional religious turn dovetailed with the rising evangelical fervor that had been spreading throughout the country, especially in the West and South, since the early 1800s. On the frontier, missionary preachers exhorted backcountry settlers, particularly Methodists and Baptists, with highly emotional, expressive professions of faith that emphasized man's helplessness to save himself and stressed a spiritual equality before God: all men, from rich plantation owners and businessmen to day laborers and factory workers, came together in an emotional acceptance of grace from God. Material possessions meant nothing in the search for salvation. Camp meetings sprang up like wildfires in rural areas and small towns throughout the South and in western frontier regions, showcasing the exhilaration of the revival spirit and inspiring dancing, shouting, and singing.[64]

Calvin, like many who attended such camp meetings, may have turned into a devout Christian, but he remained first and foremost an ambitious, hard-working businessman. Far from rethinking those materialistic roots in light of his newfound faith, he now made deliberate and—at least for himself—compelling connections between his capitalistic ambitions and his recent conversion. As he went to work one Monday morning shortly after his conversion, he gave direct voice to this rather full-throated expression of the Protestant work ethic:

> This is Monday morning. I arise with some new covenants & promises to my God and myself if I am spared. I intend to commence the business of my profession under the *Christian era*. I do intend to abandon that selfish peevishness, that restlessness, that rancor towards my adversary, that exultation in victory, and that remorse & private chagrin when defeated . . . I intend to leave off and discourage lounging in my office as time is precious but I hope to pursue my avocation with renewed diligence, punctuality and attention . . . I have always let my business *drive*

me, I never have drove my business. This neglect has done me much serious injury. It has made me often captious & Jealous towards them I consider of the highest importance . . . I have lost much time by long stays and talks with others both at my office & other places. I hereafter intend to use plain dealing with such loungers.

Or, as he more bluntly explained his deliberate mingling of faith and work: "I consider it my religious duty to be industrious."[65]

Perhaps it is not surprising that a new convert like Calvin Fletcher would experience some lapses and find his religious principles somehow inadequate to the task of navigating the emotional tug and pull of everyday life. So it went with his relationship with Governor Ray. Working in his office one Saturday morning, Calvin received an unexpected visit from the governor related to some business involving Ray's brother-in-law. It was the first time they had talked in six months. "I have said many hard things against him of which I did not deny but told him from our present situation, both members of the Methodist church we at least should be apparently friendly—That I had no political views—that I considered such views entirely incompatible with correct Christian conduct," Calvin commented in his diary. "We parted half pledging to treat each other well and so far as it relates to myself I wish that it was in my power not to mention his name again for the next 3 years—for I cannot speak well of him [but] to speak evil is highly improper."[66]

Calvin's conviction that hard work and devout faith would lead to simple and agreeable decisions ran afoul of the emotional reality that confronted him as his own father became ill later that year. Realizing that "my old father in Vt . . . is laboring under great bodily infirmities and does not expect to live but a short time," Calvin determined "with the advise & consent of Mrs. Fletcher" and his legal colleague to go visit his father in Vermont in the summer. Yet the decision clearly conflicted with the needs of his business. "I have much important business to do as a lawyer," he lamented. "I have let too many precious hours escape without much account. If I go see my father I must make somewhat of a sacrifise." As the summer trip drew closer, Calvin's conviction to take the trip wilted under the weight of his business responsibilities. On May 1, he received a letter from his father "by which," he noted, "I find he confidently expects a visit from me during the summer. I am in a great doubt what to do." Three days later, he had become "down spirited" trying to sort through the dilemma of honoring the genuine need to visit his sickly, aging father and swallowing the likely loss of business if he made the trip. Despite his "urgent" business at home, Calvin finally decided to pay his father a visit, even if it meant risking, as he put it, "all consequences of losing business & perhaps indanger[ing] the very reputation I have already acquired for punctuality."[67]

Calvin never made the trip to Vermont that summer. Dispirited by all the claims on his time and his indecision about how to resolve them, he instead rode down to Lynchburg, Virginia, to visit his brother Elijah. Before Calvin's arrival, Elijah had already begun to worry about his brother's emotional state, especially in light of the news about his sudden conversion to Methodism and what that suggested about his economic prospects. As Elijah said in a note to their father: "This is an uncommon circumstance with one of your Boys, and the first one that ever pretended to any thing like religion. It is very well if he sincerely thinks so and I doubt not [will] have a tendency to advance rather than retard his worldly prosperity."[68]

Elijah himself, while hardly devout, nonetheless did support religion. As early as 1822 he served as a member of an organizational committee to establish an Episcopal church in Lynchburg and helped raise funds for a permanent clergyman. He also served on the vestry of St. Paul's Church in Lynchburg in 1826. When his oldest children, Sidney and Lucian, were of a suitable age, Elijah made them attend Sunday school. Writing his father one Sunday morning, Elijah noted that "the bells have just rung for church, of which we have a goodly number for so small a place: two Baptist, two Methodist, one Presbyterian, one Quaker, one Episcopalian. The greater part of the people are *professors* of Religion. I must finish this and start for church. I generally attend the Episcopal."[69]

So when Calvin arrived in Lynchburg on July 14, 1829, he and his brother could at least share a general sense that religious observation meant something to both of them. But for Calvin, it seems, conversion to Methodism had brought both solace and increased volatility. He had been ill and depressed just before the trip and—just as nine years before, when he made a trip to his brother's while sick—he apparently hoped this visit might prove restorative to his health. Elijah doubtless showed him his numerous plantations and gave him a chance to get to know his two little nephews, Lucian and Sidney, and especially his one-year-old niece, Indiana, already her father's favorite.

Even though Calvin decided to return home after only five days in Virginia, the visit seemed to revive him. Before leaving for Indianapolis, Calvin told Elijah he felt better than he had in four years; he had regained his appetite and left in good spirits. Elijah's verdict, as disclosed to their father after Calvin left for home, was that "with ill health, the *Methodist* and the cares of his family and complicated business, he had [illegible] become much dejected and low-spirited before he undertook this trip. I hope, though his absence may have somewhat interfered with his business, it will ultimately be advantageous to him."[70] For his part, Calvin felt even closer to his older brother, someone he had come to admire and respect.

Such fraternal bonding led to mutual worrying over their ailing and badly indebted father. After receiving accounts of Jesse Sr.'s condition from his brother Timothy and talking with Calvin about how best to extricate their father from a lifetime of debt, Elijah bluntly informed Jesse Sr., "You have been so long in the bondage of debt that I feel anxious that you should be free from such slavery the few remaining days that you may have to spend among us."[71] Elijah's plan, based in part on Calvin's suggestions, was that both brothers would pay off their father's farm debts, which came to $150. Meanwhile, their younger brother, twenty-two-year-old Stoughton, would step in and "try to manage so as to support the family, improve the farm and make something for himself." If Stoughton accepted Calvin's plan, Elijah wrote their father, then "I should advance money to set you once more even with the world." Elijah realized his father would likely resist the plan. "You are very timid and perhaps will say that I am visionary," he noted. "But I know it can be done if Stoughton has the least turn for any such thing."[72] Later Elijah wrote Stoughton about the plan, advising him as well about the imperative to stay out of debt: "I think with good management you can support your Father and mother, improve the Farm and lay up something every year for yourself."[73]

Calvin returned from his visit with his brother Elijah rejuvenated. And he would need the additional energy and focus. On Christmas Day 1829, Calvin found himself in the middle of an extremely prominent and volatile legal case involving "a yellow woman & 3 children who are claimed by her master, a Virginian, by name of Sewell." William Sewell, a Virginian who had emigrated from Virginia with four female slaves, a mother and her three daughters, had been delayed in Indianapolis for a few days because of high water. Someone told the woman that in the northern state of Indiana they were free, so they fled their former master. He then chased them down and tried to recapture them, but slave-runaway sympathizers in the area brought the case to court on a writ of habeas corpus. Calvin and his law firm took up the case on behalf of the former slave and her children.[74]

"At 12 o'clock went to the court house where woman & 3 children, girls oldest about 10 years were brought forward," Calvin noted in his diary. "The house was full. Most of the members of the legislature were present. Great excitement among the people of the county. Their sympathies were alive for the woman & children." However, he observed that the legislators in attendance, as well as people from his own neighborhood, displayed a willingness to "countenance the horrid traffic" of slavery and "were almost clamorous for the pretended owner." After introducing all the relevant evidence in the case, Calvin got up and addressed the court "in behalf of the woman & read law." After Calvin's remarks, Sewell's attorney rose and spoke to the court; his speech, Calvin reported, was full of "much severity & abuse against persons & against me—all of which I overlook in him."[75]

On December 26, Calvin went home and awaited Judge Morris's verdict. It didn't take long. That same day he learned, much to his surprise, that "the Judge decided that a man abandoning a Slave state with his Slaves for the purpose of settling in a free state, the moment that his slaves &

himself reached a free state they were free." "This decision will produce great excitement," Calvin predicted. "What violence, what outrages may yet be committed on the poor negroes, I know not. I have discharged my duty towards them & in accordance with my own sober convictions." This was the first case on the legal rights of African Americans from the slave South in which Indiana identified as a free state.[76]

With growing confidence in his legal practice, and more settled in spirit with his faith, Calvin focused on rejuvenating his home life. He and Sarah and the family planned to move into a new home in the center of Indianapolis. Meanwhile, his household was expanding: he brought in a thirteen-year-old-girl, Dorio Crumbaugh, as a bound servant for five years to help Sarah with the household chores. Likewise, Thomas Moore, a sixteen-year-old boy, moved into the Fletcher home as a servant during the winter of 1829. Calvin and Sarah, like many other prosperous couples, presided over a fluid household comprising their own children, live-in servants, and occasional boarders, such as Curtis Mallery, a young teacher who stayed for a while with the Fletchers while he taught school in the neighborhood.[77]

In the summer of 1830, Calvin took Sarah on her first "vacation," which was partly a trip to visit her family back in Urbana. Calvin left her briefly during the journey when he boarded a steamboat one night from Cincinnati to Louisville. This boat trip caused more than a little concern for Sarah, who observed, "I never felt more anxiety about him in my life."[78] About a half-mile from land, the steamboat, Calvin reported, "received a small snag in her side & almost filled before it was discovered. I witnessed a scene of great confusion. She was run ashore and all was saved—but we were badly alarmed." The next day, Sarah visited a museum and a paper mill in Cincinnati. Despite Calvin's near tragedy, she also took her first ride on a steamboat, which made her sick. The couple rode on horseback to Urbana since the stagecoach wagons couldn't handle the rough roads at that time of the year. Seeing his wife away from home, experiencing the broader world he encountered regularly, Calvin offered an admiring, if condescending, perspective on his young wife: "Mrs. F. rides horse back with great ease & is very choice or rather proud of a good horse & riding dress," he told his father.

> I took great pains to show her Steamboats, Steam engines, *museums,* paper mills—Sunday schools—Infant schools high life & low life. Nothing improves even a woman with good common sense more than to travel—to put up at some of the best houses & stay at some of the meanest. Let her keep a Journal & observe all things as women usually do & in a Journey of four hundred miles which we took she must learn many things & more especially how to be agreeable to strangers & to keep a neat house when at home.[79]

After a four-week absence, Sarah and Calvin returned home, pleased to see that their children were all in good health. The whole trip, Calvin noted, had cost $100. At the end of the journey, Calvin took the opportunity to appraise himself, professionally and parentally. And it was an unusually upbeat, even confident, assessment. While out visiting other lawyers in Urbana, he told his father, "I had an opportunity to learn the progress of the men of my profession who were doing business there when I first went to the country & I had the conceit to think that as a business man I was equal to them." Such high standing had for the first time brought Calvin some modest but noteworthy prosperity—of which he was prideful. "I am reasonably prosperous in my worldly concerns," he informed his father. "I spend my money I think liberally—yet I am very industrious. I have been blessed with a Judgment to calculate well as to some investments I have made in lands which have raised much in value."[80]

He was even more prideful about his sons. "Our four boys are growing well," he reported. "Elijah the second one we have sent about 24 miles distant to go to school to an old friend of ours . . . James Cooley has boarded with his uncle James since the first of December and gone to school with his uncle John. There is an excellent school about one mile from James's. John & Cooley have been almost two months & have not missed but one day. They are learning fast." He further noted that while Elijah was away at school, Sarah came to visit him, especially when he became "dangerously sick with an ulcerated throat," during which time Sarah watched over him until he recovered. "She came up alone on horseback through the then almost unbroken forest. Indeed she was well skilled in horsemanship."[81]

Most important to Calvin was how manly and mature his four boys were becoming. As he fairly boasted to his father, "We have lately brought them all to eat with us at the table. The eldest is now able to water and feed my horses & I rejoice at the prospect of having my own servants or rather children to wait upon me." Cooley, his eldest, he proclaimed "a Fletcher in form and appearance" but with "an excellent good disposition— . . . generous & very affectionate—still afraid of specters & ghosts after dark," which, Calvin acknowledged, were "slavish fears which troubled me & you in our boyish days." Apparently, Jesse Sr. considered these sorts of youthful fears "constitutional" in nature, emanating "from the female branch of your own family."[82]

Jesse Sr. had obviously communicated to his son his own doubts about religion, and about Calvin's deepening Methodist convictions in particular. Far from deferring to his father's spiritual instincts, Calvin saw those misgivings only as a sad reflection on his father's dwindling faith. "You say in your last [letter] that you are in great doubt & that you do not give yourself much concern about it," he wrote his father.

> My first strong impressions as to religious matters I learned from father. They were strongly impressed on my mind. You must have felt the same then or would not have had the power to communicate to me or your other children in so forcible [a] manner . . . You since have changed your views. I believe you were once right on these matters but are now wrong or that you are now in doubt and confusion. When you had the strongest faith were the days of your happiness & greatest worldly prosperity.

As a new convert, Calvin simply couldn't accept that his new convictions would be questioned by his own father. "In this I can't be mistaken," Calvin insisted. "Should I not then stand to the faith—should I not then seek for that which gave you the greatest quantity of earthly happiness? If I am wrong tell me so."[83]

We don't know if Jesse Sr. ever told Calvin he was wrong. His health declined rapidly during the winter of 1830, and on February 14, 1831, he died. Perhaps revealingly, Calvin's diary contains a rare, nearly year-long gap from his birthday, February 4, 1831, until Christmas of that year, so we don't know how he responded to his father's death. But given Calvin's mixed feelings about his father, we can imagine it was an occasion for grief tinged with relief. Weeks later, Elijah, in a brief but heartfelt passage, communicated with Calvin after first hearing "the sad intelligence" from their brother Stoughton. "You have no doubt heard," he wrote, "the heart rending tidings from home, that a Parent whom we all esteemed and had much reason to love was no more."[84] This man, who had taught them both—and their siblings—so much about hard work, the perils of indebtedness, and the power of education, had spent most of his life fighting debt and struggling with depression and dependence on his children, especially Elijah.

Like most endings, Jesse Sr.'s death not only prompted mournful reactions but also revealed new beginnings. Within days of his father's death, Calvin, Sarah, and their four children had settled into a new house in Indianapolis that they had purchased in December. Located on the south side of East Ohio Street, the residence was much bigger than their previous home, offering additional space that their quickly expanding household sorely needed. And, in the same letter in which Elijah commiserated with his brother about the sad demise of their father, Elijah disclosed that he had just bought a plantation where Maria was keen on settling and spending summers. It was called Sweet Briar, and it would one day become the central focus of his daughter, Indiana, offering a legacy that, like the indelible stamp Jesse Sr.'s death left on the Fletcher children, especially Elijah and Calvin, would stretch far into the future.

Four

"THE BEST FORTUNE WE CAN GIVE OUR CHILDREN"

T he death of Jesse Sr. in February 1831 reverberated for years in the larger Fletcher family. Aside from Jesse's widow, no one felt the loss more keenly than Elijah, who had for years advised and helped support his father from the "distant country" of Virginia. Soon after hearing "the sad intelligence" of Jesse's death, Elijah took charge of memorializing his father's legacy, covering his numerous debts, and protecting the ancestral home and property as best he could. He also wrote his brother Calvin about what should be inscribed on their father's gravestone, remembering that "Father was the first Justice of the Peace" in Ludlow. As one of the town's first settlers in 1783, Jesse Fletcher Sr. was a local leader, serving as town clerk, selectman, and legislator in the 1790s. Like most proud sons, Elijah wanted the world to remember his father in the most flattering fashion: "I want Fathers [gravestone] to be a little nicer than any other in the Grave yard," he told Calvin.[1]

Jesse Sr. may have been a respected local leader, but he died mired in debt. Elijah and Calvin quickly became consumed with trying to pay off that debt and protect the estate. The brothers focused their attention on their youngest brother, twenty-three-year-old Stoughton, who had been living at home in Ludlow during their father's final years. Realizing that Stoughton "had been a faithful Boy to his Father . . . till his dying hour," Elijah and Calvin immediately looked to him to serve as caretaker of the farm and to oversee the repayment of debts. Stoughton began selling off his father's sheep, but doing so made only a slight dent in all the financial obligations. With a debt once estimated at $150 now grown to $250, Elijah noted, "it seems as though they never could get to the end of their debts."[2]

Clearly, the Fletcher farm was a poor one that offered little incentive to anyone to take over its overseeing and protection. So Elijah made a financial proposal to Stoughton: he would pay off their father's remaining debts himself and allow Stoughton the opportunity to make whatever profits he could by remaining on the farm. But, like so many other New England youth in this era, Stoughton had other, larger ambitions, mostly out west. "He thinks the offer I make him not a very good one," Elijah reported. Stoughton wanted to go to school and travel. And his mother Lucy, as we have seen, was stamping her feet, insisting—even in her hour of need—that the young Stoughton leave home and make his own independent life. Even Elijah couldn't argue with these youthful ambitions—the very ones he had acted upon with success a generation before—but he did not want the property to fall out of the family "into other hands." Finally, the Fletcher sons settled on hiring "a good man" to carry on the work of the farm and engaged Susan Sargent, a neighboring friend who had been living with their mother, to take over the domestic responsibilities.[3]

Meanwhile, Stoughton weighed other, more intriguing options. Both Elijah and Calvin offered to help support him if he moved to Indianapolis, where he could go to school. Stoughton already owned property willed to him by his father worth $600 to $700, and he proposed that Elijah give him an additional $500 "clear of all the debts," an idea that gave his brother pause. Ultimately, as Elijah wrote in a letter to Calvin, "as he is our youngest Brother, to give him a start I have concluded to do it. I pay him $100 now and when he fully makes up his mind not to return but to go into other business, I am to pay him the balance." Elijah hoped that getting out in the world would do wonders for his younger brother; it had done so in his own youth. The difficulties of life on one's own just might awaken Stoughton to the value of returning to safeguard the family home. "After travelling about and seeing the world," Elijah noted, "and seeing how people live and that is not the easiest thing in the world to get property, he may return." Fearing that Jesse Sr. may have given Stoughton the mistaken notion that he would simply be handed the farm, Elijah was seizing the moment to give his younger brother an important lesson in working hard, a lesson Elijah himself had learned. "He is young and healthy and, I am glad to find, smart and intelligent for his opportunity and I think pretty well calculated to make his own way in the world," Elijah observed. "I have scuffled pretty hard to make and save what I have and I owed it to my own family to preserve it for them, or at least what I give away, to give to my Mother, Brothers and Sisters who are in need or distress; or if I have any thing else to give them—they are all dear equally to me—I ought to distribute equally among them."[4]

After a "long and somewhat perilous journey," Stoughton arrived in Indianapolis in October 1831 to make his own start out west, supported in part by his brother Calvin. Upon hearing the news of his safe arrival, Elijah expressed delight. "You do not appreciate him too highly," he told Calvin. "There are few young men of better qualities. He wants what he has now, an opportunity of getting a little common education and by travelling, a little acquaintance with mankind. He ought to study writing, arithmetic, and Geography—nothing further yet awhile."[5]

Calvin agreed about Stoughton's character and prospects. In fact, he was so impressed with him that just weeks after Stoughton's arrival in Indianapolis Calvin named the baby boy Sarah had just delivered after his brother. But Calvin's perspective on his younger brother, like so much else, was seen through the prism of his own experiences and traits. Stoughton, Calvin told his mother, "has many new things to attract his attention—new

manners & new customs of the people here have been objects of speculation and remark by him. His acquaintance with the world was very limited
when he started from home but his opportunities have been & will be great
to learn mankind as they really are." Stoughton was studying geography
and on his way to becoming "a good scholar . . . if he can only acquire
habits of reflection & study—and get rid of many of his prejudices." Like
himself, Calvin perceived that Stoughton had "a naturally peevish temper"
and "must learn patience & meekness." If he could only control his temper,
Calvin thought he "will make a man of whom we shall be proud."[6]

Within months of those words, Stoughton's youthful, ambitious spirit
carried him away from his new home in Indianapolis—at least for a while—
on an even greater adventure. Early in the summer of 1832 he joined several
hundred other men on the northern Indiana border to fight the Black Hawk
War. Some four hundred mounted riflemen headed for Chicago in early
June to take revenge on a band of Native Americans led by Black Hawk, a
Sauk tribal leader who, with Meskwaki and Kickapoo support, was trying
to take over disputed lands stemming from a controversial 1804 treaty with
the United States. When some of Black Hawk's band killed several white
people in Illinois, frontier settlers, like Stoughton Fletcher, rose up to join
the fight.[7]

Stoughton seemed positively eager to jump into the conflict. He immediately equipped himself with a rifle, two blankets, a tomahawk, a knife,
a canteen, and twenty days' worth of provisions. According to Calvin,
Stoughton spent a week "exercising himself with his rifle & horse" and
could "shoot as well as the best of them." Calvin was also quick to point out
that "had my family & business permitted it, I should not have hesitated
one moment to have gone myself." Calvin's wife Sarah, whose father was
experienced in frontier conflicts, having lived on the Ohio frontier during
the War of 1812, eagerly "spent the whole week preparing S.'s equipments.
S. said nobody but mother would have done more for him." At no point did
Calvin fear for Stoughton's life, reflecting, "I do not apprehend any danger
that may befall S. in the field of battle as I believe peace will be made without an engagement."[8] During the short-lived conflict, Stoughton oversaw

the transportation of goods from New York to where the treaty negotiations with the Potawatomi were being held on the Tippecanoe River near Fort Wayne, Indiana, about one hundred miles north of Indianapolis.

For Calvin, Stoughton's brief but revealing tour of military duty conjured up a vision of all the valuable experience and potential for valor that any young man could hope for. By the time Stoughton returned home, Calvin predicted, his younger brother would have "seen more than any young man of my acquaintance during my whole life." Since arriving in Indianapolis, in Calvin's proud calculations, Stoughton had attended school for six months; fulfilled his wartime duties in Albany and Buffalo, "when the cholera was raging"; supervised the transportation of $10,000 worth of goods; and maintained a presence at two Indian treaties. Brother Stoughton, Calvin proudly noted, "had an early education" that would make him "a brave and persevering man—and as it is I look to see him do well. I shall spare no pains to make him respected and useful if he stays here."[9]

After his return home from the war, Stoughton went into business, joining a mercantile firm that was closely associated with Calvin in Indianapolis. From Virginia, Elijah voiced strong support for this path, especially since his own brother Calvin would be able to watch over their brother's progress. "His little experience in this kind of business will give his partners great advantages over him," Elijah noted. "But if they are honest men he may not suffer . . . Your brotherly advise and counsel will be of much service to him."[10]

Brotherly advice served Calvin and Elijah well throughout their lives, but especially during the next ten years or so, as they struggled with the issues of avoiding debt, navigating public life while pining for retirement, and ultimately—and most painfully—trying to raise responsible and successful children.

By the 1830s, Calvin's legal business was growing, especially the "collecting" end of it. He invested in government lands and soon needed an assistant to keep his land books and travel the state on horseback to look after his collections.[11] In January 1834 Calvin bought 1,200 acres of land in La Porte County, 150 miles north of Indianapolis, launching a long career of mostly profitable land speculation. The next month the Indiana General Assembly elected him director of the state bank. He had quickly become a wealthy and well-connected man through both his legal practice and his financial dealings.

In the spring of 1835 Calvin and his business partner Nicholas Mc-Carty purchased over three thousand acres, which, along with other recently bought real estate, were valued at $6,500. At this time, Calvin's debts totaled $1,000, with his legal business earning him about $2,000 per year. Despite this highly profitable financial condition, Calvin grew increasingly concerned—precisely because what was making him wealthy was likewise seducing him into close contact with his greatest fear: indebtedness: "I must decline purchasing real estate yet I deem it a profitable investment, but I cannot do it without running in debt," he reflected in his diary.[12]

What drove him forward with hope and—to some degree—confidence was the rising interest in the country in internal improvements: the building of canals, roads, and railroads that would more efficiently (and profitably) link various regions of the country together for the purpose of transporting goods to markets. Calvin met with the Indiana governor in 1835 to talk about the necessity of such improvements. Several railroad sites were surveyed by the legislature, especially the extension of the Wabash Canal to the Lafayette White River Canal. "The Govr. & myself agree in this that canals are the best," Calvin observed, "because the capital to be expended in their construction [is] to be left in the country." In contrast, he believed railroads would take money out of the area. And, unlike canals, which would be permanently sound, railroads would wear out in a decade or two. Eventually, he and others envisioned the entire state and region connected by canals and roads. "There will not be thirty miles in the state without a water communication or railroad," he predicted in 1835.[13] On January 12, 1836, the House of Representatives passed a major internal improvements bill linking the White River and Wabash canals and the railroad lines connecting Madison, Lawrenceburg, and Lafayette. Calvin was ecstatic, commenting, "This grand project will exalt Indiana among the nations of the earth. I have a strong desire to live to see the completion of this splendid system."[14]

But his early fervent hope that internal improvements would usher in an era of financial health could not dispel his gnawing fear of personal financial loss. As early as December 1835, with $40,000 to $50,000 of real estate at risk, Calvin worried about the "future sustenance for myself & family . . . I would not recommend it to any young man to run many risks in the acquisition of property." In his annual New Year's self-appraisal in January 1836, he noted that he had invested with McCarty between $15,000 and $20,000 in real estate, $9,000 of which Calvin had borrowed. Such risk taking, he conceded, "is very hazardous & contrary to the views I have usually entertained." But he admitted he had been coaxed into the investments because of "the great probability of a system of internal improvements," which had "influenced my rashness on this subject." He concluded, however, that "the fears, the responsibility, the accumulated cares cannot be repaid by any reasonable success & that those who should ever read this account may not venture on such an experiment." Brother Elijah, he conceded, had warned him against overindulging in such real estate investments, and so he promised himself never to fall victim to "this enthrawlment" again.[15]

By 1837 the speculative fever had become a contagion that endangered Calvin's banking operations in particular. The year before, President Andrew Jackson's Specie Circular had required all payments for public lands to be made in specie, which cramped banks like Fletcher's that financed western land speculations. A growing financial crisis in England, meanwhile, prompted English creditors to call in their loans, and simultaneous crop failures in several regions of the United States weakened the purchasing power of American farmers. In what was referred to as the "Panic of 1837" several prominent New York banks in May of that year suspended specie payments, a step that was followed by most other banks in the country. The result was a depression that lasted until 1843, hitting most severely in the West and South and prompting a demand for stricter banking laws.[16]

Watching anxiously from Virginia, Elijah commiserated with Calvin not only on the southern repercussions of the Panic, but also on the dangers it posed to his brother in Indianapolis. "I fear the Whirlwind, which has laid prostrate the southern rich cotton country and the mercantile wealth of the eastern cities will not pass *lightly* over your northwestern country," Elijah wrote. "These things I have been anticipating but must confess they have come upon us one year sooner than I expected, but their effects will be felt for many years." Calvin's decision to sell off some of his overpriced land "before the Tempest and storm came" showed "much self command," Elijah felt, as the most difficult tasks during "times of high excitement in speculation" are to maintain one's poise and "to know when to stop and sell enough to square accounts," leaving people "with property but no money" owed.[17]

Indeed, Calvin followed Elijah's advice (and, no doubt, his own instincts during the crisis) to immediately sell off some of his property. He sold his land in Michigan City, Indiana, to a man from Kentucky for $2,875, observing in his diary that "I owe debts & am desireous to have them paid." He traveled to Laporte, Indiana, and noted that the town "looks like a graveyard. All the laboring class have left the country & gone West to the new lands." On his way home from Logansport, Indiana, on "as bad a road as ever I passed," he "met many wagons movers with families—on going out we met 50 waggons coming in & met as many on our return going out."[18] Everywhere Calvin looked, the speculative fever was subverting all financial sanity. "Every man almost in this country has abandoned his business to speculate in real estate," he told his business partner, Nicholas McCarty. "The farmer has left his farm & omitted to put in a crop. The mechanic his shop & even the merchant his store & have vested all they had & all they could borrow in real estate."[19]

Elijah likewise witnessed the restless drive of the Virginians, many of whom, including a few "men of standing and respectability," were heading west, some of them to Indiana. As soon as they could sell their possessions in Virginia, Elijah said, they were gone. Whether such movement led to a genuine improvement in their circumstances was another matter.

"Some who go may better their situations," Elijah told Calvin, but "others may wish themselves back. For my part, I feel contented and probably shall never change my location." Even Elijah's wife, Maria, had caught the migration bug, with Elijah noting that she was "quite restless." Despite the fact that Virginia was enjoying relatively prosperous times, Elijah could not ignore "the immense emigration to all parts of the Western and Southwestern country."[20]

Enabling all this movement and desperate speculation, Calvin believed, were eastern capitalists. Moneylenders from the big banks, he contended, "have sold to the innocent stranger to take bad money to the lounger & rascall who had none & to one & another & all owe for the property bought. All are in the market to sell & but for the policy of the prospectors there would be crash in a day."[21] Even a few unhappy citizens in Indianapolis accused Calvin's bank of encouraging speculation and helping certain individuals amass large fortunes at the expense of poorer classes—a charge Calvin vehemently and successfully disputed.[22] By May 1837 the panic was widespread. From "a very respectable merchant of N.Y. City" Calvin learned that "there scarcely will be a solvent merchant in that city by the first of June. News has arrived that the Banks of Louisville & all the Ky. Banks have suspended."[23]

As he did with many social ills, Calvin viewed the nation's financial distress as a revealing mirror into personal weaknesses. By the spring of 1837 his own "pecuniary difficulties," he believed, had become nearly universal. Financial worries "seem not only to approach me as an individual," Calvin observed, "but the whole nation are to be afflicted." For a year he could "scarcely sleep at night in consequence of the debts & responsibilities resting on [him]." And he frequently invoked God's help in resolving his "pecuniary distress": "I desire more controle over myself—a conquest that grace alone can obtain over a heart prone to evil greatly deceitful & entwined around the things of this world."[24]

While his own indebtedness seemed controllable, Calvin continued to sound the alarm, writing in his diary, "I am in my own mind prepared for the worst." He did not live an extravagant life, he insisted, and thus had no highly valued property to surrender to creditors. "We have no carriage no Turk[ish] Carpet nor stately mansion to part with," he noted. "On the contrary as yet we possess nothing but the necessaries of life." His own family, in fact, was prepared to be self-sufficient, manufacturing its own butter and making its own clothing, even if it meant putting all of his children to "daily labor."[25]

✻ • • ✻

Invoking the possibility of putting his own children to work in the Panic of 1837 was not something Calvin Fletcher did lightly. His near-daily agonizing over the looming financial distress pained him so deeply precisely because he saw it as a dangerous threat to the prosperity and future of his children. And because his family was growing rapidly—Calvin and Sarah had eight children by 1837, some fifteen years into their marriage—he felt immense responsibility for his household. Elijah praised him for having children so early in life. "You followed Dr. [Benjamin] Franklin's advice of early marriage," Elijah commented, "that you might see your children raised and provided for before you die. It is perhaps a very good rule."[26] Calvin viewed large families as offering the best test for life in a difficult world, requiring the development of traits such as compromise and getting along that were necessary for any young person who hoped to succeed. He acknowledged that most people "are opposed to having large families" but, while not unmindful of "the great responsibility" of rearing so many children, believed the bigger error lay in "those who have but few & equally disastrous expectations raised," a situation that forced many fathers to give all their property to one heir rather than spread the resources and opportunities among all children. Moreover, raising "a numerous family together gives a fair trial of their tempers & prepares each member while in this little state where many interests are to be regarded by each, to be compromised, settled & surrendered admirably for the world—'its losses & crosses.'" In what could easily be the watchword for Calvin Fletcher's life, he emphasized the value, and perhaps even the necessity, of reliving life through his children, noting that "in the life of all my children I live a new life, in their several prosperity or adversity I participate. They each add a new checker to the scenes of my own life."[27]

Elijah Fletcher did not place himself so directly into the emotional lives of his children, but he certainly shared his brother's conviction that it was a father's job (more so than a mother's) to raise and "fit" his children, especially his sons, for a specific career and future. Elijah's two sons, Sidney and Lucian, were very dear to him, but he was aware that in choosing the South as the place to rear his family, he was not doing them any favors. "This is a bad country in which to bring up boys," he confided in Calvin. "I wish mine could be raised in the indigence and simplicity that you and I were. You may feel very happy that you are not in a slave state with your fine Boys, for it is a wretched country to destroy the morals of youth."[28] What made it a "wretched country" was the well-known tendency of young southern men, surrounded and served by personal slaves, to become arrogant, entitled, and beyond parental control, especially once they reached their teenage years.[29] Young Lucian attended a neighborhood school, but, his father conceded, even at seven years old, he was "so wild he does not learn much." A few years later, when fifteen-year-old Sidney was being prepared to enter Yale within a year or so, Lucian at age twelve remained incorrigible: "Lucian, I hardly know what to do with as [he] will learn nothing at school and thinks of little but his Gun and amusements," Elijah wrote Calvin. "I have now got him writing and copying in my office, merely to learn him to write and the use of figures." Six months later Sidney was doing quite well at Yale, while another young man from their neighborhood who had traveled to school with him—no doubt "Lucian-like" in his behavior—had already gotten into trouble and been suspended. The news prompted a revealing parental *cri de coeur* from Elijah: "Children hardly know what pain, such disgrace at school, gives their Parents nor what pleasure it affords them to hear of their good conduct." Sidney and Elijah's much younger daughters, ten-year-old Indiana and seven-year-old Betty, were doing fine, with Indiana taking music lessons on the piano and guitar and Betty attending school and "very fond of her Book."[30]

Elijah's laissez-faire attitude toward life and reluctance to intrude too closely into the development of his children left him sometimes helpless in the face of the unpredictable directions they took. "I generally keep in good spirits and preserve such equanimity of mind," he once explained. "Sometimes I am a little dejected. I have so many positions to control and manage, I cannot always keep the machinery of my affairs in proper trim." Like many southern planters, he believed in allowing a certain degree of willfulness to his children, especially his sons, who, after all, grew up learning the "command experience" over slaves. Such a noncoercive approach to child-rearing left parents with little influence when it came to wayward sons. "I try to govern more by persuasion than force," Elijah explained. "Yet there are some crooked sticks that will fit no situation."[31]

It was not only Elijah who shared educational plans with his brother Calvin; as a student at Yale, Sidney himself offered advice to his uncle on how best to prepare his cousin, Calvin's teenage son Cooley, for college. He recommended to Calvin that Cooley should "get skilled in reading, writing, spelling and math so that when he enters upon prep studies he can focus totally on Latin & Greek." Sidney underscored the educational deficit under which southern boys like him had to struggle in readying themselves for college. "There are few students that come on well prepared from the South," he wrote Calvin. "I know from my own experience that a young man can not be well prepared for a thorough course through a Northern College in a Southern school. In the South they get only a smattering of what they learn." What afflicted most southern boys, Sidney insisted—no doubt including his own brother Lucian in that group—was laziness: "For once she has you under her power it is very hard to escape from her."[32]

Like so many of the Fletchers, Sidney fully endorsed the centrality and necessity of an excellent education, especially in a democratic nation like America. "The supremacy of mind can not be doubted," he wrote his uncle Calvin from Yale in 1838, "and in a republic this fact is tenfold manifest." What mattered most, he believed, was that in "the present age of refinement," the acquisition of a good education would not only command respect, but "is the only means by which public advancement may be obtained." Ambition and self-advancement, the touchstones of the Fletcher family and the American people writ large, required intelligence and enlightenment, in part because they set a man up above the common folk. "A young man without a liberal education in enlightened society," Sidney acknowledged, "is like a fish out of water." Young men like Sidney, Cooley, and others had the choice of being either among "the respectable" or among "the enlightened." The respectable man may be an honest, hardworking mechanic, Sidney noted, but "he is the slave of the opposite class." The educated "enlightened" man "controls the other," as he has the capacity to understand and "possess" the natural world through his ability to "account for its wonders." In an American nation where there was no aristocracy of wealth or birth, there was indeed "an aristocracy of intelligence and refinement." And as a young man, Sidney was convinced, this was the time to join that "aristocracy." "Youth is the time to decorate and adorn the mind and strengthen it by study," he contended.[33]

All of these sentiments Elijah no doubt found comforting, even as he agonized over the slower progress and more limited prospects of his young son Lucian. He sent Lucian to a private boarding school but determined not to send him out of Virginia for the rest of his education. "Though I do not regret sending Sidney to Yale . . . Lucian will take a somewhat shorter course of studies than Sid, so as to complete them about the same time," he wrote Calvin. Elijah's grand plan for all his children, daughters as well as sons, was that once they completed their studies, he would "let them travel one year in the U. States and then two years in the Eastern World before they settle down in Business." That is, he cautioned, "if they conduct themselves well, so that I can trust them abroad. For should they turn out badly—as they may—I would soon withhold from them the means of extravagance and dissipation."[34]

When Calvin sent his son Cooley back east to Philips Exeter Academy in 1839, Elijah endorsed the decision but cautioned that "our boys want vigilant watching and attention. I have to advise, persuade and scold some to them. They have such a tendency to take up romantic notions and try to assume the *man* while they are but Boys." Doubtless, commanding slaves every day nurtured in boys a premature sense of superiority and manliness, a pattern of entitlement and power that few planter patriarchs could prevent from developing.[35]

Elijah had similar but more limited expectations for his two daughters. Cultivating refinement and intelligence in Indiana and Betty mattered greatly to him, but these goals were oriented more toward a private sort of accomplished gentility rather than a life running a plantation or becoming a professional of any sort. Religion and morality also played a more prominent role in the education of girls; thus, Elijah sent the twelve-year-old Indiana off to the Georgetown Visitation Convent Academy in 1840. When dropping her off at the nunnery, Elijah gave voice both to his tender feelings for her and to his vision of the larger social world he hoped she would make her own. That vision described at once a capacious intellectual world and a circumscribed society distinctly lacking any sort of power or practical purpose. Elijah pleaded with Indiana not to be "too upset that he didn't come by" one last time before heading back to Virginia. "I thought it best not to do it," he told her, "knowing how tender were your feelings and how much distressed at the thought of being separated from your Friends." He understood that her feeling "a little Homesick" was entirely natural, but he expressed the conviction that she would come to like her "new home" and would advance quickly in her studies. "It would be far more agreeable to me to have you with us, but I know it is for your good to be away for a while," he told her. "You have greater opportunities than you could possibly have here and you know how anxious your Brothers are that you should be a *Learned and accomplished* Lady. Cheer up! Do not despond."[36]

In the relatively private, ornamental world of southern ladies, Indiana and her sister Betty, through their musical training and religious instruction, were being groomed for their anticipated roles as agreeable, cultivated helpmeets to their future husbands. Near the end of 1841, by which time Sidney had returned to Virginia to manage one of his father's farms, and with still no clear direction for Lucian in sight, their mother, Maria, offered the most realistic and insightful assessment of the future of her children, sons and daughters alike:

Indiana Fletcher

When my boys were little men I thought then a great deal about their being great ones but now I am contented that they may till the earth for their daily bread. I have no doubt but they would be happier and equally as respectable. Sidney seems so perfectly happy in his present occupation I should prefer that Lucian would select the same employment, tho he is much more of a roving disposition than Sid. Indiana and Betty seem delighted with their secluded situation.[37]

In due course, Maria's appraisal—in both its hopeful and its concerned tones—would play out in extreme fashion.

In Indianapolis by the mid-1830s, Calvin Fletcher presided over a large and fluid household: five sons, James Cooley, Elijah, Calvin, Miles, and Stoughton; a servant girl, seventeen-year-old Orindorio Crombaugh; a widow, Mrs. Ansel Richmond; and Mrs. Richmond's little boy, eighteen-month-old Ansel. Like many middling and well-to-do families, Calvin not only employed servants (mostly teenage girls) to help around the house, but also took in orphans or widowed women and their children for months, even years, at a time and treated them as part of the family.

It was a family devoted to hard work and self-advancement. Early on, Calvin sent his children away to school, sometimes in the neighborhood, but more often to schools miles away where he had greater confidence in the schoolmasters. In 1834, ten-year-old Elijah was sent away to a school run by Mrs. Frances Kent in Greenwood, Indiana, ten miles south of Indianapolis. She was a preacher's wife, a "celebrated instructress." "Mother carried me there on horseback," the young Elijah later remembered. "The greater part of the way the road seemed as if hewed through the dark forest." The school was apparently the only frame building in the neighborhood. Elijah recalled being seen as a bit of a hero among his fellow students, since he came from the "far distant town of Indianapolis." His memories of his early schooling were far from rosy, however. He recalled that one of his principal teachers, William Holliday, was a man "without the least degree of love or gratitude. A more cruel, hard hearted man I never knew, minister though he was. He fairly starved, and cowhided knowledge into his scholars on study days, and then on Saturdays impudently demanded their services in sawing his wood, digging his potatoes, &c."[38]

Elijah's older brother Cooley, eleven at the time, attended an academy some sixty miles away. Again, Sarah accompanied him to school, a deliberate plan Calvin had hatched: "I make her attend to this business so if I should happen to be called off, she will have had some experience in these matters," he wrote his mother. "Besides should my boys do well I want their mother to have the credit in a great measure."[39] Sarah sometimes shared educational duty with Calvin, listening to the children read aloud and monitoring their composition efforts.[40] While Calvin and Sarah tried to display an even-tempered demeanor at home, tempers did flare on many occasions, mostly owing to Calvin's ongoing struggle to govern his own passions. When they fought, Calvin was quick to downplay the tension in front of the children. "Mrs. F. & myself have had a conversation," Calvin noted, "in relation to the exhibiting a bad temper before our children. We have concluded that they have readily adopted every bad passion we have ever exhibited in their presence & that we ought at once to cease such exhibitions before them."[41]

What Calvin most wanted his family to exhibit, beyond an unequivocal commitment to learning, was a consistent focus on discipline and devotional life. His boys helped their uncles Stoughton and Michael with the corn crop and regularly cut and prepared wood for the family's fireplace. And while he wasn't a deeply pious man, Calvin made sure his children were exposed to the moral uplift that came with regular church life. "Every Sunday when at home I go to church & if possible take my children with me," he noted in his diary.

> We have a family prayer meeting on that day at which no other but the children, my wife & self attend & what is pleasing our children do not

Sarah Fletcher with daughters Lucy and Maria

look upon it as a burthen. Every morning we assemble ourselves in the winter at 6 & in the summer before sun rise to read & pray. This we should do in the eve but for the circumstances of our children retiring very early to bed & their mother sees that they repeat the Lords prayers & I am usually absent at my office.[42]

Calvin was equally religious about fulfilling the duty of cultivating his children's taste for the world of ideas and learning. He often orchestrated an evening of family debate. One February evening in 1833, Calvin noted, "we had a debating society to please the children. Cooley was president . . . and took his seat upon the table in a little chair and returned his acknowledgments for the honor conferred. We proceeded then to elect other officers & then to passing laws." One such law fined any boy who failed to secure a gate appropriately, as a couple of the Fletcher boys had recently left the bar down on a pasture gate, allowing the livestock to run out.[43] Every Sunday Calvin deliberately cultivated conversation with his children, especially the oldest ones, quite often discussing lessons (or actual letters) from his own parents, his early life, and his "native country" in New England. He sat them down for conversations on subjects ranging from memory to "disobedience." Calvin always talked with his boys about significant books, which sometimes prompted as much concern in him as it did hope. After reading the life of Paulus Aemilius to his boys, Calvin felt "very anxious" about Cooley, expressing the desire that "he should advance in his studies & not idle away his time." As he observed in his diary, "He seems willing & even apt to learn but I fear he will not dig deep for the pure waters but will be satisfied with the first pool he comes to."[44]

Such anxiety about the character and destiny of his children occasionally found expression in rather extreme measures attempting to discern the future of the family. In early January 1837, Calvin called K. E. Burhans, a prominent traveling phrenologist, to his home. Fletcher had attended Burhans's lectures and observed with great interest his "examinations" of the heads of willing subjects. Phrenology, which had become all the rage in 1840s America, was a pseudoscience focused on measuring the human skull and the bumps on the head as a revealing window into an individual's intellect, character, and personality. Calvin wanted Burhans to do an examination of his entire family—Sarah and his seven children. Burhans arrived at the Fletcher home on the night of January 2, and over the course of several evenings, he carefully studied and measured the heads of Fletcher's teenage sons Cooley and Elijah, along with his younger boys, Calvin Jr.,

Miles, Stoughton, and Ingram. He then delivered his assessment: Elijah, Calvin's twelve-year-old, displayed "good intellects," Calvin reported, but, according to Burhans, "he is a little cunning, evasive." He may become "a good scholar," Burhans concluded, "but lacks application." Cooley, the eldest boy, at fourteen, was "very respectable" but fell in the extreme range in terms of needing approval and love: the boy, he said, "will be fond of show &c if not checked." Both boys showed a decent "firmness" of mind, though young Calvin Jr. was "too timid" and seemed relegated to "happy mediocrity." All of the children, Calvin reported, were pronounced to have "respectable intellects," with Elijah and Stoughton "calculated the best for scholars." Most noteworthy was Burhans's assessment of Calvin's quiet, unassuming wife, Sarah, who struggled with low self-esteem. As Calvin noted, with surprise and joy, "Mrs. F. ranks much higher than myself in her intellectual faculties. This I always knew but she fails in Hope which deprives her of much worldly happiness & counteracts her other energies."

No one in the family concerned Calvin more than his eldest son, Cooley. Calvin invested so much time and heart and hope in Cooley that it is sometimes painful to witness how much his paternal worry grew out of a seemingly relentless need to see the boy's odyssey through the prism of his own childhood experiences. In the fall of 1837, Calvin and Sarah allowed the fourteen-year-old boy to take a solo trip to Urbana, Ohio, to visit his maternal grandfather and great-grandmother Olive, who, Calvin reflected, "is yet alive & in all probability C. will be the only one of my children who will ever see her." What mattered so much to Calvin in Cooley spending time with Olive, it turned out, was the symbolic role she had played in *Calvin's* youth, most notably in his celebrated act of running away from home to start his life out west: "I am under many obligations to her & especially for the loan of a shirt in the summer of 1817 when I first arrived in & near Urbana O. from N.E.," Calvin remembered. "I had lossed & worn out all my clothes & I was so destitute that I had but one shirt. The use of one she supplied for several weeks till I fortunately obtained the pattern of one which she made for me." For his visit Cooley left Indianapolis in a covered wagon and was given $13 for expenses. A couple of weeks later, however,

Calvin learned by letter from Cooley that he had lost the money "while helping his grandfather Hill make cider" and could not get back home. Calvin was "mortified that his grandfather should be so stupid or weak as not to help him home without suffering him to write to me for money." In the end, Calvin contacted a wealthy friend in Urbana to quickly provide funds for Cooley to come home by stagecoach.[45]

Even more revealing, Calvin often used key milestones in his children's lives to prompt deep remembrance and reflection about his own early life and lessons learned and forgotten. For a man immersed in both shame (about his early poverty and ignorance) and pride (over his tenacious struggle to advance himself), recalling and reliving these critical moments in his own life and those of his children conjured up "teachable moments" about a well-lived life. To commemorate his son Elijah's fourteenth birthday in August 1838, for example, Calvin remembered that he had been absent at the boy's delivery—he had been attending a trial thirty miles away. And prior to that he had been visiting his father in Vermont and endured a difficult six-week journey (much of it either in a flatboat or skiff) or alone on horseback, arriving home two weeks before Elijah was born. "My prospects looked truly gloomy," he recalled, as Sarah had taken sick a short time before the birth, "the first serious sickness that she ever experienced."

> My prospects for success in life also seemed to wane at this time. I had not learned the philosophy of life, to be greatful & content with what I had, patient persevering & self possessed as to the future. My education encouraged & increased my besetting weakness *my fears* which even made me the dupe of those who took a more cool & deliberate view of present & future prospects in life. Such were my awful apprehensions that I should prove a failure, that things that passed before me gave me no valuable experience . . . Oh that I could live over this portion of my life with a suitable mentor at my side.[46]

While he couldn't relive "this portion" of his life, Calvin as a father committed himself to something just as powerful: he would become, in effect, his own children's mentor, ensuring through his hard-won paternal wisdom that his children's weaknesses and fears would be overcome and making failure—his biggest fear—much less likely. And so Calvin became extremely proactive in assessing, cajoling, guiding, and shaping the educational and occupational futures of his offspring, especially his many sons. This task began each morning. Calvin would rise at 5:00 a.m. and commence "the duties of the day." These involved reading a chapter of Scripture, making sure to explain it to the children, and reviewing the previous day's Bible reading. Then there were prayers and reading "by candlelight" until breakfast. In a particularly revealing moment, Calvin accompanied Cooley and Elijah one spring evening in 1839 to the academy, where several students were performing with prepared speeches. Cooley gave a brief speech, and Elijah read a composition on "Gratitude & obedience to parents & teachers." Calvin's notes on the evening could well have been those of a coach or teacher:

> E. had good composition. Cooley spoke with taste but too tame & too low. Both have left fine opportunity to improve & I have confidence they will do so. Both have exerted themselves more the present & past year than ever before yet do not fill all their valuable time as they should. C. has suggested the propriety of spending another year at home in work & study before he takes up a regular academic course—thinks 17 or 18 will do better than 15 or 16. I am pleased with the remarks. Elijah also seems disposed to be governed by his parents counsel. If my children grow up with such views such a desire to abide by the counsel of their father & mother they can scarcely miss doing right.[47]

Developing an acute awareness of one's own faults became for Calvin a touchstone for potential improvement. So he asked his fifteen-year-old son Elijah to submit to him in writing a list of his most glaring and troubling weaknesses. Elijah's list included the concession that he was lazy, guilty of inertia, "too fond of building airy castles," wasteful, and insufficiently vigilant against evil; furthermore, he didn't truly cultivate his memory, inadequately controlled his passions as "they mislead me," procrastinated, had an excessive appetite, and had developed insufficient self-esteem and ambition.[48] Elijah's list offered a litany of weaknesses and fears strikingly similar to those noted by Calvin's own troubled soul— which may explain why Calvin reacted with such approval to Elijah's self-searching effort.

When Calvin made plans to send three of his sons—Elijah, Calvin, and Miles—off to summer school in 1840, he did so, he claimed in a letter to the school's superintendent, despite great "inconvenience" to the work on his farm and around the household. But it was the strategic importance to his children's young lives of attending school that prompted his "sacrifice": "I am aware of the importance of the present precious moments to them," Calvin wrote. "This summer's attendance under your care will either fix habits of Vigilance and attention, or idleness and sickly capacity to acquire knowledge which will stick through life." Then Calvin proceeded to make specific requests and demands for each of his children that he clearly expected the school to honor. For Elijah, Calvin wanted the school to protect his delicate sensibilities and respect the internal discipline already in place for the sixteen-year-old boy: "I do not wish to have E. drove or censured. His sense of propriety, the certainty of public disgrace, and the mortification of his parents should afford abundant stimulous." Regarding the fourteen-year-old Calvin and twelve-year-old Miles, the demands were more straightforward: "I expect attention and progress from Calvin voluntary & insured beyond anything heretofore exhibited. If I am disappointed in this please return him. As for Miles I do not fear but he will use every exertion." But Calvin wasn't finished. He was intent on laying down rules that would provide him as much control and information as any teacher or school official might hope for: "They will return directly home at noon and night and disobedience in this particular must deprive them of the priviledge granted. What studying they [do] must be done at *School* if they can not keep up with their class, they must stay at home. They can do that they assure me if not I should [not] Send them I shall expect to have an inspection of the merit roll from time to time."[49]

For his oldest son, Cooley, Calvin consulted his young lawyer friend Simon Yandes for help in getting the boy into Harvard. Having recently attended Harvard, Yandes knew the school well and quickly convinced Calvin that it was a superior institution, despite the cold, off-putting demeanor of its students and faculty. "The means of education here are certainly in advance of those of any part of the Union," he wrote Calvin. "The New Englanders take them for all in all [they] are the first people in our country. They are an inquiring, thinking, moral, industrious people. They do not fritter away their time in an everlasting round of fashionable or unfashionable social intercourse, but tend to their business. I feel sure that Cooley after he gets reconciled to their unsocial and cold manners will admire them."[50]

Initially, though, Calvin sent Cooley off to Phillips Exeter Academy to groom him for entry into college and to provide him with some extended time far from home. The principal at Exeter, Gideon Soule, wrote favorably about Cooley, who, he said, had "made a pleasant impression upon his instructors & other acquaintances, by his frank & amiable deportment. He has perhaps sufficient ardour in his studies, & is making good progress."[51] But soon the optimism began to fade. When Cooley failed to write his father for several weeks, Calvin got worried ("I fear some accident has occurred") and then learned that Cooley had gotten sick, had "bought prints & busts" that exceeded his budget, and was talking about transferring to "a western college"—an idea of which Calvin disapproved. Regarding the prints and busts, Calvin noted, "He had no right to purchase them altho the part he contributed ($1.50) was small yet the principal is what is to be guarded against." The next day Calvin wrote an especially reproving letter to Cooley, only to be stopped by his son Elijah and his wife from sending it for fear he was being "too severe."[52]

When Cooley's grades fell from "very good" to "good" in the fall, Calvin could barely contain himself. "I feel mortified at this result but cannot help it," he commented in his diary. "If my sons have not pride, a sense of duty a regard for their parents wishes so as to maintain a proper position at such an institution I cannot help it." Cooley wrote his father about his falling grades, but his response fell short of an apology. Cooley seemed, according to Calvin, "happy as usual—makes a poor apology for his low standing." When several weeks then went by without hearing from Cooley, Calvin confided to his journal that he had perhaps placed too much heart and hope in his eldest son. "I have indulged in too much anxiety in this matter," he wrote. "I am looking forward [to] too much happiness in his success. His defeats, his reverses must be expected . . . Let me not place my heart too much on what may perish." When Cooley's grades improved a bit and he made an explicit apology for his "last bill of standing," Calvin decided his boy's problem came from "his too confiding disposition. He has expected favors without adequate labor . . . He is determined to please everybody in future & hurt no bodys feelings."[53]

Meanwhile, Calvin was beginning to rethink the future for some of his other sons, especially Elijah and Calvin Jr. Increasingly he came to believe that a life devoted to agriculture—which, of course, had been his own father's lifelong work—might be the most suitable and honorable calling for them. To Calvin, not only did successfully running a farm make practical sense, but working the soil conferred a sense of dignity that he considered essential for a man. When Elijah came home from school in May 1841, Calvin decided that working with his hands would be his son's "first trial." "His success in getting my corn plowed, my wheat & hay harvest in will mark his character through life," he determined, "& I feel anxious that he should succeede that I may hold him up as an example to the rest of my children & disappoint a few of my prophesying friends that say my boys will prove failures." Working the soil was always honorable work to Calvin Fletcher, so a young man toiling hard in the fields was destined for respectability. "I wish my sons each & all of them never to see the day while in health that they cannot do a good days work at husbandry," he reflected.[54]

Which is why Cooley so troubled his father. Unlike the other boys, who were willing to engage in agriculture, Cooley strictly pursued an intellectual life. But his uneven progress at Phillips Exeter sowed mostly worry, doubt, and, ultimately, anger in Calvin. Because Cooley, like most students living away from home, both then and now, didn't always disclose his failings and occasional excesses, Calvin fretted constantly about the boy, fearing his son had "become the creature of his own vanity." And what concerned him most were Cooley's unmanly character traits. "He has not moral firmness," Calvin concluded, and "can be misled by women & cajoled by men."[55]

While studying at Exeter, Cooley developed an interest in collecting artwork and doing some drawings of his own, even making some paintings for his uncle Timothy as well as two drawings of a factory he showed some members of the family. In the summer of 1841 Cooley made a trip to the homestead in Vermont, where he showed "some beautiful Landscape sketches of his" to his uncle Timothy as well as his uncle Elijah, who was visiting from Virginia. One of the sketches was of "the old Mansion" itself, which, Elijah told his brother Calvin, "I think so much of as to have it put in a Frame. You must not neglect to give your children opportunity for mental culture. For that purpose I now propose to you, if you cannot conveniently otherwise do it, appropriate the interest of the money arising from the money you owe me."[56] Calvin was deeply moved by his brother's offer to help fund the children's "mental culture." But despite being "grateful to God for such a brother," Calvin wouldn't accept his offer, if only because he thought adversity might be a better teacher: "Poverty more frequently proves a blessing in the acquisition of education & the preparation for usefulness than property or wealth."[57]

While his uncles and brothers saw promise and talent in Cooley's budding interest in art, Calvin saw distraction and disappointment. Cooley's plan to start a "painting school" was a future for which Calvin had "but little faith," but he decided to let him try it. All along Cooley sensed his father's disapproving eye and fear that his oldest boy was headed toward failure. Even Calvin correctly recognized his son's despair over parental disapproval, noting, "He seems to feel a little despondent & states he fears that I have lost confidence in him." As he completed his schooling at Exeter in the spring of 1842, Cooley began to wonder if he was "fitted for college," citing "his own defects of character" and worrying that "his intellects are not equal to those of the rest of his brothers." This perceived intellectual inferiority was one he had sensed for a long time and considered a "mortification" that he wanted his father to keep from "the rest of his broth-ers." This gradual but unmistakable sense of inferiority, Calvin deduced from a letter Cooley wrote him, "had deterred him from choosing a higher destiny than farming & that he believed [his father] was conscious of these defects &c." Cooley's recognition of his own weaknesses sparked an odd sense of joy and recovering confidence in his father. Calvin told his eldest son that "this awakening in him I considered one of the best symptoms of his talents" and revealed that he himself at a similar age had formed a "simi-lar" self-assessment and arrived at an opinion "as to my destiny" precisely the same as the one Cooley was now experiencing. True self-knowledge, Calvin told Cooley, "was to Know how little could be known, to see all other faults & fell our own." If Cooley "would aspire to a higher destiny than an inferior farmer or professional man I would risk the attempt."[58]

In the fall of 1842, Cooley entered Brown University in Providence, Rhode Island, at which point Calvin claimed he was going to let Cooley be his own man: "I have reconciled myself to let him take care of himself. I hope it may be beneficial to him. I have not much confidence in his classi-cal attainment—think he has not laid out but very little of his real strength in his classical studies." His opinion did not improve once he learned a few days later that Cooley had been "instructing some young girls how to draw." Calvin nonetheless sent him $152 to cover his expenses for a year. Despite his pledge to let Cooley find his own way, Calvin registered plenty of concern: "I do not feel such apprehensions as to his morals as I do to his firmness & ambition as a student."[59]

Brown University turned out to be an appropriate place for the Fletcher boys, even if their performance did not always show it. Founded by the Baptist Church in 1764, Brown always focused on the individual student rather than on any sort of abstract learning experience. It offered a remark-ably liberal, student-centered curriculum. As President Francis Wayland, the school's leader during Cooley's time, declared, the curriculum was ar-ranged so that "every student might study what he chose, all that he chose, and nothing but what he chose." Drawing students mostly from rural New England, Brown was a small place, with fewer than two hundred students in the early 1840s. All of these characteristics served its purpose, which was not only to broaden young minds but also to safeguard student morals and discipline. Like other Ivy League schools in this era, Brown was top-heavy with elaborate moral rules that were carried over from Puritan days but fitfully enforced. Despite an intricate system of fines for all manner of petty offenses, many schools had to contend with mob violence and violent disruptions—some of them direct, bitter confrontations between entitled young men and their professors. At Brown in the 1820s, students stoned President Asa Messer's house almost nightly. Harvard had a riot over bad bread and butter in 1805; during a riot at Princeton in 1807 the faculty lost control and had to call in townspeople for help. At other schools, fist and knife fights happened with great regularity.[60]

President Wayland, along with his entire faculty of nine professors (three of whom were glorified tutors), regularly visited students' rooms during study hours to make daily reports and exercise vigilance over student absences and other violations of school rules. If a student's conduct was deemed unsatisfactory, the president would inform the student's parents and "dismiss him without public censure or disgrace." Wayland's concept of college life was that of an academic family, knit together by a strict but kindly paternalism of the faculty over the mental and moral life of its students.[61]

Life at Brown drew the attention of Cooley's younger brother Elijah, who was following in the same path, attending Exeter to prepare for college. In the fall of 1842 Elijah paid a surprise visit to Cooley. Upon arriving in Providence, he found a student to direct him to the college and the boarding-house where his brother was staying. He "met C. on the stairs. [He] didn't know me." Elijah "stayed up in his room until he came . . . He almost cried he was so glad, and it was so unexpected. His questions came so fast that it was a long time before he could stop for answers." Cooley showed him the campus, the statue of Roger Williams, and the old church. Then, Elijah wrote his family, "we measured. I am the tallest and the broadest. In my eyes he was the same fellow as when he left home, only more polished in his manners. He recommended to me the study of politeness." After spending a little time with his older brother at Brown, Elijah reported to his father on what he had witnessed and learned back East: "I have seen the Yankees, and I find they are nothing more than men with heads on their shoulders. I'm not afraid of them . . . Cooley is a perfect Yankee."[62]

Reflecting on the "Yankee" world of the Boston area, Elijah marveled at the eating arrangements where he had stayed, which were a sort of nineteenth-century fast-food experience: "I boarded in a victualing house," he wrote his uncle Calvin, "where there are hundreds eating all the time and only three waiters. You may call for whatever you want, a waiter runs to a speaking tube and mentions to those below then walks to a cupboard on the other side of the house and gets it, so quick is the cooking done and so quick is it passed up into the victualing room by means of sliding cupboards."[63]

Back home in Indianapolis, Calvin not only watched and fretted over Cooley and Elijah away at college, but he also struggled with the uncertain future of his next-oldest boy, seventeen-year-old Calvin Jr. Despite urging the boy to "acquire a taste for reading the Classics," Calvin perceived Calvin Jr. as "ha[ving] none & look[ing] upon it a great hardship to study them. I have warned him of the consequences of his general apathy on the subject."[64] Calvin rightly saw that his son had a "much better business than literary turn." The very next year, Calvin Jr. was apprenticed to work in Alfred Harrison's mercantile store. Even still, his father worried about whether the boy would succeed. "I know it is a fearful business," Calvin wrote Cooley, "not one out of 20, no, out of 30, who have commenced in our place succeeded. They have all proved failures. I have laid these matters before him. I have made a great sacrifise to spare him from my farm."[65]

Then, as now, parental worry over a son's future spawned a lot of sleepless nights, but dealing with disobedience was another matter. Even as he seemed to find some emotional equipoise regarding the futures of his eldest children and that of his brother Elijah, Calvin simply couldn't hold back when any sort of apparent defiance surfaced. In June 1843, Cooley and Elijah attended the Bunker Hill celebration in Boston, part of festivities honoring the start of the American Revolution. Elijah traveled at some cost from the family homestead in Ludlow, which he had been visiting, and Cooley set aside his studies to join him for the event. Viewing this trip by his children as a "species of disobedience," Calvin nonetheless tried to reconcile himself "to what I could not help." But he worried about how attending such an event would both "exhaust" Cooley's limited funds and affect the boy's "standing" at the end of the term. He was also "much mortified" that Elijah was going, too—"but as it is I must put up with it."[66]

Calvin became even more "mortified" when he learned that Elijah was not remotely regretful for having gone to the Bunker Hill festivities. "My teacher went, my classmates went, and I went," he told his father. "I studied during my vacation and was tired out and rather unwell." But after discussing it with his grandmother and her caretaker, Susan Sargent, in Vermont, he got total support. "It cost me about $10 beside a book that I bought for a dollar and quarter," Elijah noted in a full-throated defense. "I saw Cooley and John Tyler, his sons, [Daniel] Webster, General Scott, and in fact all the great men of our country. Moreover, I beheld several scores of old soldiers. I saw hundreds of women, the fair population of the Athens of America. In short, I had a fine time and I don't think I will ever regret or repent going." Calvin responded with a severe four-page rebuke for having been influenced by others to do what he, Elijah, knew was wrong. But to the very end, Elijah denied he had been led astray: "No one persuaded me to go, but myself."[67]

The independent courses that his sons often took produced in Calvin angry outbursts and harsh reprimands. But for his brother Elijah, who experienced his own painful struggles with his sons, especially Lucian, the response to wayward conduct, while unhappy, took on a more philosophical, even laissez-faire, tone. Despite his success at Yale, Sidney returned from college in the summer of 1841 determined to work on the farm rather than follow any professional career—a decision Elijah ultimately supported, although he worried that Sidney might be returning to the farm "to lie down and be a drone," something Elijah, like Calvin, would simply not allow. "My Boys shall never spend my Estate either in idleness or dissipation," Elijah vowed. If they did, he promised to give it away to charity. "Upon this," he declared, "I am firmly resolved and I take every opportunity to let them know it."[68]

Concerned that Sidney was squandering his talent and future on the plantation, Elijah, along with some of Sidney's friends, coaxed him into attending medical college in Richmond the next spring. In short order, Sidney felt oddly out of place studying medicine, preferring the more honest, but less professional, toil as a farmer. "I am as much surprised at my present situation as any of my friends can be," Sidney told his uncle Calvin, "as it's a department for which I am by no means constituted to excel or which can afford me any gratification in practicing. In leaving Agriculture, I am transformed from a good *farmer* into a shabby gentleman." Dutifully attending the lectures at the medical college might well make Sidney sufficiently knowledgeable to become "a tolerable country Doctor," but he knew that once his courses were complete he'd be heading straight home and would in fact devote little time to medicine. When Sidney did return home, Elijah was pleased with his son's "zeal and industry on the Plantation. He is no drone." Sidney apparently used his medical knowledge "among the Servants" (by which he meant black slaves), though it was clear even to his father that he had no plans to become a full-time doctor. For Sidney, returning to the plantation represented an act of duty and obedience to his father, who had often told him that his "prosperity in life has been dependent on the benedictions and blessing of his [own] parents, and that a Source of his greatest satisfaction arises from the reflections of having done his duty towards them."[69] Although he became known as Dr. Fletcher, Sidney never actively practiced medicine.

Sidney returned to a family that was scattered to the four winds. Sister Indiana was ensconced at the convent in Georgetown, and Betty remained at home. Betty, though "not as good a Schollar as [Indiana] . . . possesses more talent and has the most amiable disposition ever I met," Sidney noted.

Lucian had been attending Yale and hoped to finish his education at the College of William and Mary. He was also already talking of making a trip out West, "which he certainly ought to do," Sidney wrote. "I shall try and persuade him to go in the Spring."[70]

Early on, Elijah saw promise in young Lucian, believing in the spring of 1841 that he might even make a better scholar than Sidney: "Though quite wild and headstrong as a child, he is grave, ambitious, and very studious as he is approaching to manhood." Unlike his fretful and worried brother Calvin, Elijah found hope and optimism when he considered his children and the future they faced. "When I look about and see so many unfortunate, wild and dissipated ones, it affords me peculiar satisfaction that mine are so far moral, affectionate, and obedient," he reflected to Calvin. "I have never been rigid with them but early taught them how to obey." He may have been hopeful, but he wasn't myopic. "They are still young," he conceded, "and great changes may come over some of them yet and my present satisfaction may hereafter be turned into regret. But I will hope and pray for better things." Even with all the unknowns and expense of educating children far from home, Elijah insisted, "A good Education is the best fortune we can give our children."[71]

And Elijah made good on that conviction in his family. Having sent Sidney, and then Lucian, to Yale, he invested considerable further funds in Indiana and Betty, both of whom studied at the Catholic convent in Georgetown. After a year at the convent, "Inda" (as the family called Indiana) attended Bishop Doane's School, a well-known female academy in Burlington, New Jersey. Established in 1837 by the Right Reverend George W. Doane, it was one of the more prominent all-girls' academic boarding schools in the nation. And, like other girls' schools and seminaries—which began to flourish after 1800—Doane's School was a small, private academy run by individual proprietors or, in this case, religious orders. The girls came from exclusively white, well-to-do families and were taught a wide range of subjects—literature, history, geography, natural sciences, foreign language, and religion, as well as those subjects thought to be indispensable to female accomplishments: music, painting, and sewing.[72]

Quite the scholar, Indiana wrote her father a letter entirely in French as a teen. Although nineteenth-century society was a man's world in terms of learning and power, Elijah grasped early on that Indiana would "excel either of her Brothers in Learning. She is shrewd and sensible, very ambitious and intelligent, but will not be very showy. It is not a characteristic of our Family to make much display—rather retiring and contented with a reserved self-importance." By the summer of 1843, the family's hopes for Lucian, in contrast, began to dim. Unlike his sisters, he was intent on displaying his "self-importance." Returning from Yale in the summer of 1843, Lucian decided he would finish his studies at William and Mary, presumably in preparation to become a lawyer. "He is somewhat vain and pedantic," Elijah noted, "and thinks he will make a great Lawyer. But there is no telling." Elijah worried that "he will not be able to maintain the ground and eminence he now assumes to himself . . . it is a critical time with him."[73]

Early signs of paternal regret can be traced back to correspondence from Lucian's time at Yale. Those communications in the spring of 1842 reveal a young man quite full of himself—"He thinks he will make a mighty man," Elijah acknowledged. "Even now [he] considers himself quite an Orator and flatters himself that [he] has a genius to thread the intricate mazes of the Law." Maturity and time, "practice and experience," Elijah insisted, "may show [young men] that many of these fancies are visionary, but unless they strive and hope for distinction they never will attain it." In the fall of 1844, Lucian, as planned, intended to leave home for the West, "where he thinks of seeking his Fortune," Elijah told Calvin. "He is not very well settled but somewhat visionary in his calculations about the Future. I am willing for him to try his luck, go among strangers and depend upon himself for a while. He will then know the better how to appreciate a home, where everything has been Plenty, Ease and Comfort." Elijah hoped he could talk young Lucian, then twenty, into paying a visit to his uncle Calvin in Indianapolis. "You sometimes like to have a young man as an assistant in your Office," he wrote Calvin. "If you could put Lucian to work and I could persuade him to stop with you, instead of going South, till he learned some good *hard sense*, it would gratify me much. Lucian is sufficiently towering—too much so for his acquired abilities." Referring to England's famous opposition statesman and eloquent orator, Charles James Fox, Elijah noted that Lucian had "many lofty *Foxian* notions and wants very much practical information. He is somewhat headstrong and thinks few know better or more than he does. I have said nothing to him about this project and will not till I hear from you."[74]

After Calvin sent Lucian a detailed and demanding letter spelling out exactly how he would have to live if he moved to Indianapolis, Lucian changed course, deciding first to sail from Norfolk to New Orleans "and perhaps locate there." Soon after his arrival in New Orleans, however, he became sick with a fever. After he recovered, he set out on his way home to Virginia, still hoping to stop by his uncle Calvin's in Indianapolis. A few months later, though, Lucian had still not visited his uncle nor returned home to Virginia. "Lucian is now somewhere in the Mississippi," Elijah glumly noted, presumably visiting with an uncle in the area. "What will be his ultimate destination I cannot say. He seems to want his own way and I am willing to let him have it."[75]

At the same time that Elijah was worrying about Lucian's wanderlust, Calvin revealed that his own son Elijah had withdrawn from college, signaling a level of ingratitude that both men recognized as a dangerous warning sign. In the face of his nephew's disregard for his educational "advantages and privileges," Elijah expressed support for Calvin's feeling of being "compelled to deprive" the boy of further financial aid. For Elijah, Calvin's son and Lucian's decision to wander off the well-laid path offered a profound and instructive cautionary tale in the precarious art of raising sons: "My determination is fixed," he told Calvin, "about the management of Boys: to be kind to them and give them every opportunity to make themselves useful citizens and an ornament to Society, if they are disposed to properly appreciate those opportunities; and if not, take the opportunities from them. Do not give them money to spend on demoralizing and destroying themselves." If his children chose not to use that support carefully and thoughtfully, Elijah believed it was his "duty to

Society" to give it instead to charity or "other needy relations who would properly value it."[76]

Like Calvin, Elijah believed in the democratic distribution of family resources so that all children could enlarge their world and opportunities through education. He, like all the Fletchers, felt committed to such an egalitarian perspective, even if it meant funding "the undeserving as much as the deserving," because "all should be equally dear to us." However, Elijah drew the line at deliberate defiance. What if one son "wantonly and willfully perseveres to distress and make me unhappy?" he wondered. "What obligation do I owe him? Ought I not to cast him off, forget him, and not be rendered unhappy by him?" He treasured each finger on his hand, he observed, but if one "became diseased . . . and threatened the welfare of the rest of the body, I ought cheerfully to cut it off and cast it away and not grieve for it."[77]

Because they so deeply valued education as a means of self-advancement and prevention of failure—in part because it had profoundly shaped their own lives—Calvin and Elijah put everything they had on the line to give their sons and daughters every advantage possible. Their heavy emotional and financial investment sometimes paid off, but, as they would painfully learn, living so much through their beloved children would also bring heartache and loss.

Five

PUBLIC LIFE

As Elijah pridefully observed the private world he had so carefully cultivated—his pastoral plantation life and the "enlightening" experience three of his children were enjoying while traveling in Europe—his brother Calvin, still agonizing over the fate of his own children, increasingly focused his attention on the public arena, a disturbing world of slavery, intemperance, and illiteracy. The brothers' families thus gave expression to two equally compelling sides of the Fletchers' American journey: an intense desire to nurture successful children for self-advancement and the felt need to remake the world in their own eyes.

For Elijah, raising children to become successful and valued citizens required both education and refinement. Like most southern planters, he associated success with a cultivated gentility reserved mostly for the elite. So he felt confident that sending three of his four children (Lucian, alas, could not be so trusted) abroad for an extravagant two-year grand tour of Europe and the Near East in 1844 would only enhance their stature as they made their way in the world. Armed with influential letters to the U.S. consulate in France from U.S. Secretary of State John C. Calhoun, Ambassador to France Rufus King, and Virginia senator William Cabell Rives, along with letters to leading French physicians, Indiana, sixteen, Betty, thirteen, and Sidney, twenty-three, took a steamship to Havre in late October and then traveled 160 miles by land to Paris. "I part with the children cheerfully (a melancholy cheerfulness)," Elijah noted, "hoping it will be for their good." Indiana, he noted, could already speak French fluently, as well as Italian, and would serve as the interpreter for Sid and Betty. Betty delighted in "describing Scenery and passing events." Like her older sister, she was focused on "improvement and little occupied by the light Frippery and Foolish fashions of the day." Thanks to their well-placed contacts in France, the girls connected with royalty; they were presented to the queen and attended a royal ball. "Bettie," Elijah wrote, "is so delighted with Paris, she wants to stay there six years. If they have health, they will have an interesting time and I hope profit by their opportunities."[1]

What he hoped would result from their two years of travel abroad was a well-rounded, cultured perspective on the world rather than any sort of professional or career outcome. Elijah was in the business of polishing, not training, his daughters. And although their older brother Sidney acted often as their chaperone, he was notably engaged in furthering his own medical training in Europe. While traveling around Europe and the Near East, Sidney and Indiana wrote dozens of letters that were featured on the front page of the *Virginian* between January 1845 and August 1846, offering personal commentaries on the art, architecture, and lifestyles of the many countries they visited. When Indiana and Betty weren't engaged in daily music practice and sketching, they attended plays and concerts and toured cities and the countryside in France, Germany, Spain, Italy, Egypt, and the Holy Land. Indiana's commentary about the exotic look of Alexandria, Egypt, on October 19, 1845, in particular reveals thoughtful powers of description, especially for a sixteen-year-old, on matters of race and gender:

> The novel and singular appearance of everything in the streets as we passed along awakened sensations which I shall never forget. The countenance, costume and look of the natives first attracted my attention—not a white face was seen before me—all either negroes, the dark mulatto,

colored Egyptians; savage looking Turks or Arabs, almost naked, with
a few clothed in costumes of the gayest colors. The women were closely
veiled, wearing jewels on their ankles as well as on their toes, which are
exposed to view by the peculiar fashion of their sandal . . . then the ba-
zaars, the narrow streets crowded with camels, dromedaries, and donkeys, made me feel as if I was a stranger in a strange land.[2]

Elijah gave his children enormous latitude to indulge their appetites
abroad, believing that his generosity was well justified by their trustworthy
behavior. He told them that if they saw "anything they wish to purchase
and can make the monied arrangement," they ought "to do it."[3]

Still, Elijah worried that the cosmopolitan experiences and perspec-
tives his children developed abroad would upon their return make the
simple rural world of their Virginia home feel like a backwater wasteland
in comparison. Before they made their way home, Elijah betrayed this
sense of cultural embarrassment: "All I want of you is when you get home
to be satisfied with home as you find it," he wrote them. "You know I
am willing to improve and not niggardly in spending money for that purpose, but you know I have not had much time, if I had taste, since you
have been gone, to devote to that purpose." Promising that their mother,
Maria, would help them find more fashionable furniture in New York and
elsewhere, Elijah was clearly nervous that the girls would return home
depressed at their simple surroundings: "I hope, I say, you will be contented with home." He solicited the girls' opinion regarding taste and improvements, promising that he would "only put in a word of *humble old
fashioned* advise now and then." His goal was to make "a genteel home in
Lynchburg for a centre and then our rural establishment we will make and
adorn as becomes simple rural establishments."[4]

While he was willing to cater to their need for taste and refinement,
Elijah went to great lengths to warn the girls against letting their recently
acquired world travels go to their heads, in part because the people back
home would see through any pretensions. "When you come home," Elijah
told them a month before their return to Virginia, "the people will not

estimate you by your finery. They will expect from you intelligence and mental adornment and not external show. They have all read that you rode on Mules and Donkeys and horses in your travels and will think you can do the same here. The whole country will think it an honor to associate and converse with you, but will not think a whit the better of you for geegaws and finery." His pride, though, could get in the way of his fear of pretensions: "Still," he told them, "I wish you to appear in neat and rich and genteel apparel."[5]

Sidney's return from his European travels led him to refocus on becoming an even more successful and profitable plantation manager. A few months after coming home, he took a trip south, looking for a sugar plantation to buy. Thinking that there were greater profits in sugar than in Virginia tobacco or wheat, and hoping "to colonize a portion of our slaves in that region, being rather over stocked with them here," Sidney looked to Florida. But he found it a "rude country," much of it "laid waste" by the Seminole Indians. He did identify a spot on the Atlantic coast called Smyrna, sixty miles south of St. Augustine, but found the land too expensive.[6]

Meanwhile, the girls, much to Elijah's surprise and delight, were "content with the monotonous retirement of this country," spending their time reading, writing, sewing, and playing music on the piano and harp they had purchased in London. "They are likewise fond of rambling about," Elijah observed, "and riding with me among the mountains." His daughters were clearly his main companions, since he and Maria appear to have crafted distant, separate lifestyles in their rather unusual, detached marriage. Maria, "not liking much the country," stayed mostly in Lynchburg, leaving her husband Elijah to supervise the country estate, Sweet Briar.[7]

Already a budding connoisseur, Indiana returned from the European trip with an increasingly nuanced aesthetic grasp of the many treasures her travels had revealed, from gilded harps and Italian architecture to Rococo Revival game tables and romantic landscapes. She especially had loved the time they had spent around Florence during the winter of 1845–1846 and became particularly attracted to Palladian architecture, the principles of which she would apply just a few years later in helping her father refurbish Sweet Briar. Beginning in 1851, that house took on the flavor of Indiana's evolving tastes. Upon her advice, Elijah refashioned the place from a simple Federal-style brick Virginia farmhouse with a shake shingle roof into an elegant Tuscan villa. Drawing on her contact with Bishop Doane, whose Italian villa near Burlington, New Jersey (where Indiana had studied at the bishop's female academy), was built in the 1830s, and her many months spent in Italy in the 1840s, Indiana confirmed her taste for the Roman style, with its arched windows and formal gardens arranged in eighteenth-century manner with marble statuary, exotic trees, and unique box hedges. At Indiana's direction, and with some help from Betty, Elijah supervised "several white mechanics" in the summer of 1851 as they erected two three-story towers, one at each end of the house. "This is a project of my Daughters," Elijah noted, "and as I rarely deny to gratify any of their desires, have consented to this." A year later, square tower wings and an arched portico were added to the façade of the old farmhouse, completely altering its appearance. "I tell Inda and Bettie they will become lonesome when all is finished and they have no more to keep up the excitement," Elijah wrote Calvin. But the girls insisted that they would be able to "amuse themselves" by taking special care of all the elaborate furnishings and decorations they had chosen themselves, mostly on trips to New York and Philadelphia.[8]

⚜ • • • ⚜

If Elijah Fletcher found contentment cultivating his relatively private southern plantation world in the pleasing company of his beloved Indiana and Betty, Calvin's Indianapolis-based family was busier and more complicated than ever, and Calvin found himself increasingly immersed in a precarious, conflicted public world. When he assessed his life on his birthday, February 4, 1844, as he routinely did every year, he stressed that he owed a regular accounting to God as well as to himself—"We should often retrospect our lives," he insisted, being mindful of "the various periods of the journey before us." In viewing his "journey," the forty-six-year-old observed with "gratitude" that his two oldest children, Cooley and Elijah, were progressing in school, and that among his older children, Calvin and Stoughton, had, like Cooley, joined a church—Calvin and Cooley were Presbyterians, Stoughton a Methodist. As always, Calvin looked upon all this with a bittersweet feeling: "This affords me new hopes & fears," he wrote, concluding that his children, if "blessed with firmness & grace[,] will be well." If they failed in their sense of purpose and gave in to wicked impulses, "they will be a reproach to their parents & ruin themselves."[9]

But Calvin could become just as engrossed in worrying about what he viewed as the wicked and ruinous developments of the larger world. Raised in an antislavery family in Vermont, Calvin by the 1840s had grown into a much more vocal opponent of slavery, especially as it evolved into an increasingly visible and divisive issue in America. It was, of course, rare to witness the ravages of slavery in a northern city like Indianapolis, so when he encountered it personally while traveling, it made a deep impression. While leaving Cincinnati on a steamboat after a business trip in February 1844, he witnessed the ugly business of the slave trade: "Soon after the boat left the wharf at Cincinnati," he recalled, "it proceeded towards the Ky. Shore & took in 4 light mulatto men & 4 women slaves—The men chained 2 & 2—all young with their ruffian driver or owner who had bot them at Baltimore & was on his way to N. Orleans with them to sell." The slave trader, he noted, had landed them the night before in Kentucky but was clearly fearful about keeping them in Ohio overnight because of the antislavery sentiment of that northern state. The slave trader's reluctance was the only positive takeaway for Calvin in what he saw, but he relished it: "I rejoice the boundaries are so well defined that public opinion is so determined against slavery as it can only exist by the rigid compacts of our land & where ever slavery is not justified that public opinion will not suffer it to exist."[10]

The problem for Calvin and other antislavery activists was that public opinion, especially in the expanding slaveholding South, did not agree with them. And in 1844, as Texas loomed large in the nation's discourse over slavery's likely extension into the territories—"the great exciting question" of the day, Calvin called it—he was left to watch with horror as "demagogues" among the proslavery states manipulated "the ignorant" into accepting the "evil" institution of slavery into the West.[11] Long a proponent of the moderate "colonization" plan, Fletcher believed that while holding men in bondage was a horrible sin, the only lasting solution to slavery was to emancipate southern slaves and return them "to their native Africa," where, under more Christian and civilized conditions, they would flourish. Advocates of colonization, like Fletcher, despite their antislavery convictions, sometimes held racist views, arguing that the movement of blacks was preferable to emancipation. As one prominent proponent of colonization put it, because of "unconquerable prejudice" by white Americans, free blacks would be better off emigrating to Africa.[12]

The presidential election of 1844 threw the volatile issue of slavery into bold relief, and Calvin found himself right in the thick of the conflict. Normally a Whig, he could not bring himself to support the party's candidate, the slave-owning Kentuckian Henry Clay. And he certainly opposed the Democrat, James K. Polk, whose proslavery pro–Texas annexation stance he found loathsome. In Indianapolis, the contest became "exciting," with occasional outbreaks of violence as each side conducted spirited torchlight marches. "All are in arms as to the coming contest," Calvin observed. A Polk victory, he predicted, would only lead to anarchy and the immoral spread of slavery, while "capitalists & men of business, the moral & religious part of [the] community"—the men with whom Calvin clearly identified—would be defeated by "forregners who are ignorant of institutions & [represent] the insolent ignorant part of [the] community." Given his antislavery leanings, Calvin found himself approached by supporters of a third party, the abolitionist Liberty Party, to help campaign for its presidential candidate, James Birney. A week before the election, Calvin met with Birney supporters—a coalition of Quakers, participants in the Underground Railroad, and roughly two hundred abolitionists—in nearby Hamilton County. Sympathetic with their goals—especially their fierce commitment to an immediate end to slavery—Calvin nonetheless remained reluctant to take such an active, public role in the election, especially since he wasn't convinced that campaigning for the Liberty Party would produce anything other than an unwelcome result: a vote for Birney would simply steal votes from the Whigs, all but guaranteeing a victory for Polk and the Democratic Party. When some of the abolitionist activists tried to persuade Calvin that Birney's candidacy harmed both major parties equally, Calvin was unmoved. "I could not open [their] eyes as to the imposition of Birney & other imposters to aid a party who avowed war with Mexico to get Texas," he wrote in his diary.[13]

To make matters worse for many Whigs like Calvin Fletcher, the fast-growing immigrant population of mainly German and Irish settlers did not warm to the elite, heavily Protestant tone of the Whig Party. Indeed, like most Whigs, Calvin believed that immigrant voters, plied with liquor and politically inexperienced, would unthinkingly support the Democratic Party. On Election Day, Calvin observed, "the newly naturalized Germans rushed to the polls to vote the democratic ticket." "The ignorance, the want of schools, the deficiency of men of integrity & intelligence," he noted, "renders it almost unfit for self government." On the evening of Election Day in Indianapolis, bonfires in the streets lit up the night air, while the political activists set off cannon fire. The next day the outcome had not been announced, but Calvin sensed defeat: "I prepare for the worst & suppose or rather prepare my mind to meet an event I have so much dreaded." He was right to feel such apprehension: while Polk secured a narrow victory over Clay in the popular vote—with Birney receiving only a tiny fraction of support—all twelve of Indiana's electoral votes went to Polk.[14]

Little did he know it, but Polk's victory would coincide with a personal loss as well for Calvin. Around election time, Calvin received a letter from his son Elijah announcing that he had dropped out of Brown University. Wishing "to strike out . . . for himself" without putting his father to further expense, and apparently prompted in part by an upcoming poor grade report, Elijah traveled to Philadelphia to stay for a while with a former roommate of Cooley's until he could determine his next move. Elijah's sudden departure from college, Calvin declared, was "an act of disobedience which I can forgive as a parent" but which "cannot be blessed as it is against the holy commandments of God." He was also deeply "melancholy" about the impact of Elijah's decision on his brothers, as well as its implied judgment of Calvin and Sarah's parenting values. "It has caused me to review my treatment to my children, my advise &c.," he wrote. "I fear I may have committed errors & shall endeavor to revise my mode of treatment in some manner." His biggest fear was that he had somehow failed to "subdue his [Elijah's] temper sufficiently" and restrain Elijah's "romantic notions & view of the world which I thought would wear off in proper time." All this devastating personal news happened just as the "eastern mail" arrived bringing the official news that New York had gone for Polk. "This news disconcerted me . . . & I soon sat down," he recorded. "The same mail brought the letter of E.'s departure from Providence. To both of these dispensations may I submit—one a private affliction & the other fraught with forebodings of national calamity." Alone and ill-prepared, Elijah, Calvin feared, might now be driven "to do something immoral & wicked to get a living." For his country, he sensed that "immoral & wicked" things were already afoot.[15]

By the spring, Elijah had reconsidered and returned to college, sparking new faith in his father for the boy's future. But for the nation, in Calvin's view, there was no such hope, especially when it came to slavery. When the House of Representatives admitted Texas into the Union on January 31, 1845, Calvin saw the moment as Judgment Day: "I fear it is to hasten the punishment for the national sins & the greatest is negro Slavery." Although he tried to reconcile himself to the decision—such an expansion of the country would, after all, offer greater commercial potential—allowing slavery into Texas left him hopeless: "I shudder at the consequences yet God may intend to punish us on the one hand & relieve these poor creatures on the other."[16]

Soon Calvin began to take issue with respected religious institutions that were backing away from the slavery issue. He and his banking colleague, J. M. Ray, became disturbed when Presbyterians meeting in Cincinnati in May refused to support the numerous antislavery petitions that were put forward and instead "virtually accepted slavery as a legitimate Christian institution." Calvin told Ray, "I could not cooperate with any denomination" that "[sanctions holding] millions of human beings in bondage & make[s] it a penitentiary offense to learn them to read the bible." The slave question also provoked a rupture among the Methodists, prompting additional anxiety in Calvin. "The subject is now being agitated in the various churches," he wrote, "& I think will result in a final separation of all the churches north & south."[17]

In the midst of Calvin's anger and fear over the direction the slave-holding American nation was heading, his personal world received another sudden, if not unexpected, jolt: Lucy Keyes Fletcher, his beloved eighty-year-old mother, died at the family home in Ludlow, Vermont. She was, Calvin observed, "worn out of old age." Several years before Lucy's death, her son Elijah reported to Calvin her declining mental faculties, writing, "Her memory [is] gone and quite childish." Their brother Timothy, who had visited Lucy that same summer, found her condition "quite melancholy," observing, "I hoped once more to have seen her with her original vigor of mind, and not as a second child." Upon her death in the spring of 1846, Calvin remembered Lucy as small but "very shrewd, enterprising." That last word meant a lot to Calvin, as he firmly located the roots of his own independent, ambitious spirit in his mother. She had, he proudly observed, a "most unbounded confidence in her children *provided* they would leave their native town & go ahead & especially if they would compete for places of honor & an independent fortune . . . Such was the confidence in the success of her children she urged her last son the 15th child & only one left at home to go out & compete for the honors which lay before the bold & enterprising."[18]

Brother Elijah joined in the mourning, noting that "while I live [I] shall remember it with a sorrow that cannot be soothed." Ever the distant caretaker of the family home in Vermont, Elijah promised to keep "our mother's wardrobe carefully preserved" and to distribute it to all the living sisters and daughters. The furniture, he said, would be untouched, and the farm "should be the common home of us all or our children. No money can purchase it and all propositions to purchase from Friends or enemy will be promptly rejected."[19]

Perhaps in response to his mother's death, Elijah began making plans for his own final days. He told his children that summer that he had picked out his burial ground and gravestone. It was to be on the round top of a prominent hill near his Sweet Briar plantation. Elijah told Sidney that he wanted "a plain White marble obelisk 20 feet high," enclosed with fine cultivated trees, shrubs, and flowers. Furthermore, he ordered, "All my children should meet there once a year and prune and trim and cultivate it." Aware that for a vigorous fifty-six-year-old man such a preoccupation might seem strange, Elijah could only say that he contemplated death and his legacy "with pleasure." "I meditate upon those events," he told Calvin, "as composedly as my daily occupations[;] having lived a blameless life with the best intentions, the future has no dread to me."[20]

If Elijah mourned his mother and pondered his own legacy, Calvin had neither the time nor the inclination to plan his final days. Instead, he found himself drawn quickly back into the public arena, repeatedly confronted with issues dear to his heart and the nation at large. Having already lent his support to the abolitionist cause, especially in urging protection for editors of abolitionist newspapers, who were increasingly under attack from proslavery mobs, Calvin joined hands with ministers who were willing to preach openly against the sin of slavery. His good friend, the prominent minister and activist Henry Ward Beecher, who pastored the New School Second Presbyterian Church in Indianapolis, overcame Calvin's initial hesitancy about speaking out on slavery. With Calvin and a prominent U.S. circuit court judge listening from the pews, Beecher forcefully declared slavery a sin and warned against the looming American aggression in Mexico as an act of dangerous arrogance. After the sermon, as Calvin and other antislavery supporters had feared, several church members asked for letters of dismissal against Beecher. With such division in the church and Beecher's own mounting personal debt, he soon sought out another opportunity and the next year took a position as minister in the Plymouth Congregational Church in Brooklyn, New York.[21]

The annexation of Texas not only prompted fears about the expansion of slavery, but also sparked a war with Mexico, which saw the annexation

as a completely invalid power grab by the American government of territory Mexico viewed as its own. President Polk's claim of the southernmost
Rio Grande boundary in 1845 in effect provoked the dispute with Mexico.
In July 1845, Polk ordered General Zachary Taylor to Texas; by the fall
some thirty-five hundred U.S. soldiers had assembled on the Nueces River,
prepared to take the disputed territory by force. Immersed for months in
the newspaper accounts of this mounting threat in Texas, Calvin worried that "our nation are aggressors." Like most antislavery activists in the
North, he was firmly convinced that behind the aggression in Mexico lay
the relentless drive of southern slaveholders to acquire new territory under
the guise of "Manifest Destiny," the notion made popular by the 1840s that
Americans had a Providential mission to expand their democratic institutions across the breadth of North America.[22]

As with the Polk victory in 1844, the developing Mexican War took a
personal turn for Calvin—and once again, it involved his son Elijah. After
returning to college for a year, Elijah announced late in May 1846 that he
was leaving for the "Far West," heading for Missouri, where, as Calvin put
it, he would "enter the broad world." Despite being offered opportunities
to study law; clerk in a mercantile store, like his younger brother Calvin; or
work on the family farm, Elijah "could not bring his mind to settle on any
of them."[23] "He is the first child I have had leave me to enter the world without my care & means of support," Calvin noted. "It is not small matter for
a young man of 22 to commence for himself as he now does." Eventually,
Elijah received the blessing of both his mother and his father before depart-
ing home on June 1, 1846. He journeyed first to Independence, Missouri,
where he was able to find work outfitting traders headed for Santa Fe and
Mexico. Despite his dramatic leave-taking from the family home, Elijah
held no hard feelings for his parents. In fact, as he wrote Calvin from Independence, he felt great affection for them. Acknowledging that he had often
"committed many wrongs . . . been impudent to mother—and sometimes
to you," he observed, "I never received a reprimand from you." Everything
his father had done for him, Elijah realized, had been "dictated by feelings
of love." "Oh, father," he wrote, "how many times I wanted to go to you and

tell you all how I felt & pour out my whole soul to you and tell you every secret thought, and I was afraid of you (why I do not know), I was suspicious and above all a pride of heart would arise—and thus I continued to muse my own unhappiness."[24]

Comforting to his father as those sentiments may have been, Elijah's work and future prospects conjured up all kinds of concern. "I am going to Zacatecas [Mexico] with [Reuben] Gentry, a trader and a gentleman," Elijah wrote Calvin in June 1846. "I am to drive a carriage and will not be back for one year at shortest. I shall then likely return home & see you if I live."[25] Needless to say, such uncertainty about their son's welfare produced anxiety in the Fletcher household. After weeks of no correspondence, Elijah made contact once again with his family in early July, assuaging some of their parental fears. "I felt much concerned about him," Calvin revealed in his diary, "but am somewhat relieved by this letter." Later that day, Calvin learned from his son Miles, who had just received a letter from Elijah, that Elijah had visited Fort Leavenworth and was helping outfit some of the new recruits bound for California and Santa Fe—both battlegrounds in the Mexican conflict. Predictably, Elijah's deepening involvement in the developing war with Mexico only added to his father's apprehension: "If he goes to Mexico at this period," Calvin noted, "I think he goes into danger as the war renders the 2 nations hostile." Into the fall of 1846, Calvin and Sarah grew increasingly worried as news emerged about General Taylor's bloody battle in Monterrey. Not having heard from Elijah in six weeks, Calvin reported, "We fear for Elijah . . . who is now on his way to Zacatecas & think probably his safety may be effected by this battle." Two weeks later, Elijah wrote his parents with news that he was suffering from dysentery and, more concerning, offered bloody depictions of what he had been witnessing. The morning he wrote, he told his parents, "a Spaniard died. They scooped out a hole of sand & laid him in." Calvin feared his son would be caught up in a war that "seems to rage with Mexico with greater intensity & its settlement is uncertain. E. will be surrounded with a rough population."[26]

By the spring of 1847, Elijah's situation had grown even more precarious. The traders he had traveled with were caught up in a violent insurrection at Taos that led to the massacre of the territorial governor. Ten days later rumors swirled in the American press that General Taylor had fought a "severe battle with Mexicans" near Buena Vista in northern Mexico. Some 267 American officers and soldiers were killed, and nearly twice as many Mexicans died in the battle, a pivotal, hard-earned victory for Taylor.[27] Because initial stories in the American press claimed that over two thousand Americans had died, Calvin called the battle "the greatest Slaughter that has ever occurred in any engagement where the Anglo Americans have been engaged." "I moan this bloodshed—This inhumanity of man to man," he lamented. "I trust it is mere rumor." From Lynchburg, Calvin's brother Elijah expressed alarm as well for the safety of his nephew and namesake. "I have felt no little uneasiness about your son in Mexico," Elijah wrote Calvin, "and it would give me great pleasure to hear of his safe return to the bosom of his Family and Friends."[28]

Elijah's safe return would not come easy. He found himself in Zacatecas "surrounded with hostile Mexicans" fresh from the blood-stained battle of Buena Vista. His boss, Reuben Gentry, was taken prisoner along the road between El Paso and Chihuahua. Pretending he was a subject of Great Britain, Elijah managed to avoid capture. Upon learning of his son's clever and possibly life-saving subterfuge, Calvin was at first upset: "I think it wrong & to me it forbodes evil & they must if detected be counted as spies. I do not wish my children except in an extreme case to be placed in such a condition." Calvin eventually tempered his criticism, calling his son's escape "almost miraculous" and applauding how he had "maintained his integrity in the midst of corruption." On July 26, 1847, Elijah's—and the family's—drama finally ended: "This eve as we were eating supper E. arrived—[he] looked well," Calvin reported in his diary. "It should be a matter of rejoicing & gratitude to God that he has been brought home." It had been fourteen months since Elijah had left his home in Indianapolis—"and these months," he accurately observed, "were the most perilous and eventful of my life."[29]

Amid the trauma and uncertainty of Elijah's exploits out west, Calvin had to say goodbye to his eighteen-year-old son Miles, who, like his older brothers, had decided to try his hand at college back east. Ironically, Calvin sought to discourage the boy from attending college, believing that he had proven his worth in helping out on the family farm, where he was greatly needed. Calvin even enlisted his son Calvin Jr. to keep Miles at home, but the effort backfired. Calvin Jr. instead wrote his father that Miles had "done more than any of us to help you, and did it cheerfully too, and has recd. less reward . . . If I am not much mistaken it is your desire to help us equally, on that score it is his turn to come."[30] Several weeks later, Miles was packed up and ready to go. Calvin and Sarah accepted the departure with a measure of sadness and hope. "We regret to part with him," Calvin noted. "He has been a reasonably good boy. What he knows he knows well." All the Fletcher children sent farewell gifts along with Miles—from nine-year-old Billy, "a half dime"; from six-year-old Stephen Keyes, some "dried cherrys"; and from everyone "an apple a piece." Sarah gave him "a can of honey." Their goodbye scene, as Calvin recalled it, was both muted and moving: "We conducted Miles to the gate & the children parted with him & I rode to town, shook hands & left him. I paid his passage, $13 to Wheeling. I trust his life may be precious in the sight of the Lord. I cannot preserve my children when with me but God has been good & gracious in this matter when they were present & absent."[31] Upon arriving in Providence, young Miles remembered the sad farewell, whose formality had betrayed a suppressed affection. "I felt very bad on leaving home," he wrote. "I could hardly bear to shake hands with mother but the time had come and I had to go." For Calvin, the weight of so much leave-taking in his family had sunk in: "I feel lonesome as Miles, Calvin, Elijah & Cooley, my four oldest have all left me for the present."[32]

He may have felt lonesome, but he was hardly lethargic. Living a life forged on the anvil of self-improvement while supporting such a large family and trying to remake the larger world according to his own values made Calvin Fletcher a very busy man. As the presidential election of 1848 approached, he made a firm commitment to support the antislavery Free Soil Party, and its candidate, Martin Van Buren, the former president. He did so because he thought it "the right side of the question to vote against extending" slavery into any new territories. "I have examined the question in reference to my duty as a freeman & Christian," he noted, "& I have come to the firm conclusion never to countenance slavery in any shape." Calvin continued to claim that he preferred not to "meddle with public matters," but when it came to slavery, it was "a matter of sheer duty & necessity. The good sense of the community have determined that not another inch of free territory shall be made slave domain." Congress, he believed, should act "to exclude this curse on our land."[33]

Like his antislavery crusade, Calvin's fierce adoption of the temperance movement represented a commingling of personal experiences and larger social values. A growing movement of mostly Protestant ministers and social reformers since the 1820s, the battle against alcohol was waged by more than eight thousand local groups with well over a million followers by 1840. Calvin's personal connection to the temperance movement began when he worked at a small tavern as a young man in Urbana, Ohio, shortly after leaving his Vermont home in 1817. Several thousand soldiers recently discharged from the War of 1812 lived in the area, and he saw firsthand what alcohol did to them. "I was then acting in the humble capacity of barkeeper at a little tavern & can say that scarcely without exception every man would get drunk & the last pay they drew was used in dissipation," he later remembered. "They soon scattered & died & scarcely one returned to the useful departments of life."[34]

Active in the movement from the late 1830s on, Calvin became a prominent spokesman for the temperance cause by the mid-1840s. Written off at first as "a humbug farce," his temperance advocacy soon enlisted the support of several Indianapolis businessmen, and in June 1845 he was asked to deliver a major address to the Noblesville branch of the Indiana Temperance Society. His opening declaration was nothing less than a personal credo: "Life," he said, "is a scene of difficulty, perplexity, anxiety, a warfare which demands the use of the best faculties with which man has been endowed. To lose one of our senses, seeing, hearing, tasting, feeling, smelling, is esteemed a great misfortune. Also to lose any faculty calculated to destroy the moral sense, the ability to compare good with bad . . . would be truly deplorable & anything we do to lessen the availability" of those senses "may be called intemperance." His message was clearly aimed at youth. Young people, he believed, unthinkingly expect a long life "full of enjoyments." But that leaves them ill prepared for the real, and mostly difficult, journey that lies ahead. Not only can unforeseen financial problems or sudden illness shorten a life, the "useless frivolous pursuits" that "so often captivate the young" prompt imprudent choices: "See the circus rider, the play actor, the horse race, the fiddler for the menagerie, the gambler," Calvin exhorted the crowd. "They seldom live out half their days . . . No, they seldom pass 35 or 40 & then come to some violent end & rarely leave any one who will own them. Their whole history is summed up in this—*They have led intemperative lives*." In Calvin's perspective, anyone who gave in to habitual anger, revenge, or deceit lost all ability to reason—and these flaws "are weaknesses as much as getting drunk."[35]

While he pushed for local and state laws prohibiting the sale of alcohol, Calvin tried to enforce within his own family the same sort of broadly conceived temperance spirit regarding all forms of excess. When Jonathan Harrington Greene, a renowned former professional gambler from Cincinnati, came to Indianapolis with a powerful anti-gambling presentation, Calvin attended the event with his oldest son Cooley. "Green the Gambler" made a big impression on them, so much so that Calvin was prompted to challenge his four oldest sons to sign a pledge never to play cards "either for amusement or for gain." Away at Brown University, both Miles and Calvin Jr. responded respectfully but warily: "Now for my part I do not know one card from another," Calvin Jr. wrote his father. Plus, he couldn't imagine that if his principled life and common sense hadn't kept him from learning to play cards, "no promise could."[36] Signing such a pledge, he argued, would make him feel obliged to list "every vice, every kind of folly and extravagance, and everything that is forbidden by my duty to God and man." Assuring his father that nothing in his response "is intended as impudence," he questioned the entire notion of the pledge, at least as it related to him. "I hoped that all these things were tacitly understood e'er I moved one inch from home, at least I supposed they were, and cannot bring myself to think . . . you do not now have confidence in me," he wrote. Not wanting to appear disrespectful, Calvin Jr. a few weeks later agreed that he and his brother Miles would sign a pledge, noting, "It may not be worded to suit you, but it is all that I think necessary." The wording was simple: "Neither of us ever intend to play cards. Calvin Fletcher, Jr., Miles J. Fletcher."[37]

While only partly successful with his own family, Calvin tirelessly devoted himself to stamping out gambling, drinking, and "houses of ill fame." He spoke at public meetings aimed at suppressing gambling and offered up resolutions, most of which were swiftly adopted. In one meeting, twenty or thirty "gamblers & their adherents" showed up to make a noisy protest but found themselves in uncongenial company and "were soon silenced." At the courthouse a temperance group met by candlelight in December 1846 to battle what they called the "vicious," a group Calvin labeled the "disaffected [and] the ignorant" who were "opposed to good order." Ten citizens gathered that evening at the Hall of the Sons of Temperance and unanimously passed resolutions to suppress all gambling, drinking, and prostitution in the community.[38]

Even if he had strong fellow activists who supported his temperance cause, Calvin experienced significant pushback from within the community against his zealous crusade. His side ("the moral part of the community," as he put it) lost several votes over the question of selling liquor to the "wicked." He knew he was "marked for the vengeance of those who hated order," and, in fact, in one memorable election in 1847 he became the subject of ridicule for his "anti-Gambling exertions," with the result that the "wicked" voted him in as "fence viewer." This position, whose job it was to assess damages when livestock broke into another person's property, was clearly seen as the most tedious, least important local office. "I will perform the office cheerfully," Calvin noted solemnly in his journal.[39]

More hurtful was his own brother's reaction to Calvin's relentless temperance activities. A few years later Elijah reported to Calvin the fanatical efforts of the "Temperance Friends" in Lynchburg, Virginia, and their "warfare upon all the local authorities that did not favor their views," including a demonstration to unseat all the civil officials who favored granting licenses to taverns for selling liquor. As it happened, Timothy Fletcher, a brother of Elijah and Calvin who also lived in Lynchburg, was one of those officials the temperance demonstrators were protesting. But, Elijah noted, "as it was thought they [the temperance protestors] were rather stepping out of their sphere and carrying the matter too far, a reaction took place," and Timothy won reelection to the magistracy by an overwhelming vote. "Thank you for making Timothy so happy," Elijah concluded. Probably more disturbing to Calvin was Elijah's description of his "charitable Hobbies—Religion, Temperance, Abolitionism, Education," which, he noted, were "all most praiseworthy and commendable." Calvin took exception to the word "hobbies" and was particularly defensive about his abolitionist zeal, arguing that he was simply engaging in "moral suasion with the old Slave states till they may either voluntarily manumit their slaves or some amendment by the Constitution to release them."[40]

Elijah's humorous dismissal of his brother's "hobbies" reveals as much about his own detached, laissez-faire worldview as it does about Calvin's reforming zeal. And Elijah was keenly aware of the differences in how the two men spent their time in public versus private arenas. "You are probably by nature more social and not altogether of that retiring turn," Elijah observed.

> You have from an early period mixed busily in the varied active pursuits of life, always having many warm, attached friends, and promoted to stations of honor and trust . . . You are constituted with a zeal for the welfare of mankind that renders you peculiarly fitted for public employment. You have gifts . . . I have not gifts that would make me useful in many things like yourself. I was destined for an unobtrusive, retired life, the sphere of my usefulness to be more limited than yours.[41]

There certainly seemed no limit to Calvin's reform instinct. Given the pivotal importance of education for the entire Fletcher family, it is perhaps unsurprising that Calvin also embraced the common school movement with so much determination. Less controversial than temperance and abolitionism, the common school movement came wrapped in a spirit of economic vitality and community improvement. "Can there be a question of greater, or more vital importance to the prosperity of our State?" Calvin asked in an op-ed piece published in May 1848. The push for free and better schools, he argued, should appeal to "the intelligence, the philanthropy, and patriotism of the Press of Indiana." By voting for "Free Schools," Calvin insisted, "you will elevate the character of our State, and thousands yet to be, will bless your memory."[42]

By the mid-1840s, Calvin had become a complete convert to the educational reform movement, initiated a decade earlier under the leadership of Horace Mann, which focused on bringing local school districts under a more centralized town authority and making school attendance mandatory, curricula uniform, and teacher training more professional. Backed mostly by evangelical Protestant reformers like Mann, the common school movement emerged in part as a reaction against increased Catholic immigration and the desire to prevent Catholic schools from receiving tax money. While Calvin certainly bought into the anti-Catholic, anti-immigrant elements of the movement, he was mostly focused on the need to bring good, qualified teachers out West to places like Indianapolis.

The city had been growing quickly, providing opportunity and profit for those in banking and government, especially after 1825, when the state's capital moved to Indianapolis from Corydon. As early as 1835 Calvin adopted the town's boosterism, confiding in his diary, "The past seems a dream, a delusion. I have witnessed a total wilderness converted into a flourishing city." Calvin was thirty-seven, and Indianapolis, only fifteen years old itself, had grown to about seventeen hundred people. By 1840 it was one of a few real urban centers in Indiana, with a population over three thousand. And its growth would continue: by 1850 over eight thousand people lived in Indianapolis.[43]

The city may have enjoyed a thriving population, but it certainly wasn't showcasing the kind of educational achievement that Calvin and other civic leaders felt a progressive city required. In 1840 one in seven Indianapolis citizens couldn't read, and by 1850 that level of illiteracy had risen to one in five. In some southern counties (Jackson, Martin, Clay, and Dubois), barely half the population was literate, and only one in three children in the state attended school. Indianapolis didn't establish a free public school until 1853.

Such circumstances of a growing but barely literate population prompted educational reform in progressive thinkers like Calvin. He was particularly enamored with the plan of former Vermont governor William Slade, who visited Cincinnati in 1846 in order to set up an organization to send "properly qualified teachers," all of whom were women trained in New England teachers' colleges ("normal schools"), to schools in the West. When the Indiana legislature called for a convention to be held in Indianapolis in May 1847 aimed at promoting common school education, Calvin chaired the organizing committee. Governor Slade addressed the group, Calvin proudly recalled, declaring that "our highest priority as a nation" depended "upon the intellectual and moral elevation of the masses of the people, and . . . the importance of a *good common school system* in order to attain this important object."[44]

Author and reformer Catherine Beecher joined Slade in proposing that six or eight female teachers be sent out to Indiana. Calvin eagerly welcomed the idea, agreeing to temporarily take one such female teacher into his own family—room and board being their only form of payment. In the summer of 1847 the first crop of transplanted New England teachers arrived in Indiana. Early one morning in June, Calvin, along with other key members of the common school organizing committee, met the "9 young ladies" at the Palmer House in Indianapolis. They were mostly Baptist and Methodist women who had "voluntarily left their friends & relatives to become teachers in the West—not seeking compensation but to supply the destitute places [in] a state where at the present there will not be more than 5 out of 6 [who will] learn to read & write."[45] Samuel Merrill, a prominent civic leader and friend to Calvin, claimed the transplanted female teachers "are said to be accomplished and the prospects are that they will be well provided for first with schools and then with husbands."[46] One such teacher was Keziah Lister, an intelligent and lively thirty-year-old woman from

Maine who quickly caught Calvin's eye as a remarkably effective teacher and a clearly kindred spirit. He called her "an extraordinary woman" who could "more effectually win the hearts of her pupils than any one I ever saw . . . She seems to have been a God send & blessing to this place."[47]

Despite considerable opposition to free public schools—voters were leery of the cost and the centralization of authority—Calvin overcame the resistance. In city elections in 1847 the voters approved a modest tax for the establishment of free schools, a major victory for Calvin and his fellow common school reformers. "I can leave no better inheritance to my children," he later observed, "than a moral, intelligent, religious community & I cannot be an indifferent spectator to these matters & to the interests of this my adopted state."[48]

If he was successful in bringing free, compulsory public schools to Indiana, Calvin faced a more daunting struggle when it came to influencing the educational and career goals of his own children. With his sixteen-year-old daughter Maria studying at a Providence, Rhode Island, prep school, his educational expectations, while modest, still mattered. But a report from her teacher, John Kingsbury, suggests that female education of the time aimed more at producing pleasing and obedient girls rather than fostering academically ambitious ones. Kingsbury told Calvin in the summer of 1849 that Maria's progress was good, as she was "dutiful and obedient, respectful and desirous to please," despite obvious "deficiencies in some of her elementary studies," such as penmanship, spelling, and writing. Cooley visited his sister later that summer and reported to his father a similarly gendered appraisal: Maria, he observed, was now "wonderfully altered and much improved. She wears long dresses, looks and acts like a lady . . . She is much beloved."[49]

When it came to his sons, Calvin sought to nurture a nuanced combination of high achievement and explicit devotion to improving *themselves;* his sons must pursue, he wrote them, "self education like their Father." As much as Calvin pushed his children to commit themselves fully to their studies, he also felt curiously abandoned by his sons off at college, who were so caught up in their own worlds that they ignored his needs—in terms of both labor and personal attention—back home. While attending Brown University in 1847, Miles and Calvin Jr. felt compelled to respond to their father's worry that they somehow intended to "desert" him. "Do you think we have no desire to aid you?" Miles wrote. "Do you think we would spend the money so hard earned by you without repaying your kindness? By no means."[50] As he often did, Calvin wanted his sons to work tirelessly at their studies and yet wondered if such a devotion to college also betrayed an effeminate temperament, compared to that cultivated by the manlier world of farmwork. Caught between the plowboy life in which he was raised—and which he still revered—and the educated world he came to admire, Calvin sent mixed messages to his sons at college, especially as he was missing their company and their labor at home.

He was even willing to shame them into accepting his perspective on school versus work. Calvin Jr. essentially caved to his father's plea to return from college and work at home: "You say, 'my sons do not seem to have courage to get a self education like their Father, and if I can indulge them otherwise I shall,'" Calvin Jr. wrote his father in September 1847. "Now Father, I don't know whether you think I have any pride or feeling. When I read that sentence I feel ashamed of my self to think that I have been here 18 months. I abhor the idea and detest the place. I have no desire for study no pleasure in any thing." Frustrated at the cost of funding the college education of so many sons, Calvin wanted to ensure that Miles and Calvin Jr. completed their schooling before, he wrote, "I ever send another child from my house to get an education." To that statement, Calvin Jr. took exception, forcefully criticizing his father for implying that he and his brother Miles might be robbing their younger siblings of a good education:

> Now Father it is *wrong—criminal* in me to stay one day here and have my brothers and sisters deprived of the advantages I enjoy . . . Never shall a brother say to me, "You, sir, were the cause of my being an ignoramus—of my being deprived of going to college." . . . I have already had my share and am now ready to give place to them, and am at your service at

any moment. My chief desire in this life [is] to assist you, to help educate the younger members of the family.[51]

His brother Miles took on the "effeminate" charge directly. "You say that the boy in the plough patch," Miles wrote, "who could neither read nor write but could water a hundred cattle and take care of as many hogs was worth a hundred boys who had become effeminate by a collegiate course of four years. What encouragement then is there for me if at the end of my college course I shall be worth only one hundredth part as much as I was when I lived in the plough patch?" Far from wanting to come home simply out of duty, Miles had something to prove to his father: "I shall dig on and show you that at the end of four years I have not become effeminate but that I can do anything you please to set me at."[52]

For other young men in this era, the impulse to prove their manliness found expression in movement and adventure. After the discovery of gold nuggets in the Sacramento Valley in early 1848, the California gold rush of 1849 sparked a huge movement mostly made up of men dreaming of wealth. Once the news of the discovery spread, thousands of prospective gold miners journeyed to San Francisco and the nearby area in search of gold, spiking the nonnative population of the California Territory from about one thousand before 1848 to over one hundred thousand by the end of 1849.[53]

In this powerful public event, Calvin Fletcher insisted on having no role. Even though he himself had sought a new life and followed his dreams by leaving home for the West, the allure of California and gold was nothing but a chimera to him. "The California Gold has no little attraction," he declared on Christmas Day 1848. Even though he knew many young people in Indianapolis who seemed "determined to start for that country," Calvin disapproved of their aim. "I think those who go must spend their lives in bad company," he maintained, and instead of finding wealth, "the greater proportion must live in poverty." It was the hard-working farmer and mechanical laborer, he believed, who "will get the gold." Digging for gold, he insisted, "has but little attraction to the honest laborer generally."[54]

But there was nothing false about the allure of the California gold rush to the sons of Calvin's brother Elijah. In June 1849, Elijah reported that Sidney and Lucian had gone to California, one via the Gulf of Mexico and Panama and the other around Cape Horn. "Sidney always seemed anxious to travel and explore the Western part of our Continent and the excitement in California hastened the undertaking," Elijah told Calvin. "Lucian has gone as a real gold Hunter, joining a Company in Richmond who bought a fine Vessel and freighted her, starting from The Capes of Virginia 1st of April." Elijah lamented the decision, at least Sidney's, to head west, writing, "I regretted somewhat Sidney's departure, for he was a man of business and much assistance to me. But like you, I let them when arriving at years of discretion carve out their own destiny." Calvin, however, saw nothing promising about his nephews' westward wanderlust. "I think this is a doubtful expedition," Calvin noted in his diary. "I fear they will never return to him. He has but 2 sons & at the age of 60 to have them leave him with all his cares seems hard. But so it is. There seems to be stirring incidents going on in the old world."[55]

Predictably, Sidney returned quickly from the gold rush, coming home at the end of 1849 after three months of very modest earnings from the gold mines. While in California, according to his father, he had "endured much hardship, seen much of the world and returned better contented, perhaps, with a comfortable home." Sidney concluded that northern California could never be a "desirable Agricultural country" owing to its limited rain. He returned in good health, but, Elijah conceded, "the hardships he has undergone make him look much wasted." Thankfully, his father noted, Sidney was now "devoted to his Farm, the only place where he is happy and contented."[56]

Lucian, also predictably, stayed behind, determined to dig until he got rich, despite encountering hardship and sickness. Like so many others, he failed to make any money in the mines; after a few months, he relocated to Stockton, California, where he intermittently practiced law. His occasional letters home mentioned his desire to return to Virginia. Lucian's failure in the gold fields was both a personal tragedy and a common occurrence

Tusculum, Elijah Fletcher's Lynchburg home

among western adventurers. As Elijah observed, "few of our Californians have returned lately but none that have gone from this part of the country have met with much success." Finally, in early November 1851, Lucian made his way home after being detained in Panama with a debilitating "Fever." He "has been much of his time indisposed since reaching home," Elijah observed. Lucian's western adventure would not be his last one, and it signaled the beginning of a father–son estrangement that would not end happily.[57]

All of these events only strengthened Elijah's resolve to focus on his more successful and obedient children while cultivating his pastoral retreat at Sweet Briar. He gave Sidney the Tusculum plantation that had come to him from the heirs of William Crawford, his father-in-law. Elijah was clearly pleased that Sidney was now devoting himself to managing the plantation. "Farming is the only vocation in life that pleases him or which nature seemed to adapt his taste," he wrote his brother Calvin. And Elijah fairly delighted in regaling family members about the wonderful trips his daughters frequently made to New York City, where they picked up fashionable furnishings for their Sweet Briar home back in Virginia. They especially enjoyed visiting family in Ludlow. "They are all Fletcher," Elijah proudly noted, "charmed with the Old Farm in Vermont, as well as all our Family, and they possess not a particle of the foolish southern prejudice against Northern people and Northern habits."[58]

Like their brothers, Indiana and Betty also thought of adventuring west, but only in the context of touring or visiting, as they always needed a "gallant," a male chaperone, to accompany them. In the fall of 1848, Elijah reported that the two girls were planning a winter trip, accompanied by Sidney, either out West or to Cuba, New Orleans, and then back home via Charleston. Elijah saw travel not only as a broadening experience but also as a welcome opportunity to visit far-flung family. "My Daughters," he noted, "have often told me that they value their [travel] opportunities far above any wealth I could bestow upon them." Thus Elijah felt especially neglected when it came to getting to know Calvin's children, particularly when the oldest child, Cooley, in 1849 planned a "sojourn" (actually foreign mission work) in Switzerland but made no plans to stop in Virginia. "Can not Cooley make me a visit before leaving America?" Elijah asked his brother. "It seems strange that I should never have had the opportunity of seeing any of your Children, though you have many times promised me a visit from some of them."[59]

Elijah himself preferred the quiet and solitude of life at Sweet Briar, while his wife Maria mostly managed the house in Lynchburg, but he also enjoyed taking the entire family to reunions in Vermont. These journeys became much easier with train and steamboat travel. Before that, it could take several weeks to get from southwest Virginia to the Fletcher "mansion" in Ludlow, Vermont. With a strong horse, good weather, and the best of roads, it took four to six days to travel just from New York to Boston. But by the 1840s and early 1850s more than thirty-seven miles of turnpikes, or toll roads, had been built in New England. Furthermore, these new roads were far better constructed and maintained than earlier roads, allowing faster travel. Stagecoach lines now stretched across the Northeast, with fresh horses spaced out every forty miles or so. Steamboats created much faster passenger travel on the rivers, along with carrying enormous amounts of cargo upstream. Finally, after 1830, the railroad dramatically sped up travel. In good weather, with well-rested horses, a stagecoach could perhaps travel at eight or nine miles per hour. The small locomotives of the 1830s traveled at twice that speed. And by the 1840s, railroad tracks had spread throughout the most populated regions, especially the Northeast, greatly diminishing travel time. A trip from New York to Boston could now be accomplished in less than a day.

Even still, there were surprises and scares. When Elijah and his family returned home from one such reunion in August 1852, he promptly wrote a detailed report on that same trip home to Calvin, because he knew his brother and others "might feel some little anxiety to know how we fared on our way home," having no doubt read in the papers about a major disaster involving the steamboat, the *Henry Clay,* on which they had traveled part of the way. Launched in August 1851, the *Henry Clay* was a side paddle-wheel steamboat that ran between Albany and New York City. Elijah and family boarded the vessel at Albany on July 28, 1852, on their way home from the reunion. Just before 3 p.m., as the *Henry Clay* neared Yonkers, New York, a fire broke out onboard, quickly engulfing the midsection. The pilot immediately turned the burning ship—with five hundred passengers aboard—eastward to reach the nearest shore, a mile away. It crashed into the sands at Riverdale, New York. Some passengers at the front of the boat were able to jump to the shore, but those at the back were trapped by the raging fire in the boat's midsection and either were burned to death or drowned. All told, some seventy-two people were killed in one of the era's most notorious steamboat disasters.[60]

If travel helped bring the Fletcher family closer together, regular, thoughtful correspondence was the true adhesive. Both Calvin and Sarah insisted on their children writing letters to family members when away from home. For Sarah, writing to her children and expecting letters back helped inculcate virtue, discipline, and morality. While away for health reasons in Onondaga, New York, on Lake Superior in the summer of 1853,

Calvin and Sarah Fletcher, 1844

Sarah wrote to two of her sons, Stoughton, twenty-two, and Billy, sixteen, who were in need of counseling on the essence of a "virtuous man." "If a man," she wrote, "has acquired great power and riches by falsehood, injustice, and oppression, he cannot enjoy them, because his conscience will torment him, and constantly reproach him with the means by which he got them. The stings of his conscience will not even let him sleep quietly, he will dream of his crimes; and in the day-time, when alone, and when he has time to think, he will be uneasy, he is afraid of everything." A virtuous man, even if poor, will have his virtue "as its own reward," which always serves as a "comfort." Sarah directed this message especially at Billy, who had been struggling with volatile teenage emotions and an uncertain sense of self. "Billy," she wrote, "I want you to stick to your virtue & religion." And she wanted him, too, to write her thoughtful letters from the heart. Very few of Sarah's friends and acquaintances staying in the area, she told the boys, had received any letters from friends, despite being "very anxious to hear from home. [And] they are perfectly astonished at the number of letters I have received & written." In an accurate and revealing comment, she declared: "I tell them we are a writing family & believe in keeping up a correspondence with each other."[61]

But when ill health hit, communication necessarily slowed down as family members had to focus on the stricken individual and, all too often, on the mourning of immediate family. Frequently, it would take weeks, and sometimes months, *after* a painful loss for news of the death to be fully conveyed to loved ones elsewhere. That is how it happened for Elijah Fletcher and his family when, around September 1, 1853, Elijah's wife, Maria, became very sick with a "bad Fever," possibly typhoid, while vising her son Sidney at his Tusculum plantation near Lynchburg. Ten days later, on September 10, 1853, Maria died. As her nephew wrote, she was now gone "to her long home, never to return, and paid the debt we have all got to pay sooner or later." Elijah couldn't bring himself to discuss the death with his brother for nearly three months. "We have had mourning and affliction in our Family since I wrote you last," he finally told Calvin. "Death has laid a heavy hand and made a great raid in our social circle, and though the lot of humanity, it is not the less distressing and grievous to lose one we have long been connected with in the joys as well as conflicts of life's busy scenes." Maria's death devastated Indiana, reportedly to the point that she couldn't speak of it for a great while.[62]

Illness—typhoid, cholera, and dysentery, among others—struck nineteenth-century families of all ranks and sometimes prompted unexpected loss. In the summer of 1854, Sarah traveled with Calvin to the Fletcher homestead at Ludlow for a family reunion. Most of their activities involved visiting, card-playing, strolls along familiar childhood paths, trips to the cemetery, and the careful avoidance (not always successful) of politics and religion. Soon after arriving in Ludlow, however, Calvin fell quite ill with "the desentary" and began taking "the naucious calomel" ordered by a local doctor. Afflicted with bloody discharges, he was slowly nursed back to health over the course of two weeks, thanks to Sarah's round-the-clock care. "Mrs. F.," he later noted, "watched me as if I were an infant . . . For several days I felt it was uncertain if I should recover."[63]

Exhausted from the constant caregiving, Sarah tried to resume her burdensome household duties once they returned to Indianapolis on August 12. But a month later she fell ill. At first, Calvin was distracted, as he was once again caught up in volatile public issues. With the ongoing tension over slavery's extension into the territories, Calvin and other antislavery activists looked to the Kansas Territory, working to ensure that "free soil" settlers would prevail in the region and prevent the evil institution of slavery from getting a foothold there. On Sunday, September 24, 1854, Calvin planned to go to the Second Presbyterian Church in Indianapolis to help take up a collection to build churches in the Kansas Territory. But the night before, at 1 a.m., Sarah awoke with "a violent pain in the abdomen" and thought it could be some uterine infection or inflammation of the bowels. It was almost certainly an acute bowel obstruction, most likely from colon cancer.[64] Calvin called in their doctor, who seemed unsure how to assess her swollen abdomen. From the beginning, Sarah's "great distress" made Calvin wonder if "her life was in danger," and so he decided to stay home from church. That day the doctor came again and applied "a mustard poltice," but she got no relief. "I spent the day with her," Calvin noted in his diary, "& told her I feared her recovery doubtful." Later the doctor gave her some morphine for the pain, which did help, but Calvin nonetheless alerted his children that the end might be coming, though he advised all to maintain "prayerful firmness."[65]

Sarah struggled in and out of consciousness for a few more days. Then, just before dawn on September 27, she awoke from her stupor and Calvin decided to call in the children for a final farewell. "They all came round her bed," he noted. "She shook hands with each & when she came to take Albert's [hand she] seemed much agitated. He cried. She motioned him to be calm." Only eight years old at the time, Albert had been taken out of school and had spent the previous two days of his mother's rapid decline "terrified," watching from the "vine-covered apple trees" just outside his mother's windows. "I couldn't understand that it was possible for her to be taken away," he recalled years later.[66]

Sarah began vomiting large volumes of a liquid "resembling blue ink," a sign of internal hemorrhaging, their doctor announced. Even near the end, Sarah "observed her accustomed neatness . . . even to the last moment she would & did make great exertion to prevent vomiting . . . or [spill] even a drop of water on the bed clothes." Just as the clock struck six in evening, "she breathed her last just after the setting of a most beautiful sun of one of the most delightful days that ever shone," Calvin noted. "Our house was thronged with the poor & rich who deeply sympathized with us in our loss, great loss." Only Cooley and Elijah were absent—they were notified via telegraph the night of her death.[67]

"We all felt and looked like a shipwrecked band," Albert remembered. "Mother was no longer there with her benign and worshipful and placid face. Her chair next to mine was vacant, and we sat around the dining room weeping. To me, and I think to all the children—the younger ones, the end of the world had come . . . Mother had gone and all future life [was] at a standstill and useless." For Calvin, Sarah's dignified death was instructive to them all: "We did not know how to live till she showed us how to die," he wrote. According to Albert, Calvin gave a brief speech before his "stricken" family about "what Mother would have us do, the kind of lives she wanted us to live, and to become useful and helpful, courageous and true." Calvin's talk, Albert noted, forcefully reminded everyone of Sarah's "rare character" and "roused us . . . from our dreamy despair."[68]

None of the Fletcher children missed Sarah more than Albert. His observations in "Memories of My Mother," composed just before his death in 1917, drew revealing contrasts between the parenting styles of Calvin and Sarah. According to Albert, "*fear* was constantly present when Father was near; and calmness, and a feeling of punctiliousness and caretaking was with me when Mother was directing me. Mother was so absolutely religious in all her doings and sayings . . . that *whatever* she did had to me a meaning of sanctity and devotion." Albert remembered his father in a much starker light: "Father was stern and demanding, relentless in case of lapse from strict duty and behavior, and there was no Mother to intercede . . . Father

made things *move*; he praised or blamed or punished but, with all his ability, he hadn't the faculty of making the home happy."[69]

$$\mathcal{X} \cdot \quad \bullet \quad \bullet \quad \bullet \quad \mathcal{X}$$

Losing a beloved spouse pushed Elijah and Calvin in different directions.
For Elijah, the "grevious" loss of Maria drove him even further into a life
of retirement and solitude, sweetened only by the near-constant compan-
ionship of his devoted daughters, especially Indiana. But his contentious
estrangement from Lucian made him more withdrawn. Never a man who
loved the public arena, Elijah separated himself even further from political
life after Maria's passing. In contrast, when Sarah died, Calvin, if anything,
responded with a fresh sense of urgency and activism. After a period of intense mourning, he became increasingly caught up in the difficult issues of
the day—slavery, temperance, education—as well as the daily struggles of
his many children. And then, in yet another example of the commingling
of the public and the personal, Calvin found a remarkable teacher from the
common school movement who renewed his hope in more ways than one.

Six

CALAMITIES

When Elijah learned about Sarah's death, his reaction was brief but heartfelt. Reading about the loss "of your estimable wife," he wrote his brother, "was as melancholy as unexpected. To my daughters the sad intelligence was very affecting, for Aunt Sarah was a great favorite with them." And Elijah remembered Sarah's kindness to Calvin during the recent family reunion: "When she was so kindly nursing you at the old Mansion last summer, little did I expect she would be the first to be called home."[1]

For the Fletchers, as for most families then and now, the "unexpected" happened with great frequency, especially concerning their children. And if Calvin wanted to wallow in sorrow over his wife's passing, he had precious little time to do it. Early in 1854 Calvin composed a list of all the changes in his family, much of them concerning to him: That year Calvin had turned over most of the farm management to Calvin Jr., a decision that proved both necessary and troublesome. Stoughton, now twenty-three, had worked for several months as a conductor on the railroad, but gave that up to work in a bank. Calvin's oldest and most irksome child, Cooley, now living in Rio de Janeiro, trying to make it as a writer and barely surviving on his father's reluctant handouts. Elijah had become a Methodist minister, previously preaching in New Bedford, Massachusetts, but now struggling to stay afloat, especially with an unhealthy wife. His younger brother Miles, now twenty-six, taught at nearby Asbury University. The volatile Billy, who turned seventeen years old in 1854, was preparing for college, but in a mostly indifferent fashion. Likewise, Maria, twenty-one, was failing to distinguish herself at a normal school in Lancaster, Massachusetts. The youngest children—fourteen-year-old Stephen ("Keyes"), twelve-year-old Lucy, and eight-year-old Albert—all attended neighborhood schools, but were sick much of the winter.[2]

When it came to his children, nothing upset Calvin more than financial weakness, and in his eldest, thirty-one-year-old Cooley, he faced the ultimate test of his patience. Beset by "great pecuniary troubles" for years, Cooley, now married—and, worse yet, to a spendthrift woman he had met while engaged in foreign mission work in Switzerland—spent a year in Rio giving lectures on cotton production in Brazil and mixing with Brazilian dignitaries (subjects on which he eagerly provided commentaries to his father). In the fall of 1854 he left Brazil, once again in financial trouble. Writing his father from Concord, New Hampshire, where he filled the pulpit for an absent pastor for a few Sundays, Cooley tried to steer a course between begging and entitlement: "I am struggling to get a living," he wrote, "and what perplexes me is that I have constantly to make the question of money come into my Master's work. I do not at present pay my way." Although still in the service of the charitable American and Foreign Christian Union—which had sent him to South America—Cooley was still unable to meet his expenses. Despite his financial plight, he managed to find emotional support from his visiting brother Miles. Everything Cooley said, Miles reported to their father, could be completely trusted, since he was "a most zealous active conscientious Christian. There is a fervor and a depth of piety in his character, not often met with." But, Miles conceded, Cooley had lost all sympathy with Calvin's "plans and arrangements" and "openly denounces them all. He says right before his wife . . . that you think you must make us all march through the same hard road that you had to march: that land is the golden egg."[3]

Calvin's son Elijah, who was serving as a Methodist pastor in War-ren, Rhode Island, likewise struggled to support his own family, especially given his wife's medical expenses. After a visit with Elijah and family, and sensing an opportunity to use Elijah's financial dependence to make his own case as well, Cooley took up his brother's cause: "Is it not supposed," Cooley pleaded with Calvin, "that we have some principles about us & in us, which should entitle to effectual aid those who are in a business and calling which does not consist in California gold digging . . . though our labors are as hard perhaps more wearing to the body than any other profession?" Elijah, Cooley intimated, would gladly have left New England for Indianapolis with his sickly wife had he received any encouraging word from Calvin for him to return.[4]

All such arguments fell on deaf ears. Both sons, but especially Cooley, an increasingly annoyed Calvin believed, were simply "living beyond [their] income." Calvin had sent Cooley $700 for his "traveling expenses" in returning from Rio, but even that proved insufficient to Cooley's needs. "I view it as disgraceful to me & to my child not to maintain himself & family," Calvin bitterly noted.[5]

A month into his grief over losing Sarah and in the middle of his strug-gle with Cooley and Elijah over their fiscal failures, Calvin got served some very unexpected, troubling news that doubtless conjured up entirely dif-ferent feelings. On the morning of October 30, 1854, Calvin's teenage son Billy, who had been attending high school in Indianapolis, walked into his father's study and announced his departure, noting that he was "17 years 2 months & 11 days old," precisely the age, down to the day, that Calvin himself had left his ancestral home in Ludlow, Vermont. Calvin reported that Billy "wanted me to let him go & see if he could not support himself; for he did not want to be a burthen longer to me." At first Calvin pleaded for time. Once Billy was "qualified to teach school then I would let him go," he argued. The advice went unheeded. That evening Calvin returned from work at the bank and learned that Billy had left the house that morn-ing and had not returned. Fearing he had suffered an accident, the family began hunting for Billy. Calvin sent Miles and Albert downtown to look for their brother, but they returned having heard nothing "from him or of him." Hoping that "he will not disgrace his parents and family," Calvin went to work "with a heavy heart." After two more days of hearing nothing of Billy, Calvin tried to suppress his anguish: "I feel so but must bare it . . . The anguish of mind he must feel going away after the death of his mother & without a more specific permission."[6]

Finally, four days after Billy ran off, Calvin received a letter from his son, who was in Michigan City, Indiana. As it happened, another young friend had left home and Billy had joined him. A few days later news arrived from an H. W. Chamberlain of Sheboygan, Wisconsin, who informed Calvin that he had employed Billy as a grain dealer and asked Calvin "if [Billy's] employment suits me &c." Over the next few weeks, Calvin determined from letters from Billy that his son would have a hard time making ends meet, which was a good thing in Calvin's book: "I judge he has to work hard. This will be good for him. I want him to try the romance of life. It will better prepare him for the sad realities." On Thanksgiving, though, he learned that Billy had in fact walked off with $65 in gold belonging to his mother. Billy seemed somewhat regretful over the stealing "but not conscious of the folly he has committed." "The going away as he did might seem right enough," Calvin observed, "but the taking the money savors of criminality . . . His romance has misled him." Since the boy appeared to have simply taken off without a supply of clothing or any funds, Calvin claimed some "regret." Had he only known how "determined" Billy was, he reflected, "I should have provided money & clothing. We all feel mortified & cast down about this act. It seems an act of great disobedience."[7]

A few days later, Mr. Chamberlain reported to Calvin that Billy had abandoned his job and jumped on board a ship that would soon be headed for Buffalo. Billy, according to Chamberlain, "had become dissatisfied & not disposed to perform his contract" and now had "hid in the hole of the ship." The young man's conduct struck Chamberlain as unstable. Calvin was crushed. It was one thing for Billy to leave home as a young man to discover the larger world; it was quite another, in Calvin's mind, for him to conduct himself so dishonorably: "I left home & my father by his consent precisely at the same age," Calvin wrote. "I never violated any contract for wages tho' I made some I thought hard." Immediately, Calvin decided "to send for the boy that had not man enough & spirit of honor & sense of obligation to perform his contracts but [was] disposed to dishonor me by such fickleness." So he sent Miles to fetch him.[8]

A week later Calvin returned from work to find Billy at home. He had apparently changed his mind and gotten aboard the last boat of the season. Miles missed his brother: he had traveled by land and arrived in Sheboygan only to discover that Billy had returned the day before. While upset at the $250 in expenses incurred in sending Miles by train to retrieve the boy, Calvin seemed pleased that Billy had come back home, and, apparently, in the right spirit. "I had a talk with Billy as to his late bad conduct," Calvin noted. "He seems repentant." Realizing that Billy had "fled" simply because "he wanted to do something for himself," just as he himself had done in 1817, Calvin focused on the bright side: "He has excellent talents & no child could do better."[9]

Probably the most disturbing word Calvin used to describe his son, at least from his parental and personal point of view, was "fickleness," denoting a lack of firmness and clarity of (virtuous) conviction. If he thought Billy's conduct betrayed a moment of "fickleness," Calvin felt overwhelmed in contemplating the failures of his oldest sons, Cooley and Elijah. In December 1854, Elijah sent his father a letter saying he had resigned from the ministry because of his wife's ill health and was returning home to Indianapolis. This news produced regret and depression in Calvin, who saw it as an "apparent failure." "He & Cooley have both abandoned their parts during this year," Calvin noted bitterly in his diary. "I look upon it as fickle tho' they have apparent excuses . . . Fickleness in position after a man assumes the place of husband & father for the few first years fixes the character usually for life." Calvin had hoped for and trained his sons to be "efficient & useful" men who would invite him to the "homes they had made by their own exertions instead of retreating on me." Now he was left to endure an ongoing stream of unacceptable "excuses" about his sons' failures to carve out independent careers.[10]

As he worried about such failures in the winter of 1854–1855, Calvin's penchant for loneliness and depression resurfaced, especially since he was now a single man. And in those often sad, private reflections, he thought of Sarah, who represented anything but failure. "In my lonely moments," he noted one Sunday night just before Christmas, "I cannot but bring up before my mind Mrs. Fletcher. Her usefulness, her kindness, her affection, her great labors, all come up before me as well as the thoughts, her last hours & her cold, cold silent grave." On his annual birthday self-assessment in February 1855, Calvin again unburdened himself of his lonely anguish: "One year ago today we were an unbroken family," he reflected, but since September 27, "we have been for 4 ms . . . left without her. Oh, how dreary & lonesome have been many moments since."[11]

As much as he missed Sarah and frequently celebrated her memory, Calvin was not a man who would live out his days as a lone widower. While believing in the power of the individual, he craved the close bonding and unflinching loyalty that came with a good marriage. So it was perhaps not surprising that within months of burying his beloved Sarah, Calvin found himself drawn to another woman. And, perhaps equally predictable, that woman was one he had come to know and deeply respect in his years of devoted commitment to education. Keziah Lister, a New Englander, was one of the teachers sent to Indianapolis by the Board of National Popular Education in 1851. An extremely successful and popular teacher, intelligent and widely read, Keziah grew up in Farmington, Maine. She married George Lister, a doctor, who deserted her and moved to Texas. Keziah, an abandoned—but not legally divorced—woman, arrived in Indianapolis in her late thirties, and by the early spring of 1855 she and Calvin began to court.

This courtship began with warm letters from Calvin, ostensibly about school matters—"Mrs. L.," as he called her in his journal, was now the principal of the local school—but clearly aimed at winning her heart, not her head. But when Keziah didn't respond promptly to his letters, he began to worry like an unrequited lover. "She has imagined that there is some delicacy in the matter not perceived by me," he recorded in his diary, "that

Calvin and Keziah Fletcher, 1856

there is some coquetry necessary." This left him with an "unpleasant" feeling, especially given their years of close contact and deep respect. Unaware of exactly how to approach her in this new, deeply personal fashion, he realized that he might need her direction in how to proceed in matters of the heart. "I know she is a lady of great sensibility & may have seen things I could not."[12]

What brought them closer together into a more explicit romantic relationship were "Mrs. L's" religious sensibilities. "Mrs. Lister told me her late religious feelings," Calvin noted early on in their relationship. "I admired them. Oh, that I was better, more holy, more devoted." In yet another "interview," Keziah and Calvin discussed religion: "Mrs. Lister has in her modest lady like way given her opinion of several Religious matters. I think her a spiritually minded excellent pure woman. I wish she had better health & more physical strength to carry out her excellent purposes of life." A few days later, he wrote: "In eve talked with Mrs. Lister on subject of religion.

I feel better by our interviews. She is truly a good woman." They talked as well about matters of money, old age, and youth. By April, although nothing had been announced, Calvin felt assured that their marriage "is consecrated by God." What's more, he felt that Keziah, whom he frequently referred to as a "friend," could bring welcome change to his life and make him a better person. "I feel more like living a new life," he noted. "I am admonished by one of *my best friends* as to my peevishness or fretfulness & recommended to cease from such evil practices."[13]

But building a new life with his best friend prompted criticism within the Fletcher family. When Calvin sat down with some of his children to discuss the relationship and looming marriage, he encountered both encouragement and considerable unhappiness. Since he was considering leaving the Fletcher home and living with Keziah or building a new house for his new life, he wanted to be understood and, of course, supported. But he realized that his wish for "harmony" would not come easy: "It is a dangerous step at best," he conceded. While Elijah offered general support—"Whatever course you may deem proper to pursue, I am determined to do all in my power to render you happy"—other children expressed worry and doubt. His daughter Maria reported that her aunt Susan Hill and others, Calvin noted, "had made comments on a subject of great delicacy [that] . . . would embarrass me." Still, he concluded, "[I] shall not let such things disturb me." Miles, on behalf of Stoughton and Calvin Jr., told him, "You have children who love you dearly & who are willing to do anything for your happiness, yet they are men—have human frailties, and human feelings." These otherwise-loving children, he continued, would not take lightly any news that their father "might take a step that would disgrace the family." It wasn't getting remarried that was disgraceful, he observed, but simply having to call "any woman 'mother' or 'Mrs. Fletcher' as your wife. We could not bear to see one of our own brothers or sisters in any way controlled by a step mother. We could not love a step brother or sister as we should. We could not bear to see any woman live in comparative comfort & ease upon the products of the labor of an affectionate mother who literally worked herself to death."[14]

Lying behind the family resistance to Calvin's proposed remarriage was something more significant than simply children reacting negatively to a new woman. The "disgrace" so often hinted at pointed to the legally uncertain status of Keziah Lister. Her husband, Dr. George Lister, apparently a drunk and a deserter, had never legally separated from Keziah and was living somewhere in south Texas. Unwilling to let this mysterious man cast a shadow over his marital prospects, Calvin sought legal advice on how best to handle the "legal entanglements" of his beloved. In July Calvin sent his brother Stoughton to La Grange City, Texas, where Dr. Lister lived, and "there [made] an arrangement to disembarrass her" and "get legal relief for [his] loved friend." Calvin had Keziah put together an affidavit notifying Lister of her intention to divorce him that was published in the La Grange *Whig* for thirty days. When Lister didn't appear to contest the divorce—he was depicted by a Texas friend of Calvin's as "very dissipated in his habits . . . a profligate and debaucher"—the divorce was granted on October 30, 1855. Calvin spent $100 to cover Stoughton and the court's expenses.[15]

Two days later, on November 1, 1855, Calvin boarded a train to Fortville, and then went on to various connections via Muncie, Cleveland, Syracuse, Albany, Worcester, Boston, and Portsmouth before arriving November 3 in Hallowell, Maine. At the depot, he recounted, "my esteemed one" met him with a smile and "took me to her beautiful & happy cottage where I met her mother." They proceeded to get a marriage license at the courthouse, where Calvin made out a deed for the settlement of $7,000 for Keziah, and in return she conveyed her lot and house to him. While Calvin viewed the lot and house as a very modest substitute for a dowry, he still agreed to pay the annual taxes on the premises and keep them in good repair, giving Keziah's mother use of the place during her life, after which it would fall to the new Mrs. Fletcher if she survived Calvin. Calvin was careful to note that Keziah in no way dictated these arrangements to him, nor, according to him, considered them of much importance. "This endears her much to me," he noted.[16]

On a snowy morning the next day, they rode to church, where the Reverend Edmond Squires preached on "the marriage part of Cana of

Gallalee in the most happy manner." At 6:00 that evening they were married by Reverend Squires with only a few attending—the minister's wife, Keziah's mother, and Keziah's niece. On their wedding day, Calvin was fifty-seven and Keziah forty-one. The newlyweds returned to Indianapolis on November 9, with Calvin clearly happy about "the Providences that attended me—the good health & comfortable condition of the one I loved so well." He was also very pleased by the reception they got from his children, "who," he pridefully noted, "said they at first dreaded to see a stranger occupy the place of their good mother, yet if the world were to be searched the like of Mrs. Lister, their new mother, could not be expressed or found." A few weeks later, Calvin received encouragement as well from his brother Elijah, who expressed pleasure at learning that Calvin "had made [him]self happy in taking a new Partner to share with [him] the cares and troubles of life." "I cheerfully salute her as a sister," Elijah wrote, "and hope I shall ere long have the pleasure of a personal interview."[17]

In preparation for his new life with Keziah, Calvin bought the Alfred Harrison home on North Pennsylvania Street and, in fact, had already moved into the house in October 1855. His son Miles, who had recently left teaching to study law, moved with his own family into Calvin's previous residence, the Wood Lawn house, southeast of town. And, to add to the fluid living arrangements in the Fletcher household, Calvin's daughter Maria got married just a few weeks after Calvin and Keziah. Her husband, Cyrus Hines, had first befriended Maria while attending Brown University with her brothers Calvin Jr. and Stoughton before moving to Indianapolis in 1854. Calvin described him as "a widow's son, very small tho well made & intellectual & moral." It is perhaps revealing that Calvin had remarkably little to say in his diary or letters about this marriage, other than to simply note the day before that "Mrs. F. & Maria preparing for wedding tomorrow at 6 P.M." He does briefly mention the wedding, but only to say that after the ceremony everyone sat down "to an old fashioned supper," at which time he ate oysters for the first time.[18] Clearly, his daughter's marriage did not carry the significance for Calvin that his sons' marital decisions did. As much as he valued women's education, he could not bring himself to imbue the lives of his daughters with the same importance as those of his sons. It's also possible that because Maria's wedding took place very close in time to his own marriage, Calvin was simply too preoccupied with his "dear Companion" to think much about Maria or her new life with Cyrus. Maria joined her youngest siblings, Keyes, Lucy, and Albert, in moving into the new Fletcher house.

Calvin's house and spouse had changed, but his interests in and commitments to the larger world had not. He remained a stockholder and board member of the Indianapolis and Bellefontaine Railroad, which was chartered in 1848 and passed through the Fletcher farm northeast of Indianapolis. When it was finally linked up in 1853 with the Ohio and Illinois lines, Fletcher proudly called it "a great thoroughfare . . . one of the greatest events to Indianapolis that has occurred since its settlement to cause its further rapid advance."[19] The very month he remarried, Calvin was re-elected president of the State Bank. Despite precarious speculation and numerous bank failures, the State Bank survived until its charter expired at the end of 1856, at which point it was converted into a private institution, the Indianapolis Branch Banking Company. While he made a very comfortable living at the bank, Calvin expanded and profited as well from his numerous landholdings. During the mid-1850s he added to his farms in Marion, Morgan, Johnson, and Hamilton counties, financing the purchases through sales of land in northern Indiana. Given his wide-ranging activities and advancing age, Calvin decided to turn over much of the responsibility of managing the farms to his son Calvin Jr., though he continued to closely watch—and often criticize—the transactions his son made, especially regarding livestock expansion. And every fall, Calvin made a point of personally working in the fields to help bring in the harvest.

The Calvin Fletcher household began 1856 with "the smallest family we have ever had"; beyond Keziah and Calvin, it consisted of seven people: son Stephen Keyes (Keyes), fifteen; daughter Lucy, thirteen; son Albert, nine; grandson "Dima" (Elijah's boy), who was temporarily staying with them in the wake of the death of Elijah's wife the previous fall; Mr. Smith, a hired man; Maria, a Dutch servant girl; and an orphan boy, Johnny Ray, son of Calvin's deceased business friend, James Ray. To commemorate their new life together, Calvin and Keziah had a daguerreotype made on January 10, 1856.[20]

By now Calvin could take comfort in the realization that most of the resistance to "Mrs L." assuming the role of stepmother had dissipated. But there were a few holdouts. One was twenty-year-old Ingram, who found it hard to think of Keziah as a mother-like figure in the family, even though he respected his father's choice for a wife: "I think father has taken one, the only one, that could so well fill the vacancy," he conceded. But dealing with a new "mother" did not go down easy with Ingram: "I admit that the thought of having another mother, was cutting—'sharp as a two-edged sword,'" he wrote Keziah herself. Despite his doubts, he concluded, "Father has always succeeded in life; therefore I trust, unboundedly in his judgment. Perhaps I love him too much, if there is such a thing."[21]

A new home and new wife—eventually embraced by all—might have given Calvin new hope, but darkening the horizon were the failed records of his two eldest sons, Cooley and Elijah. In his diary and in letters, Calvin spoke directly and often to the issue. "Last week was gloomy," he noted in late January. "I saw my 2 oldest sons broken down failed—& will ultimately retire on their father's accumulations. How many more will follow their example I know not. It is the natural easy way. My children like others will follow the easy way. He [who] rows upstream & drops the oars falls back. I look for this."[22] A few weeks later, when he was commemorating his birthday, it was this paternal gloom rather than any sort of individual celebration that set the tone for his annual self-reflection.

His second-oldest boy, Elijah, now thirty-two, was struggling with chronic illness and an inability to make a living as a pastor either in Rhode Island or back in Indianapolis, where he had returned in 1856 with his wife, Eunice, and their small boy, "Dima." Eunice died of consumption within a few weeks of their return to Indianapolis, which left Elijah a single parent with no means of support. "He left N.E. in debt," Calvin noted, "& we have paid for him some $800 of old debts." Like Cooley, Elijah "seemed to think that the persons at home should license them to use up the years' labors or diminish the means already made."[23]

It was Elijah's older brother, Cooley, however, who prompted the most anger and frustration in Calvin. Although Cooley, now thirty-three, had developed a significant following for his foreign missionary work, especially in Brazil, he continued to depend on his father for financial help, as he had for years. Calvin could not resist tallying up all the generous aid he had given to his entitled son—"from 1839 to 1848 or 1849 he was at constant expense for his education, 3 years fitting for college, 4 years in college one or 2 years at Princeton Theological College—1 year at Geneva. In all I must have spent from 1st to last some $15,000"—and all this during hard times, Calvin observed. "But," he noted, "I eat no idle bread. I worked & God blessed my labors. He and E. were, however a great tax to us. His poor mother also worked like a slave to provide for them."[24]

What was worse, in Calvin's mind, was that Cooley had married very badly. Calvin was quick to blame the pair's financial problems on Henrietta Malan, whom Cooley had wed in Geneva, Switzerland, in 1850. Licensed to preach as a Presbyterian after graduation from Princeton Theological Seminary, Cooley journeyed to Switzerland to prepare for his foreign mission work. He became engaged to Henrietta, the daughter of a renowned minister, Dr. Malan. Before the marriage could take place, Dr. Malan requested that Calvin provide certification that Cooley was a legitimate child. Calvin took exception to such presumption from an elite European family: "I scented & requested him not to marry into such a family—that he came from a king killing or king hating family . . . It was my better judgment that an American lady would be preferable. He could have united with the best families if he desired—But I fear his vanity led him."[25]

And hers. Indeed, so upset over his son's begging for financial help and his daughter-in-law's grasping demands on his estate, Calvin could not decide which party was more culpable for the couple's failed life. "His wife's high expectations & his own extravagant views led him into great poverty & he has no doubt suffered much," Calvin bitterly noted. "His making debts abroad & drawing on his father to pay them has been done without considering his covenants while I advanced some 12, or 15,000 for his education & travels. He promised if I would help him thro' he would rely on his own resources. The moment he got married he demanded support. His wife seemed to be misinformed." More than "misinformed," she grew belligerent when Calvin and Sarah refused some of the pair's financial demands. "His wife wrote me one of the most abusive vulgar letters that ever was written to me," Calvin declared, noting that she had claimed that she and Cooley had been "ill treated by the family." Furthermore, she wanted her angry letter "read . . . to every child I had" so "she could make my ill treatment known" to all of them. Outraged at this conduct, Calvin and Sarah burned the letter. Given Cooley's financial straits and such a craven wife, Calvin could only assume the worst: "I apprehend he is a broken down man." And nothing better demonstrated a "broken down man," he believed, than when such a weak person brought trouble home. When Cooley and Elijah returned home in the spring of 1855, they immediately began making "unreasonable & unexpected demands on me," Calvin lamented. "[They] have brought their troubles *home to roost* . . . I have found them not deeply impressed with gratitude for the favors already done them—but feeling but little or no obligation, yet demanding more."[26]

When it came to "the present trials of Cooley with a wicked wife," Calvin couldn't help himself. Deeply devoted to unwavering principles of self-advancement and financial self-control, he reacted to his son's weaknesses the only way he knew: by angrily admonishing him—and his other children—to grow up the hard-earned, self-reliant way he had. Though honest, this message was nonetheless guaranteed to fail when addressed to young men seeking help and trying to find a way forward with their lives. In the midst of his tragic conflict with his oldest son, Calvin had a revealing moment of self-recognition: "I sometimes fear my way is too harsh for my children that I may alienate myself from them."[27]

Calvin's disdain and upset over his dependent, grasping children certainly did not extend to all of his sons. But his insistence that they all find their own way while showing him due gratitude caused such friction and unhappiness among his sons that twenty-one-year-old Ingram decided to make his move right away. In July 1856 Ingram announced he was leaving home for Lake Superior, the same area he had visited with his mother three years before. As was true of nearly all coming-of-age moments in the Fletcher family, Ingram's departure from Calvin's household was compared—in Calvin's mind—to his father's own leave-taking back in 1817. So when Ingram made his decision, Calvin presumed that Ingram viewed this moment "as taking the world for himself." Calvin even wrote a note, "a memoranda," for Ingram to take with him and on which, presumably, he was to meditate. "Most of his country men who leave home," Calvin observed, "go out with a full belief that they are going to make a fortune & better their condition. I have told him not to go out with such motives. If he supports himself for 5 or 10 years without calling on his father & gets a good reputation he will do all I expect. Seek to be useful & learned rather than to be rich or influential. Not to be alarmed or agitated if others get suddenly rich." And then, of course, Calvin could not resist brandishing his own success story: "I left home at 17 & lived some 14 years & never spent an idle day or day for amusement as I could now recollect & it was with toil & care that I arrived at 28 years without a house of my own."[28]

Ingram was doubtless unsurprised by the fatherly advice he got, but he *was* taken aback by the realization that his own father was in fact ushering him out the door that summer. Reflecting on the departure months later from his new home in Wisconsin, Ingram wrote his father that "I was happy to think that I was so soon to assist you at home . . . I need not say that I was surprised at your disposition of my future—I was astonished." And he remembered especially the specific advice he got that now was the time to make his move; to wait was to court disaster. "The evening that you and Stoughton talked to me in the yard and gave me to understand that 'I would curse the day if I did not launch out,' I confess was one of gloom," Ingram recalled. "It was the darkest hour I ever experienced! But as it was my father's advice, I determined not to stay at home and 'suck my fingers' as it would have been said . . . *Hints* are enough for *me*."

But Ingram, now several months away from his departure and living in Ashland, Wisconsin, wanted to clear the air as to why, in fact, he had left home: "First my father wished me to take care of no one; secondly, I found that my brothers were unhappy . . . [with] each other as well as their father's motives, and not willing to come to a parley. Such was the state of things when I returned [home] . . . I was greatly, sadly disappointed." Given this emotional dysfunction in the family, Ingram decided it was "advisable to go where I was not known; and built on my own merits," since his stature previously "was attributed to my father's character or my brother's influence." Now, in Wisconsin, he reasoned, if he became well regarded, "it will not be because 'my father is rich' or 'my brothers wise men.'" And if he failed, Ingram noted, "I do so on my own responsibility."

"Launching" into the world at twenty-one was the right thing to do, Ingram concluded, but he didn't want to lose sight of—or his sense of comfort with—those family members he had left behind. "I may never behold again the faces so familiar," he wrote his father, "yet I desire to hold a seat at the shrine of each ones heart." Although he was willing to enter into "the great contest with the world," he was not ready to buy into the Darwinian world of sink or swim, live or die. "Face the world I must; and if thus I am forced to do without a kind or encouraging word from a brother, amen to it. It only proves that they have lost the love that was once so pregnant in their bosom, and there planted by a sainted mother now in glory."[29]

Revealingly, Calvin took a more detached perspective on the Fletcher sons' "diaspora." He disagreed with Ingram's notion that it was "a bad matter that the family should not remain together." After consideration, Calvin had concluded that such repeated launchings of his offspring to new places "is no doubt right." Assuming a sort of familial "manifest destiny" position, Calvin declared that "God has ordered this new hemisphere to be settled. My children no better than others must contribute their part. This was the case of my own father's family. It has proven right." After some harsh words that same summer with his son Miles regarding the sale of lands, Calvin repeated this "let them go" philosophy: "I have resolved unless something very clear turns up to let my sons go from me early."[30]

Friction and doubt marked much of the dynamic between Calvin and his sons, but he certainly had admirers within the family. Brother Elijah seemed quite taken with the few nephews he met in person. He wrote very favorably back to Calvin about the good visit he had had with Calvin's son, Stoughton, early in 1856. The twenty-four-year-old had visited his Virginia uncle and made "a very favorable impression . . . [I]f he be a fair specimen of the rest of your sons, " Elijah observed, "you have reason to be proud of them and I am sure they will be a comfort and blessing to you." More than that, Elijah urged Calvin to take comfort in the mostly proud legacy that his numerous children would leave behind. "You have a prospect that your progeny will make your name common and familiar and respected throughout your state and the world at large," he wrote. "It must be very gratifying, too, that among so many, all are by nature perfect in body with minds above the common and an energy and disposition to make themselves useful and highly respected citizens."[31]

"Useful and highly respected" might have been a clichéd phrase, but it was a hard-won feeling for both brothers, especially when it came to Elijah and his dissolute son, Lucian. One day in the fall of 1856 an eerily familiar-looking man showed up at the home of Calvin Fletcher. "A stranger called & made himself known as Lucian Fletcher," Calvin noted. Lucian had been living in western Virginia but was now headed to Missouri. To Calvin, it was clear that the thirty-two-year-old standing before him was "a profligate young man" who had wasted his legal training and the large fortune that his father Elijah had spent on him. And it was equally clear what brought Lucian to his uncle's door: Lucian's father, Calvin reflected in his diary, "has thrown him on the world & refuses no doubt to aid him further." As best he could tell, Lucian "has now adopted a roving hunting life." Calvin showed him some schoolhouses in Indianapolis, presumably to suggest that Lucian take up some teaching opportunities rather than wander off west again. When Calvin asked him why he didn't go back home to work with his father, Lucian responded that despite being in "declining" health, "his father was a man of stern habits—would not give up his business to anyone."[32]

On this point, Lucian was doubtless right. Elijah, especially at this stage of life, was most interested in focusing on what was good and what brought joy and contentment to him, and he had distanced himself from those people—like his reckless son—and issues—like corrupt politics—that led only to unhappiness and difficulty. "Life is but a scuffle at best," he wrote Calvin, "and [we ought to] content ourselves with the thousand blessings we enjoy. I am not over anxious about the things of this world. To take care of what Providence has cast to my lot is my duty, but I do not worry or fatigue myself much in doing this." Rather than agonizing over Lucian's profligacy, as no doubt Calvin would have done, Elijah simply detached from him, let him go. In contrast, he delighted in involving himself in the lives of his other children, especially his daughters.[33]

Tellingly, while Elijah "scuffled" along, focusing on what brought him joy and happiness, Calvin simply could not let go of anything—whether errant children or fraught politics—that he believed needed improvement. In the fall of 1856 the nation looked west with apprehension to the new territories, especially Kansas and Nebraska, where slavery would either expand or be thwarted by "free-soil" forces. The battles in Congress alarmed Calvin, especially the "caning of Sumner," when the fire-eating slave-holding senator from South Carolina, Preston Brooks, assaulted the venerable Massachusetts senator on the floor of the U.S. Senate in June 1856. The attack on Charles Sumner, Calvin claimed, was "an outrage scarcely to be born," and signaled, he feared, "the death knell of our republic . . . it can't last long."[34]

With the fate of slavery in the territories to be determined by "popular sovereignty" (a majority vote of those settlers in the region), Calvin anxiously watched in the summer of 1856 as Kansas erupted in violence between the two forces. Later that summer, the "bleeding Kansas" conflict turned into street theater in Indianapolis. On July 15, a procession of young men took to the streets dressed up as the proslavery "Border Ruffians" who had provoked bloodshed in the territory. The Indianapolis *Locomotive* described the burlesque procession as "a long line, numbering . . . two hundred, dressed in all possible costumes, and burlesque arms, and emblems. Their leader was dressed like the devil with forked tail, carrying a banner with the inscription, 'my work follows me.'" Much of the Fletcher household attended or participated in the event, with Billy, Ingram, Keyes, and Johnny Ray joining in the burlesque company. A torchlight parade with a balloon ascension capped off a day that featured both festive activities and angry protests.[35]

For Calvin, the protest was all that mattered. In his eyes, the upcoming election between the Democrat James Buchanan and the Republican he supported, John C. Fremont, was a critical moment for the country, a point he emphasized to his slave-owning brother in Virginia. "No middle course could hereafter be taken by any member elected to congress," Calvin wrote Elijah. "He must be a pro slavery man or a free state [man]. No more *Dough faces* as they are called." The next day he noted: "I laid awake & thought of [my] Dear bleeding Country."[36]

With the fate of slavery in the territories to be determined by "popular sovereignty," Calvin anxiously watched as Kansas convulsed. A prominent Free-Soiler came to the Indianapolis courthouse square and spoke to a crowd of antislavery men that included Calvin, arguing that the state of affairs in Kansas had become "most melancholly—men, women & children in distress & many murders." Calvin's view of Buchanan's Democratic Party—as populated by men who were "made with force & fraud" while any "truthful statements of the oppression, murder & destruction of our fellow men by the slavery party in Kansas is laughed to scorn"—only deepened his despair about where his country, as a slave nation, was headed. "I fear that we have so far participated in the wickedness of Slavery that God intends we shall suffer by it," he reflected. On Election Day, Calvin worked the polls. "Our best citizens stood on the ground all day," he recorded later, but as he saw it, "the farmers are low & poor & ignorant," especially the Irish immigrants. "Some of the better class of Germans worked with us. The Irish & ignorant slave state men against us with many [demagogues]." Fremont polled well in Indianapolis and Marion County, but Calvin correctly predicted that the Republican ticket could not prevail in Indiana. Buchanan's Democratic Party won the state and the general election. "Ignorance and whisky seem to be the nursing mother of Democracy," Calvin lamented, leaving the republic to be "saved by Grace only."[37]

※ • • • ※

From his rural retreat in southwestern Virginia, Elijah Fletcher did not necessarily see the republic as being in danger. If he did, he kept it to himself and probably thought about it in quite different terms—that rabid antislavery zealots (not unlike his brother) were pushing the nation toward an irreconcilable crisis. Elijah's world focused much more on private matters.[38] In that retired and solitary sphere, Elijah delighted in discussing comparatively innocuous matters, such as the various "sojourns" his daughters would be taking. Indiana and Betty embarked on a trip to Cuba at the beginning of 1857, returning by way of New Orleans and stopping in Indianapolis to pay a visit to their uncle Calvin, a visit Calvin recorded with affection in his diary. According to Elijah, the girls returned home "highly pleased with their reception" in Indianapolis "and much gratified to find their relations occupying so eligible a position in society and so prosperous and well to do. Their representations of your wife," Elijah told Calvin, "were highly flattering."[39]

Elijah, now sixty-seven, had become a bit of a recluse. He took rambles around his various farms, especially with his daughters, but otherwise, he stayed close to home. Each year or two he did enjoy making the long journey to Ludlow for a summer family reunion. And as the summer of 1857 approached he hoped to go to Vermont, especially if he could see his brother Calvin and Calvin's new wife, whom he had not yet met—"an additional inducement to go," he pointed out. But if he did go, he wanted to travel directly to Ludlow with his girls "without calling and stopping in the cities. I hate very much of the money annoyances and confusion attendant on the transfers and Hotels of the cities." All he could promise was to seriously consider the trip, but he insisted there would be no guarantees. For, as he confided to his brother, "I like my home, my own room, and my own bed so much it requires some resolution to leave. I even dread going to Lynchburg and many times, when I ought to go on business, will put it off from day to day and week to week, till compelled to start."[40]

Elijah Fletcher, ca. 1855

As it turned out, Elijah did not make the trip to "the old Mansion." And when Calvin gave him a hard time about it, noting that their days were numbered in terms of final visits to the ancestral home, Elijah would have none of his brother's "gloomy thoughts." "If no body would tell me that I was old and upon my last legs," he wrote Calvin, "or [were there] no warning circumstance around to indicate it, my feelings and spirit would not induce me to think it. They are as buoyant and ardent as many years past." Still, he admitted, small things were now slowing him down, and any injury or illness seemed to take much longer to recuperate from. Nonetheless, Elijah insisted he would be looking forward "with a cheering hope" to meeting up with Calvin at the "Mansion" next summer.[41]

Less cheering was his worry about their brother Timothy, who was helping family friend Susan Sargent to oversee the family home in Ludlow.

Susan believed that Timothy was "quite unwell," Elijah observed to Calvin, as he had not left his room for a week because of a swollen, painful head and "a discharge from one ear." "Such symptoms are unfavorable for one of his age," Elijah concluded. He ended his long letter to Calvin by noting that despite the financial ups and downs (and mainly the latter) of the past year, he was pleased that Calvin's bank would survive relatively unscathed. In his own plantation world, he said he had made only a small provision for the winter but that his "numerous family of domestics have little fear of want, so long as Master lives they feel safe." Indiana and Betty had decided to stay with him for the winter instead of heading for New York, as they often did. Their apple crop was a failure, he reported, but the corn had turned out well, and soon plowing for the next year's crop would begin. Finally, he wondered if Calvin knew that the *National Intelligencer* in September had described Timothy as an "F.F.V. [First Families of Virginia] of Vermont, now of Virginia," especially for the "order he keeps of not permitting his kin at their reunions at the Old Mansion to talk of *Abolition, Religion or Politics.*"[42]

This letter, dated November 12, 1857, was the last communication that Calvin was to receive from his brother Elijah. On New Year's Day 1858, a cold wind awakened Calvin at 1:15 in the morning. He got up and fastened the blind, then went to the bedroom in the southwest corner of the house and lay down to look out the window toward the south. At about 2:00 a.m. he saw "a most beautiful star, a little down in the south from the zenith. It was brilliant & of a good size. It seemed another indication, another invitation to be grateful to God, to be of courage—to be in faith for the new year." A few weeks later Calvin celebrated his sixtieth birthday. With some eight children and seven grandchildren around him (among them Miles, Maria Hines, Ingram, Keyes, Lucy, and Albert), he ate dinner, feasting on succotash and turkeys brought from the farm. After dinner, with Maria playing the piano, they sang songs, including one Calvin Jr. had composed for his father's birthday. Then Calvin and the boys went into a room, and he read the history of the several anniversaries of his birthday since 1835. Ingram was decked out in his Native American "voyage clothes," which amused everyone. (A few years earlier, after a trip to the Great Lakes, Ingram had become enamored with the Native American customs and attire he had encountered in the region and had returned home dressed as a "native," much to the shock of everyone). Cooley could not attend but sent a note of congratulations from Newburyport, Massachusetts. Observing that his father looked "in appearance in strength & in spirit younger than most men in the U.S. at age 45," Cooley affirmed the belief that it was God who had allowed Calvin to live so long and who gave him "strength for days to come."[43]

Exactly two weeks later, Calvin received letters from Virginia, one of them from his niece Indiana. The story she told began innocently enough: On January 30, she wrote, "my Father left me for Lynchburg. When he rode away, it was a mild summerlike afternoon, but the next morning the weather changed very cold, raining, & severe wind." The storm worsened, she said, and about a mile from town Elijah "was suddenly taken very ill, disliking to stop at a Strangers house, he succeeded by fast riding, in reaching the Mulberry Farm" three miles from town. There some "kind hearted people" applied "hot bricks" to his hands and feet, but for four or five hours he lay immobilized. Finally, he consented to sending for a doctor, who arrived at 11:00 p.m. "& at once relieved him." It wasn't until 1:00 p.m. the next day that Indiana learned about her father's illness, but she rode over within two hours to be with him, having dispatched a messenger for her brother Sidney. A day later, "Papa" was better and had been brought by carriage back to Sweet Briar, where he was anxious to be once more. After taking some "mild medicines" that removed "the oppression about the heart" that he complained about, he improved over the next week, suffering no pain at all and becoming quite cheerful. Indiana said he "remarked that he was afraid he would get well too soon & that we would not think he had been sick."[44]

Indiana and Elizabeth sat up with Elijah every night "to attend to his slightest wants & to be with him when he awoke." He was progressing so well that they were inspired with "joy and gratitude for his rapid recovery." On February 11 and February 12 Elijah stayed up most of the days writing notes, reading the papers, and talking "in his usual bright, cheering way," and he rested quite well. On Saturday morning, February 13, he got up at his usual hour, Indiana recounted, "dressed himself, partook of his accustomed breakfast, gave orders to the servants for their days work &c. Sidney had gone to visit a distant part of the plantation, whilst I remained in his room. He remarked that he wished to accustom himself gradually, to the cold, before going out, & asked for the keys to go down in the Cellar." Indiana tried to convince him not to go, given the cellar's chilly cold, but Elijah went anyway, "doubtless to ascertain what groceries were necessary for the Servant portion of our family, for he had not been able to think of their wants, during his illness." After returning from the cellar, she wrote, "he sat with me at the fire, whilst I read to him a paper I was holding at the time." They talked about the news, and then she set out his shaving "utensils," and he began shaving while she read a journal nearby. After about ten minutes, she noticed he took "an unusual long breath," and, she wrote, "as I looked up I saw his head drooping. I instantly arose & held him in my arms, calling him, calling Sidney & the Servants. As I can remember, they all came in, camphor &c was applied, but nothing availed & in a moment, without a sigh, he raised his eyes, beaming with ineffable love, to me, & like one 'who lies down to pleasant dreams,' breathed his last, in my arms!" He had most likely died of a stroke.[45] "It has cost me many tears to write this," she told her uncle, as her grief left her with a "broken, crushed heart."[46]

Indiana's letter was brought to Calvin while he was at work at the bank. Later that evening, he struggled to grapple with the depressing news: "A great man has fallen—an affectionate brother gone; the family circle broke." Elijah, he said, "was the last one whose death I would have expected. How poor judges we are—how frail, frail."[47]

Calvin had no time to wallow in sadness over his loss, as he learned in a letter from Sidney that same day that his help was needed to come to the aid of Elijah's profligate son Lucian, who had fallen into trouble in Cincinnati. Early the next morning, Calvin and Keziah boarded a train for Cincinnati to look for Lucian. He was reported to be "in a rather dissepated condition" and "had a negro girl somewhere in Cincinnati." Calvin and a detective scoured the city's jails and "all other places" but found no trace of Lucian. Calvin and Keziah returned to Indianapolis empty-handed.[48]

But a few days later Calvin learned that Lucian had arrived in Indianapolis. He had been in Cincinnati, as it turned out, when the Fletchers were looking for him, but had gone into hiding because Lucian had heard that the police were looking to apprehend "the colored woman & children" who were traveling with him. So Lucian fled to a nearby Quaker community, which later brought him to Indianapolis and took in the "colored girl" and her children. "Lucian seems much affected at the loss of his father," Calvin reported, and was clearly "destitute." So Calvin bought him a pair of pants, paid his hotel bill, and sent him to work on the family farm with Calvin Jr. Calvin wrote Sidney that Lucian had been found and that he might buy the young man a farm in the area and "let him hold it . . . in trust." "I do not think him entirely lost," he reported. "[He] may yet recover." Sidney responded that he had made every effort possible to help his brother, but with no success. Calvin then offered to pay Sidney $200 for a year to keep an eye on Lucian while Lucian "live[d] in some little village at a hotel." The idea was that if in a year's time Lucian became "a steady man," a more generous arrangement might be made. With Lucian working with Calvin Jr. and Keyes planting apple trees in the family orchard, Calvin felt there was hope: "I think his father's death may have a salutary effect on him," he concluded. The woman, Sidney observed, had been taken by Lucian "to a free state and she is by law Free. Let her go. She is absolutely able to take care of herself."[49]

Despite the hope Calvin and Sidney may have held out for Lucian, the young man was clearly reeling not only from his father's death but from the harsh message Elijah sent him from the grave: his father had written Lucian completely out of his will. As Sidney put it, "he need not look to his father's estate for anything." Early on, Elijah had made a clear decision about Lucian. His will, drawn up in the summer of 1852, conveyed his house, lot, and furniture in Lynchburg to his wife Maria (who died the following year); his Sweet Briar plantation, furniture, and silver plate to Indiana, twenty-nine, and Betty, twenty-six—as well as the Lynchburg house after his wife's death; and the remaining property to Sidney, Indiana, and Betty. Betty attempted to move on from her father's death, marrying W. Hamilton Mosby of Lynchburg in 1859. Indiana stayed behind as the sole owner and caretaker of the Sweet Briar plantation.[50]

Enraged by his father's decision to exclude him from the estate, Lucian stormed into Calvin's house waving a copy of his father's will and asking what his uncle could possibly do to fight it. Calvin noted that Lucian had "forfeited no doubt the respect of his father by his profligacy," though he did sympathize a bit with his failing nephew: "It may be it was all right for him [Elijah] to restrict his bequests but to deprive him of all hope of all expectation, is lamentable indeed." Calvin would have preferred a clause that if Lucian could "reform in his habits," then he would be granted access to some of the estate. "But I confess," Calvin concluded, "I have but little compassion for a disobedient trifling child, son or daughter, infant or adult who views life a farce & all that parents have done was a piece of mere selfishness . . . Such children have never prospered to my recollection."[51]

By late fall of 1858, Lucian had run out of prospects in Indianapolis and returned to Amherst County, Virginia, where his brother and sisters lived. Calvin had mixed feelings about seeing him go: "He had been a source of care to me & nothing but the love I bear to his deceased father & my belief in cultivating the natural affections induced me to undergo & retain him." Calvin paid him $15 a month for eight months, "more than he deserved," Calvin observed, "but no more than I owed his father & to the relation we sustain." Calvin told Sidney and his sisters "that they should forgive & treat [their brother] kindly." Sidney responded positively, sending $1,500 to Calvin "to be invested for Lucian in a farm." Somewhat surprisingly, Sidney seemed "pleased to find him [Lucian] so rational &c," giving Calvin and his family "great credit" for helping his troubled brother out for nine months. A few weeks later Lucian returned to Indianapolis; Calvin reported that, though he looked well, Lucian gave "a melancholly account of the plantation left by his father & the slaves." Apparently those slaves "well raised & instructed" by Elijah had come to "feel all the love of liberty" and were now upset at the prospect of "a new generation" of masters less interested in their well-being than Elijah had been.[52]

Alas, Lucian's own well-being soon came into question. Within a week of boarding at a neighborhood tavern, he got drunk, which greatly distressed his uncle. Now the $1,500 investment of his siblings, Calvin feared, "will be of no use. I am at my wits end almost to know what to do." Calvin Jr., who had worked with Lucian on the farm, came to his father's house to discuss the troubled man. "He has become a drunken bad young man. I [have] done all I could to reclaim him," Calvin concluded. The very next day, Lucian appeared at Calvin's house at five in the morning, "no doubt drunk." Later that evening, Calvin heard that Lucian had gone into the city "drunk & crazy." Calvin gave him some money to go to Canada, where his black mistress and children had recently moved. "Hope he will go," he noted. It is not clear if Lucian used the money to go to Canada. The next news Calvin heard about him came six months later in the summer of 1860, when he learned from the Virginia newspapers (which, thanks to his brother, he had been reading for years) that Lucian had gotten into a fight and stabbed a man at the Amherst Courthouse. Calvin noted that Lucian was "badly shot himself & would likely die . . . He has been a bad boy & when here acted one time hostile to me. But my boldly looking him in the face he cowered." Lucian, as it turned out, lived on to continue to frustrate and anger his brother and sisters.[53]

While he watched, mostly from a distance, the sad unraveling of Lucian, Calvin was leaving no stone unturned in trying to keep his family together and as happy as possible. During the Christmas holidays in 1858, he brought together his eleven children for a family reunion in Indianapolis, an event highlighted by the taking of the daguerreotype of the whole family—save, revealingly, his relatively new wife Keziah, who doubtless stayed out of the picture out of deference to the still-wounded sensibilities of Calvin's children over the loss of their beloved mother. A daguerreotype cost from $2 to $5 in most towns and conveyed a sense of status and recognition that not just any family in nineteenth-century America could afford.[54]

As he began the new year, Calvin could point to as much hope as despair when considering his children. The despair and doubt fell, as always, on his eldest sons Cooley and Elijah, as well as on Calvin Jr. and Miles. Cooley, now thirty-five, Calvin lamented, "has an extravagant, unfortunate house & does not rule his own household when it requires such a governor. He is insolvent but is trying to escape from debt." Elijah, now a thirty-four-year-old pastor at Wesley Chapel, had managed to escape debt "after many years of embarrassment." Calvin Jr., thirty-two, had crafted "a career of extravagance" by "buying things without paying for them—machinery & let it lay out in the field & rot—make debts & not pay them—sell good stock which would command money for other stock of an inferior breed—buy 500 cattle when prudence would only demand 100 or 150." Likewise, thirty-year-old Miles, who was managing the family's land business, had now fallen into debt as well. Calvin described this latter son as someone who "supposed he had the world in a sling but found his strings broke & sling false" and was now desperately "trying to retrieve his character & live economical. I believe he will reform."[55]

But he gave passing to high marks to his other children: his recently married daughter Maria Hines, now twenty-five, and son Stoughton, twenty-seven, he considered "prudent"; Ingram, twenty-three, had proven himself "an economist" and Calvin "ha[d] hopes of him"; Billy, twenty-one, studying medicine in New York City, also had a promising future; Keyes, at eighteen, looked to be "a steady man but likes now to eat"; Lucy, a sixteen-year-old, was a bit "obstinate" and "indolent" but had "sufficient ability to be a lady of intelligence"; the youngest, twelve-year-old Albert, had "great amiability." And, of course, Calvin reserved his greatest praise and hope for Keziah, "Mrs. F." God, he claimed, had greatly blessed him in "giving me such a friend. It will be my delight to make her happy & I can't do it more so than to reciprocate her affections not in costly apparel but in congeniality & sympathy with her." He and Keziah occasionally had more sobering heart-to-heart talks during which they discussed each other's "deficiencies." "She thought me too oppressed with business. I told her I thought I wore that as easy as possible," Calvin reflected, noting that obsessing about money and belongings "had not been the great aim of life. We closed the day with commending ourselves to God & his grace."[56]

Indeed, though often consumed with political and family issues—many worrisome, some tragic—Calvin found great joy in some of the noteworthy moments of progress of the day. He was especially excited in the summer of 1858 by the successful laying of the transatlantic telegraph cable, which the *New-York Tribune* reported "will form one of the great events, indeed, an epocha in the age," he reported, "the communication between the Eastern & western Continent will be no ordinary event—One of the wonders of the age." On August 17, Indianapolis celebrated the lines after President James Buchanan and Queen Victoria exchanged messages through it. According to the Indianapolis *Locomotive,* "the city was all a blaze with the jollification on the successful laying of the Atlantic Cable," with parading military companies, fireworks, cannonfire, and bonfires all over town. From his house, Calvin "could see all the fire works & hear the shouting . . . I feel truly greatful to God for permitting me to live to witness so great an event—that 2 nations of the same language, sympathies & religion mainly should be permitted thus to speak face to face by & thro this wonderful agent, the Ocean Telegraph."[57]

Increasingly, though, the news of the day prompted worry and fear in Calvin. On October 18, 1859, he learned of the unsuccessful raid led by radical white abolitionist John Brown on the federal armory at Harpers Ferry, Virginia. Brown's effort to incite a slave revolt throughout the South electrified the country. Brown was captured, tried, and found guilty for treason, murder, and attempting to spur an insurrection. Watching events unfold from Indianapolis, Calvin worried that the "fanatical undertaking will unite slavery more close[ly] & separate the slavery & antislavery sections of the country." Sympathetic as he was to John Brown's beliefs, Calvin nonetheless worried that the whole issue of slavery was now being played out through "the imprudence of fanatics [and] that the chords [of union] will break." Calvin and Keziah read Henry Ward Beecher's sermon on the capture of John Brown, noting that Beecher referred somewhat "charitably" to the slave states, saying they were to be "pitied." The truth was, as

Calvin saw it, Brown "was made crazy by the oppression of the slave states in the Kansas matter where Brown had a son wickedly murdered." Driven insane by his desire to liberate the slaves, his "crazy" plot to free them ultimately "shows the weakness & fear of the slave states." When a telegraph on December 2 announced the hanging of John Brown, Calvin viewed it as a sad and frightening result of several evils and overreactions: "The north sympathized with an old crazy man whose insanity had been caused by the outrages he received in Kansas." Brown had violated the law, Calvin conceded, and no amount of suffering in Kansas could justify his actions. But now he feared that Brown's plot and hanging would only fuel more "ill will & bad blood between north & south." "It is plain the Southern people are great cowards & live in fear & dread of their slave," he concluded. Calvin was unsure what would happen as a result of the raid on Harpers Ferry, "but something under providential direction is to grow out of it."[58]

Calvin may well have wondered if providential direction was at work in a much more personal and unhappy way months later when he received news at the bank one day that his twenty-five-year-old daughter Maria Hines had fallen quite ill after the birth of her second child. Maria's husband, Cyrus, told him that Dr. Woodburn "had just informed him that Maria could not survive long—that the fever (childbed) had taken a stronghold & [she] could not survive but a short time." Late that afternoon, with Calvin at her bedside, Maria appeared anxious but was able to talk. "She said she was fraid she was going to die, that I had been a good father to her— that she had always thought if she was going to die she would have a great many requests to make," Calvin recorded in his diary. "But as the time had approached she could not think of many to make" other than to ask her maternal grandmother to help raise her new baby son, Fletcher. Later, her brothers filed into the room as they "supposed she was dying." A few hours later, Calvin reported, "she was sinking fast . . . just able to speak rather incoherently. She soon began a sort of melancholly hum like a child lulling itself to sleep rather loud but gradually lower for a half hour." Soon her voice became nearly inaudible; Keziah joined Calvin sitting next to her bed and "in 2 or 3 minutes [she] ceased to sing & her breath ceased without a

struggle or sigh." Maria had died from septicemia, a bacterial infection induced, as often was the case in less-than-sterile conditions, by childbirth.[59]
During the first half of the nineteenth century, roughly one in eight mothers died in childbirth. "Thus God has removed the first of the 11 children
he gave me," Calvin wrote. "Maria has accomplished [the] mission she was
sent to perform, to become a wife, a mother of 2 children & to die. God
doth all things well blessed be his name." Calvin telegraphed Miles and
Keyes to come right away. The next morning, his keen sense of loss turned
even deeper as he linked Maria's early death to her mother's passing, a loss
that Calvin still mourned. "The chain is broken, the whole undivided family were severed by the death of their dear mother in Sept. 1854," he said.
"Now the 1st of her children has passed into the spirit world to accompany
her, I trust . . . we must all soon follow."[60]

Calvin placed Maria's casket in the main parlor where she had stood as
a bride just four years earlier in December 1855. "She was & is entitled to
the best room in the house," he said. Later that day her body was "encased
in ice" to preserve the remains until the burial. At 5:30 the next morning
Calvin got up and entered the parlor, where "poor Maria had remained
alone all night. She is in the presence of the likeness of her sainted mother
on the wall looking down upon with an eye of compassion & pleasantness,"
he noted. "Poor girl—poor child. I regret I had not talked [to] you more on
the state you now have entered."[61]

※ • • • ※

While Calvin grieved this personal loss, the turmoil and fear of the larger
world resurfaced in an especially threatening way. By the fall of 1860 the
sectional tension between the antislavery North and the proslavery South
had deepened to such an extent that the newspapers were filled with talk
of various southern states, particularly South Carolina, threatening to se-
cede if the next president turned out to be, as it appeared quite possible,
Abraham Lincoln. Hardly an enthusiastic advocate of the awkward, plain-
spoken Illinois senator, Calvin nonetheless supported the Republican as

the best hope to thwart the slave-power conspiracy in the South. But early on, Calvin couldn't bring himself to believe that secession was anywhere on the horizon. "I can't think it possible that such an event can occur," he noted in late October. "The Slave States would be [in] the most miserable condition to do any such thing . . . Their real & personal estate & credit would sadly depreciate at once in such an event." Most proslavery southerners who threatened secession tied the threat to Lincoln's election. Calvin dismissed such threats as "feeble," "mere vaporing—the gas cannonade of only a few desperadoes, political mountebanks."[62]

As the firestorm of reaction to Lincoln's election progressed in the South, antislavery activists in the North like Calvin started to adjust to the reality that secession was near at hand. By early December, Calvin had had a political epiphany: "I have today made up my mind," he wrote on December 7, 1860, "that South Carolina will go out of the union & that Georgia, Alabama, Mississippi, Florida & Texas will go with S.C." Reading the papers, he learned that in Washington the southern delegates seemed to be in an uncompromising mood, even if most Americans, as Calvin sensed, felt strongly in favor of *union*. Slavery, he was convinced, was doomed—"but how & when & how long & how much we are to suffer for this cause no one can tell. We are in the hands of God who will do all things right." By Christmas Eve, southern secession seemed to him to be "a fixed fact." The South Carolinians, in particular, "seem to court a fight & unless they can consecrate the act by shedding of blood & get up a military fever they will soon die out."[63]

On the night of December 30, Calvin hosted a big family dinner. Present were his sons Miles, Ingram, Billy, and Keyes. Billy had just recently graduated from the New York College of Physicians and had returned to Indianapolis to practice medicine, an accomplishment that lent a festive air to the gathering. But after dinner, the subject turned to the looming danger facing the nation. His sons, Calvin noted, "proposed the subject of war, stated it was inevitable." Miles claimed that Washington, D.C., would be taken by the South before Lincoln could even be inaugurated in March, and so the ceremony would have to be conducted "somewhere else." And then they all wanted to know the answer to one compelling question: "If I would consent that [any] of my sons if required, should enlist to fight the South. This I declined to answer, stated [I would] be governed by the circumstances when they arose not before. I was for peace & if possible avoid bloodshed."

The next day, the last of 1860, Calvin saw from his reading of the morning papers that the South seemed bent on violence. He deplored bloodshed, but he could no longer see how it could be averted: "What will be our condition, what our sufferings to be recounted on the last day of the next year—*The 31 of Decr. 1861*—no one can tell. No one can now know what dire calamities await as a nation or as individuals."[64]

Seven

WAR AND
LOYALTY

T he question about war that Calvin and his sons talked about over dinner in late December 1860 would soon be answered. Fresh from graduating medical college in New York and having returned to Indianapolis to practice medicine, twenty-three-year-old Billy Fletcher enlisted in the Sixth Indiana Regiment, serving as an aide to commander Colonel Thomas T. Crittenden. On January 14, his twenty-year-old brother Keyes, who had just returned from Greencastle, Indiana, where he had worked in a hardware store, joined a Zouave regiment, a light infantry volunteer company. Calvin Fletcher himself did not believe in violence as a political tactic, but everyone in his family saw the looming civil war as a compelling test of manly virtue and an honorable, just war against the hated enemy of slavery. More than once, though, the larger Fletcher family, like the nation, would find itself painfully divided.

Early on in 1861 Calvin moved from doubting the likelihood of secession to seeing war as nearly inevitable. Poring daily through numerous papers—in addition to the various Indianapolis papers, he read the Cincinnati *Gazette*, the Louisville *Courier*, and the *New-York Tribune*—Calvin watched as other southern states (Georgia, Alabama, Florida, and Louisiana) joined South Carolina in secession. What was worse, the munitions and outposts of these states, except for Fort Sumter, had now fallen into the hands of southern extremists. "It looks now to me for the first time that blood shed & a protracted war must ensue," Calvin noted on January 14. He also feared that the border states would go with the South. "If so," he wrote, "it will be truly sad . . . I pray God may avert the War. I believe it is beyond the power of man."[1]

Calvin became a reluctant supporter of preparations for war as he witnessed his son Keyes drill every Monday and Wednesday evening with his Zouave regiment. Decked out in a new uniform—blue jacket with gold lace, baggy trousers, orange leggings and shirt, a white belt, and a scarlet cap with tassels—Keyes received military instruction in tactics and practiced gymnastic exercises. When Calvin's friend Bishop Ames came to visit, he told Calvin that his own son Eddy, prompted by Keyes's decision to join the Zouaves, had also enlisted. Believing that Keyes wanted to put his considerable energy to work for the country, Calvin could only hope that the Union's war needs "would not injure these young men."[2]

On February 11, newly elected President Abraham Lincoln arrived by train in Indianapolis. Calvin witnessed the event on Washington Street, where the train appeared around 5:00 p.m. The military and fire companies were out in full regalia to see the new president, along with some ten thousand people. Keyes stood in uniform with his Zouave regiment. The governor made an address and "Mr. L. replied to it," Calvin noted. The dangerous ambitions of the South continued to weigh heavily on his mind. Like most northern Republicans, Calvin viewed southern objectives as the ambitions of its craven slave-holders writ large: they were determined to export their evil institution of human bondage into the West. But now that the nation had "elected a President from the free state of Ill. & vice president from Maine [Hannibal Hamlin]," he declared, "the power of the south must decline. The struggle & death throes will now show themselves. May God give wisdom to the new incoming administration . . . the free states have the physical & moral power." Like most antislavery advocates in the North, Calvin firmly believed that the South had become ungovernable, except by force or threat: "I hope it will be found if true that a Southern city can't be governed—That Tyranny is the rule or mob—A republic cannot exist in a slave state."[3]

While the nation edged closer to violence, young men like Billy Fletcher had to make career decisions. In early April Billy was offered a position as a doctor in the Indianapolis "Insane hospital." The pay was a modest $800 a year. "It is quite as much as he deserves," Calvin claimed. But instead of jumping at the offer out of gratitude, Calvin observed, Billy treated the prospect as "a sort of temporary burial place." Looking back at his own experience, Calvin noted, "I rejoiced to make $85 the first year I came here by the practice of law & gave $8 of that away to aid in building the 1st Presbyterian Church."[4]

Before Billy could decide about his new prospect, the larger world jarred him and his circle of family and friends into a new reality: on April 12, at 4:30 a.m., Confederate cannons launched an attack on the federal installation of Fort Sumter in South Carolina. With limited and inappropriate munitions available in the fort to retaliate—the fort had no fuses for its explosive shells, rendering them useless—the Union forces were forced by the next day to surrender and evacuate. The Civil War, in effect, had begun. In Indianapolis the news prompted a day "of great excitement," according to Calvin. "Men doing nothing but walking up & down the street greatly angry at any one who intimated a favor to the South." When two local newspapers editorialized in sympathy with the secessionists, local citizens issued threats. With the attack on Fort Sumter, the gauntlet had been thrown down. "No man," Calvin declared, "will be allowed after this to express secession sentiments. The South cannot visit or have intercourse with us. It must be cut off."[5]

As "excited" as Calvin appeared by this early flash point in sectional conflict, the personal reality was much more complicated and, in fact, scary. As it happened, two of his children, Keyes and Lucy, were visiting their Virginia relatives at the time Fort Sumter was attacked, and Calvin worried greatly about their safety in "enemy" territory: "I fear the Rail roads will be torn up in Md. & Va. & it will be troublesome for them to get back or that they will be exposed to violence." Calvin telegraphed his nephew Sidney in Lynchburg to have Keyes and Lucy returned immediately. Keyes needed to be with his volunteer company but, awaiting any definitive news of combat, had accompanied his sister to Virginia. "I feel bad that K. is not here to join his company of Independent Zouaves," Calvin said. "They marched to the Fair ground."[6]

Keyes and Lucy reached Lynchburg on April 12. William Hamilton Mosby, the husband of their cousin Elizabeth, met them at the depot. The next day Keyes traveled to Sweet Briar, where he found his cousin Indiana and his uncle Timothy. It was there he learned about the attack on Fort Sumter. "The news nearly made me sick," he wrote his father, "for I was remaining in hopes that things would be settled in some way that we would have no fight." Like many northerners, Keyes had hoped that South Carolina would remain an outlier in the struggle over secession. With Fort Sumter, he feared, everything had changed: "Virginia will go out of the Union." Fearful about staying much longer in the South, Keyes and Lucy a few days later took the train home. Ingram picked them up at the station and brought them back to Calvin's house. Their father noted that "K. looks well, Lucy very bad. K. had not slept for 4 or 5 nights." With Keyes back home, Calvin "laid the necessities of the country before him—that it now seemed there was no other way than to conquer a peace." Meanwhile, women throughout Indianapolis had collected over one thousand blankets for the soldiers. Calvin saw seven different companies arriving from all over the area—"from Lafayette very raw looking boys," he noted.[7]

Because of his trip to Virginia, Keyes had missed out on getting into his Zouave company: it was full by the time he returned home. Instead, his friend Ed Ames, son of Bishop Ames, took his spot. Determined to prove his patriotism and manly spirit, Keyes had his father approach the bishop with a plan for Keyes to take back his spot from Ed. Calvin told the bishop that "he [the bishop] had but one son. I had 9. If he desired his son to withdraw from the company, K. would take his place." But Bishop Ames declined the offer, saying he felt it was his "duty" to let his boy remain in the company.[8]

Writing from the border region of New Albany, Indiana, just across the river from Louisville, Elijah reported that the war spirit was high and that if Kentucky seceded, his little town would become a dangerous hot spot. "Actual hostilities have brought out latent patriotism," he wrote, adding that at the church he pastored the "treasury was as empty as a whisky barrel at the close of an old fashioned election day." While he did not want to abandon his post at New Albany, Elijah recognized that the church was filled with Confederate supporters and that across the river in Kentucky, "nearly all its support . . . has come from the South." But, he insisted, "we are staunchly for the Federal govt." A few days later he informed his father he had enlisted in the Home Guards. "We are doing no packing up—only praying and keeping our powder dry," he wrote Calvin. Calvin agreed with his son that no longer was there any tenable position of neutrality over the war. "It is certain that Maryland, Ky nor any other state can assume a neutrality," Calvin acknowledged. "There can be but one opinion; that is, if any state refuses to aid the general government it amounts to treason."[9]

Calvin's convictions about the war were tested the very next day. Governor Morton called him to his office to request he lead an important mission to procure munitions from anywhere in the North to help arm Indiana soldiers. He was to leave that very evening for the East Coast and, later, Canada. "This news startled me," Calvin wrote. "I felt heart sick—I viewed myself totally incompetent for a great exigency." Pointing out that at sixty-three he was too old and totally unqualified for the task—"I was not a practical mechanic, nor was I acquainted with arms or munitions of war of any kind"—Calvin tried to back out of the assignment. The governor was not persuaded. What was needed, Governor Morton insisted, was "a man of sterling integrity" whose work would never "be tinctured by fraud." Calvin Fletcher was that man.[10]

Calvin went to talk with his partner, Thomas Sharpe, who agreed that their business demanded their full attention, and besides, "the Governor might find a younger man." Sharpe paid a visit to the governor to try to plead their case against getting involved in the war effort, but Morton would have none of it. Unless Calvin was willing to make a direct "absolute refusal" to the governor, the request would not be withdrawn. In the end, Calvin concluded that "if my country called & no other one was acceptable . . . I must serve." Calvin went home, revised his will again, and then hired his son Miles to travel to New England to check out all the munitions factories there while Calvin prepared to travel to Canada. He was to look into all kinds of artillery—guns, carriages, caissons, and rifled cannons. By early May Calvin had made his first deal: he brokered an agreement in Montreal to buy one thousand "minie or Endfield Rifles" to be imported from Belgium at $20 each. By May 8 he had returned to Indianapolis after one thousand miles of wearisome travel. "This journey & trip cost me much anguish & a great sacrefise," Calvin noted. "I am too old to take new responsibilities on me."[11]

Meanwhile, Billy's involvement in the military drew the Fletcher family even closer to the war. Enlisted in Indiana's Sixth Regiment, Billy trained at Camp Morton until May 30, when the troops finally were called into action in western Virginia. Billy described the scene: "The days had been growing longer and hotter at Camp Morton, and the boys were getting restive under their hard drills and strict discipline. At the announcement of 'Marching Orders' it seemed as if each man was suddenly struck with insane excitement, hats were thrown in air—cheer upon cheer given—officers were carried upon the shoulders of the men—even old Col [Hiram] Prather was insane enough to attempt an insane speech." Billy's company was called into line hours before dawn, and he recalled the moment vividly:

> The night was beautiful—and star-packed, and our camp fires were dieing into the last few flickering flames—20 rounds of carterge were distributed to each man & at 3 A.M. we were ready to march—while the band played a part of the plaintive march in the "Gentle Shepard," the Fife Major [Billy] took a stroal along the new vacant sheads where we had campt so long—the old Cow stalls were silent—here and there an old hat was thrown or a pair of breeches hung . . . it was almost 4 A.M. May 30th before the command—March! was given—and the day was blooming in the east. We marched down towards the sleeping city.

Marching down Meridian St. and F. Maj. felt almost sad. The band was playing "Then You'll Remember me"—when he past his fathers house; no one was moving—the shutters were shut and the F. Maj. could see no kind face or eyes suffused with tears . . . At the Depot a few persons were gatherd—by curiosity to "see the soldiers go" it was yet early, not 6 o'clock—and the F. Maj. looked around for a resting place—and a breakfast.[12]

The "F. Maj.," as Billy referred to himself, found breakfast that morning with his brother Stoughton, who was living in the nearby Woodlawn family house. Then the Sixth Regiment departed for western Virginia. Billy worked three weeks as a camp surgeon and then became Colonel Crittenden's personal aide. When Billy and a friend volunteered to do some reconnoitering and drew plans of a rebel camp near Laurel Hill (now West Virginia), he became highly valued as a scout. From a location near Camp Madison, Virginia, Billy told his father that they captured men every day and made them take the oath of allegiance to the federal government. Increasingly, his stories involved bloodshed. "Yesterday," he reported, "I was out with a squad and ordered a man who was crossing his field with a rifle in his hand. I being in command ordered him to 'Halt!' which he obeyed by turning and firing at me as cool as could be—and then ran. I ordered men to fire—which brought him too—white with fear." Calvin learned from Ingram that Billy was acting "rather daring as a scout." "I feel fraid of his adventures," Calvin remarked. He admired his son's courage but feared the boy's "discretion," feeling that he was taking unnecessary risks. Billy's commander, Colonel Crittenden, told Miles about his brother's heroics in the field. With conflicting rumors about the location of the rebels near Laurel Hill, Crittenden felt it necessary "to send some cool, clear headed, courageous man" who was also skilled at sketching to map the encampment. "I knew that W. B. Fletcher filled the bill," he stated, even if "it tugged at my heart strings to let him go."[13]

Billy saw the assignment as a pivotal moment to prove his manliness and courage. As he proudly reported to his father, "When I left home I determined never to write to you until I had proven myself to be a *man in arms* and not a coward. I believe I have now done so." Billy revealed that he had been involved in a major clash several miles inside enemy lines: "One of the most brilliant skirmish battles I ever read of—the Canon would fire—the shell burst—our boys rush yelling like Indians into the woods fire and fight—then fall back crying 'Rally to your logs', in this fight but one of our men was killed and two wounded." During this conflict Billy was with a party of men who were hiding behind some logs in a meadow and firing across the road at rebel soldiers. A fellow soldier, "a mere boy—but brave as a lion—was lying behind the same stump with me," Billy reported, and "he asked me to load his revolver (one he had taken from a rebel the day before) saying, 'Dr. I am going over the pike into the woods and shoot a secessh with my pistol.'" Ten minutes later Billy saw the boy cross the road and head into the woods. "Soon we heard the crash of a Mississippi Yager— and a man scream three times—very soon we concluded that Anton [the boy] was shot and we determined to take his body." Billy and some of his comrades rushed into the woods and had gathered up the dead boy when some two hundred rebels fired upon them and a "charge of cavalry" came "thrashing through the woods." "We never let go our brave dead but fought our way out and reached the camp in safety," Billy concluded.[14]

Two weeks later he would not be so lucky. On July 30, Billy and his friend Leonard Clark were out scouting near Cheat Mountain, a high and rugged ridge along the Alleghenies in eastern West Virginia, trying to de-termine the enemy's position. They were instructed to ride their horses as far as the Confederate picket lines and then proceed on foot. Dressed in everyday clothes rather than army uniforms, they quickly saw evidence of rebel forces. Before they could get to safer territory inside the woods, they ran into a rebel ambush and were forced to surrender. Thanks to a ploy with a corncob pipe, Billy burned the map and papers in his posses-sion. The two men were marched under guard to a nearby camp, where they were handcuffed and eventually sent to Huntersville, Virginia. Rebel soldiers treated Billy as a spy and questioned him about Union troop move-ments. At one point, he and Clark were marched out to a field as if they were to be shot, but inexplicably, they were returned back to their quarters. For days nothing was heard from or about them.

Miles, who had been in the most direct contact with Billy, searched for his brother in the rugged terrain, looking to find any information on him or any of his belongings. Back in Indianapolis Calvin tried to assess the "intelligence" he was getting from various sources and to begin to make peace with a possibly tragic outcome: "Telegraph from Miles that Billy's fate uncertain &c. I have made up my mind that if in the line of duty to save the country I must submit to his loss." The next day a friend's son, who was in the army in West Virginia and who had seen Billy before he "disappeared," reported that Billy "was rather reckless." "I regret that in his character," Calvin noted. "I fear he used strong & extravagant expressions." When Miles returned from his own scout and brought to Calvin Billy's sword, rifle, and trunk, Calvin became completely demoralized. "It may be he is killed," he concluded. "It is the fate of a bloody war. I have come to the conclusion to trust for his deliverance . . . History shows that civil wars are usually long, bloody & desolating." After learning that Billy had gone missing, Calvin's son Elijah counseled that he remain calm before jumping to conclusions based on his sons' reports. "Do not allow yourself to be anguished by any impulsive or indiscriminate advice of the boys," he told his father. "It is as natural as the beating of their hearts that they should be deeply incensed & intensely excited. And when [they] are so, it is a natural consequence, that they would say & do ill advised things."[15]

Amidst all the uncertainty, Calvin found himself trying to interpret information from all kinds of sources, useful and otherwise. On August 21, he got a visit from a soldier named James H. Durham, a musician in the Ninth Regiment, commanded by Colonel Robert Milroy, who knew Billy. Durham claimed, Calvin noted, that "Billy has been or will be hung." The man was drunk, however, and Calvin pushed him off on Miles, frustrated and worried about the implications of his purported message. "The subject," Calvin conceded, "harasses me too much to talk about it." Another man who had been to Virginia and had contacts with rebels holding Union prisoners claimed that a "Secessionist" contact had witnessed Billy and

Clark being carried off in chains on the railroad headed for Richmond. "This is the first plausible information of Billy's whereabouts," Calvin declared. "I had supposed him dead." But then a week went by with no further information, leaving Calvin to conclude once again that his son must in fact be dead.[16]

A few days later, however, it became clear that Billy was alive as various "Secessionists" approached both Miles and Calvin offering their services to have Billy released, "if," Calvin reported, "I would make what I supposed would be dishonorable terms to me, my son, my family & country." What was "dishonorable," of course, was the very idea of making any sort of deal or trade of prisoners with rebels he viewed as contemptuous "traitors." But it was the only way out for Billy, and soon Calvin was instructing Miles to "endeavor to get Billy released from his imprisonment in the Rebel Camp" but not, he insisted, to go "beyond the law usages & custom of the country." Make any offer "that reason, justice & honor would allow but no more," was Calvin's carefully worded plea. Miles traveled to West Virginia and "presented a flag at Lee's Camp" to get Billy exchanged for a prisoner at Columbus, Ohio. He failed. Calvin was not surprised, reflecting that "No reasonable person would suppose that Billy would now be released [only] to bring back the exact intelligence of the rebel forces about which he would know much." Miles telegraphed his brother Stoughton from West Virginia asking what he ought to do next. Stoughton wasn't at home, but Elijah told Miles to come home. Meanwhile, Calvin was furious to have been left mostly out of the loop. "I refused to give any advise as he [Miles] went without consulting me," he noted bitterly. "If his deceased mother could have spoken, she would have told him consult your father, consult your father—that I was yet worthy I thought of that respect. Miles is rash."[17]

Just as the Fletcher family was embroiled in a struggle to extricate Billy from a rebel prison camp, twenty-year-old Keyes was making a forceful attempt to join the war effort. In fact, both Keyes and Ingram desperately wanted to enlist, and to decide the issue, they tossed a penny. Keyes won five of seven tosses. By mid-October, he had enlisted as a private in Company E of the Thirty-Third Regiment, encamped outside Lexington,

Kentucky. Keyes left with his father's blessing, based on their mutual belief that no firm patriot could fail to see the urgency of the cause. "He says that he feels it a just war," Calvin observed, "that all that is dear & near depends on the result of the struggle, that if we lose our liberties as a family we will regret we made no greater effort, offering & sacrifice for our dear country." Not serving, Keyes and Calvin both argued, would lead to a "just reproach for not going to the aid of our country." Just as fervent for the Union cause, Ingram claimed it would be "disgraceful that out of 9 sons but one goes to the battle field."[18]

Meanwhile, Billy himself was writing Calvin from his Richmond prison urging his father *not* to let Keyes or Ingram go to war. But Keyes's determination to serve his country and his father's belief in the virtue of such a sacrifice trumped Billy's understandable fears for his brother. "So as a matter of duty to God & country," Calvin concluded, "we give up Keyes & trust in that kind parent our Heavenly Father to go with protect & return another so dear to us." Early the next morning, Keyes prepared for his journey to Kentucky. As he left the Fletcher house with blankets, money, and a revolver, Calvin, like many a father then and now watching his son go off to war, could only hope for the best: "He said he would see me again. Poor fellow, his father's heart goes out after him. I regret his general education is not more enlarged."[19]

It did not take long for Keyes to see combat. Within ten days he wrote home about the battle of Camp Wildcat, an hour-long skirmish in which he served as sergeant of the commissary (ammunition) department. A few weeks passed, though, without any word from him, which only aroused more worry back at home. "I am greatly concerned about Keyes," Calvin noted, realizing he was now in an advanced position near Cumberland Gap—"the vital point to the enemy. I feel now more concerned for him than for Billy who is now languishing in prison in Richmond."[20]

Calvin's apprehensions over Billy may have lessened in part because Billy's letters from his Richmond prison suggested that he was not suffering too much and, in fact, was finding his niche as a medical professional. Billy reassured his father that all the prisoners were in very good health, each had one quilt, and none were yet hurting from the cold. In fact, Billy seemed mostly concerned that northern newspapers had exaggerated the suffering of the prisoners. "I hope the cries of the restless rabble of the north about the 'poor prisoners' in the Tobacco houses of Richmond—will not shake the policy of our Government—or drive them into any hasty action," he wrote. "I know some who are willing to rot in prison—grow grey in dungeons, or wear chains a life time—or die any death, rather than have an exchange that would do harm to the cause or be humiliating to our country and all the poor cowards are heart sick and want to give up every thing—will be of no use to any country or government and are as well out of the way." Billy's letter was published anonymously in the Indianapolis *Daily Journal* as an editorial titled "The Right Spirit," with the newspaper claiming his sentiment "breathes exactly the right spirit for the time." Part of the letter was republished in the *New York Times* on December 1.[21]

While still imprisoned, Billy was "paroled" to the city of Richmond to oversee all the sick and wounded under care there. "This gives me much pleasure," he wrote his father, "not only because it takes me out of prison but I can do so much for those who are suffering." Unlike all the other doctors who "selfishly went home as soon as an opportunity offered leaving our poor fellows to the hands of strangers," Billy declared it his "duty" to stay behind and take care of all the "unfortunate victims of Bull Run and Balls Bluff . . . I have made up my mind to stand by them to the last." Working out of a comfortable office on Main Street, Billy said his health was "remarkably good" and his "wants are all supplied." In what had to feel like both a point of pride and a moment of sadness for his father when he read these lines, Billy noted that "I have today refused my first opertunity of release to do what I feel to be my duty." Fellow prisoners agreed that Billy Fletcher served with noteworthy selflessness. In early January 1862, Miles met with Alfred Ely, a former prisoner at Richmond. Upon learning that Miles was Billy's brother, Ely remarked, "Your brother is the most remarkable young man I ever knew. His cheerfulness and encouraging words have saved many of us from death." Apparently, Billy had not been as healthy as he had claimed, for Ely noted that Billy had "endured and suffered more than any of us. When he was brought to our prison he was so weak and emaciated that he had to be carried; now he is fat enough for two doctors."[22]

Miles continued his effort to liberate Billy from the Confederate prison. On January 3, he rode to Fort Monroe, Virginia, with a peace flag, expecting to make an exchange for Billy, but learned firsthand that Billy's promise to serve his patients before himself was a heartfelt conviction. Miles went home empty-handed, as Billy had insisted that another prisoner, a Lieutenant Hart from a different regiment, be released in his place. "Billy permitted Hart to return instead of himself," Calvin observed. He was clearly impressed and moved by his son's decision: "It is *a sublime sacrifice.*" Calvin was not even put off by Miles's fears that a successful advance on Richmond might lead to all the prisoners being murdered: "This I do not dread," Calvin insisted. "God will take care of those & provide a better world for such as meet that event after such noble sacrifice."[23]

As he often did, Calvin personalized the dramatic moments and proud accomplishments of his sons, seeing in Billy's "noble sacrifice" his *own* unsung heroism during the cholera epidemic that had swept through the Midwest in 1850. For nearly a month, Calvin recalled, he had not left home but stayed there nursing the sick and burying the dead. "I nursed & buried some 20 to 30 almost alone & my dear wife, now deceased, aided me & both had touches of the dreadful disease," he remembered. "A few German families who could not talk English suffered & died like sick sheep." All these "dangerous labors," Calvin claimed, now afforded him "great gratification. So I say God has a great compensation in store for those who do their duty"—a group that doubtless included himself.[24]

Billy's prison odyssey finally reached a climax on January 28, 1862, when Miles informed the family through Stoughton that he had been released and had arrived at Fort Monroe from Richmond the night before. "This is truly happy news," Calvin noted. "I have written to Lucy, Elijah & Albert to give the glad tidings." At 9:00 a.m. on February 2, Billy arrived back home in Indianapolis. "Billy looked well," his father reported, "had grown larger & more robust, cheerful & happy." He had been imprisoned for six months. He told his family he had escaped twice and been recaptured, the second time being wounded in the process. That evening Elijah joined Ingram, Keyes, Calvin, and the rest of the family to celebrate Billy's return. And he was quickly the toast of the town: "Billy has been waited on by gentlemen & invited to deliver addresses at Masonic Hall . . . the Ames Institute . . . & the Ladies Soldiers relief society also," Calvin recorded. Later in the week, all of Billy's brothers living nearby (Elijah, Calvin, Ingram, and Keyes) got together in their father's library and spent the day "hearing Billy relate his adventures," with Elijah and Calvin Jr. making notes for an address their brother would soon be delivering. On Friday night, February 7, Billy gave his "lecture," which attracted a very large crowd—over seven hundred people—to hear his war and prison experiences. He reportedly spoke in a "modest, conversational style that was captivating."[25]

Billy may have been a bit of a celebrity in town, but living at home, under Calvin's strict discipline, he was no hero. In fact, dealing with his father's relentless expectations left Billy "restive" and resistant to his father's "parental advice," even if it was offered only in "kindness." To Billy, his father's demanding views about the necessity of honoring his advice and avoiding debt seemed like "an invasion of his rights." Depressed that his counsel was "not appreciated but rejected with scorn or as an improper interference," Calvin decided he and Billy ought to avoid "all intimacy & treat each other civilly only." In a matter of a few testy days, Calvin told Billy that he "best leave his father—seek another home, another field while we now feel kindly to each other." Elijah tried to intervene in this unhappy family atmosphere by suggesting that if any mature son under Calvin's roof did not appreciate his father's guiding hand, he should leave without condemnation: "He [Billy] has a right to ask your advice," Elijah wrote Calvin, "you have a right to give it—or withhold it as you see fit. But he has no right to be offended because you deem it expedient to remain silent; nor have you a right to be angry because he sees fit not to follow your counsel."[26]

While Calvin struggled for his sons' total respect, he continued to fight an angry personal war against the South and the slave-power conspiracy he so detested. In particular, Calvin was intent on protecting all Fletcher family property against claims by his "traitorous" brother Timothy, now in his sixties, who, like his brother Elijah, had long ago moved to slave-holding Virginia. (There was no similar concern over the intentions of Elijah's daughter Betty, since, as a married woman, she could not, except in rare circumstances, own and sell property; Indiana, Calvin presumed, would likewise soon be married.) So when a bill was introduced into Congress that would confiscate the northern property of individuals supporting the South, Calvin contacted Indiana governor John Wright urging him to become a forceful proponent of the legislation. Governor Wright did so, focusing, at Calvin's bidding, on the Fletcher family as a perfect example of why such an unyielding confiscation bill needed to be passed. In early April 1862 Wright spoke before the U.S. Senate, observing: "Fifty years ago four brothers left their father's home in the Green mountains of Vermont, and two of them settled in Virginia [Elijah, followed by his brother Timothy]; the remaining two in my own State [Calvin, and later his brother Stoughton]." Noting that Timothy and one of his nephews had strongly promoted "the existing rebellion" while "the brothers in Indiana," in contrast, had sons serving in the Union Army, Wright argued—at Calvin's urging—that the family homestead in Ludlow, Vermont, proud home of "their revolutionary father" and currently owned by "traitor sons," should be immediately confiscated for the use of the federal government. What animated "these loyal men," Calvin and Stoughton, was simply the hope that "exemplary punishment shall be inflicted upon those who have disgraced their heroic ancestry, and with parricidal hands have struck at the existence of the Union which gave them property and protection."[27]

The Confiscation Bill, passed by Congress July 15, 1862, and signed by President Lincoln two days later, focused on the issues of treason, property confiscation, and the emancipation of slaves. In terms of confiscation, the penalty for southern sympathizing by owners of northern land was immediate forfeiture of such land after sixty days' warning. The bill was considered "one of the most drastic laws ever enacted by Congress," and initially Lincoln resisted it. As it turned out, the confiscatory provisions of the law were only occasionally enforced, and only a small amount of property was ever seized.[28] Timothy's claims on the Fletcher homestead, despite Calvin's efforts to legally repudiate them, went away only with his death, not because of the confiscation law.

Calvin would remain, though, an inveterate hater of "secesh" traitors. He had heard—and believed—too many war stories about the brutal behavior of rebel soldiers, many of them from his soldier sons, Billy and Keyes. And he felt "the story of their wrongs . . . are more than human nature can endure." While some northern politicians tried to win converts in the South by "plaster[ing] up *secession*" as somehow an understandable political decision, Calvin would have none of it. He viewed secession as deserving, as he insisted, "a retribution of greater severity than our public authorities are disposed to give it. It is a rupture or attempt to destroy the government that history should record with all its deformities & costs of life & treasure."[29]

It would not take long before the war effort brought home to Calvin the "costs of life" in heartbreaking fashion. On May 10, 1862, Calvin was summoned from the bank by Governor Morton with a request that he join the governor in traveling to Pittsburgh Landing, Tennessee, for additional munitions. Once again, this was a trip Calvin wanted to avoid, and this time he was able to offer his son Miles as an effective substitute. "Was happy that Miles had returned & agreed to go with the Governor," Calvin wrote in his diary. That evening Calvin and his young son Albert went down to see the governor and Miles depart on the train at 8:40 p.m. "I felt relieved," Calvin noted, "for I disliked to decline going," but "the next 10 days regulating the farm & setting out a hedge" were more important to him. "May God grant a useful trip to get home our sick & wounded," he prayed. That night Bishop Ames and Calvin "sat under the pines & conjectured the future of our rebellion," Calvin noted. "We both think the rebels are doing much towards liberating their Slaves by burning the late crop of cotton, sugar &c & declining to plant this year's crop." They were also quite buoyed at the news that the *Monitor* and the *Merrimac*—the first ironclad warships—would "soon go into action."[30]

But at that very moment of reflection—"just as I closed the above sentence, about 10 a.m.," Calvin wrote—Albert came running into his room with news that a man wanted to see him immediately. "A. seemed to be impressed with some sad news was to be delivered to me & I not understanding it as he did, told him his sudden entrance scared me & not to be so abrupt." Calvin rushed downstairs only to find the governor's secretary, Holloway, "with tears in his eyes." The story Holloway told came from Governor Morton. He and Miles had left Terre Haute about midnight, Morton reported, "and on taking [their] places in the car" and having a brief snack along with "much merry conversation," they laid down to sleep. Miles's head was toward the forward end of the car, with their other travel companions, General Noble and Dr. Bobbs, facing the opposite way. And then Morton reported the following:

> I had but fallen asleep, when a heavy jar, as if the train had struck some heavy obstruction, roused me and I sprang to my feet. Professor Fletcher [Miles taught at the Greencastle Seminary] raised up on the seat and threw up the window just over where our feet had rested and near where I was standing and put out his head, very little as I thought. At that instant a dark object glanced past the window and his chin dropped on the window sill. I immediately caught him and drew him out of the window, when his head dropped to one side and I perceived the blood and his fatal wound. I laid him down with his head upon his carpet bag as he had been lying before, but he never spoke, struggled or moved. At the end of a few minutes, say three or four, he gave a few gurgling groans and all was over.

"Your son was my friend in whose society I took great pleasure," Morton added, "whose usefulness to our state can scarce be estimated, and in whose future success I had the greatest confidence. I knew his clear, penetrating mind, his indomitable energy, and how wholly his heart, hand and purse were devoted to his country in this struggle through which she is passing."[31]

Miles Fletcher

Calvin was devastated as much by the suddenness of this event as by the finality of Miles's death. He had had a "warning" when he lost his "dear wife & daughter," but Miles's death was "an unexpected dispensation, the most serious affecting my near personal relations that has ever overtaken me." That evening Calvin went with Ingram to the depot, where Miles's body arrived on a special train. "I stood where I parted with him 24 hours before & as the sad ring of the train met my ears what a contrast met my eyes from the warm hand I pressed as he went out & the sad enclosure I noticed in the baggage car as it rolled past me!" he remembered the event. They set the casket out in the most prominent room in the house. Calvin noted, sadly, "He was safe in his father's house, the last respect I could pay him."[32]

The cause of the accident, a coroner's jury determined, was a boxcar that had been moved to the main track as a prank played by a soldier on leave. Apparently, after taking a ride on the boxcar, he was unable to stop it until it had rolled onto the main track, where it sat unreported until Miles's untimely opening of his window onboard the moving train.[33]

The news of Miles's death shocked and devastated his brothers. From New Bedford, Massachusetts, Cooley told his father, "Grief has entered our hearts." Miles was a brother, he claimed, whom he had come to "love & prize" highly. Keyes, from the battlefield near Cumberland Gap, learned about Miles's death from his commanding officer, Colonel Coburn, who walked up to Keyes's quarters one night and asked Keyes if he'd heard of Miles getting hurt, bringing him a *Cincinnati Gazette* with the particulars of the accident. "Can this be so?" Keyes wrote. "We know not the hour nor the day . . . I feel it so *deeply* being *away* so far from home & knowing that my brother is *buried* before I have heard of his death."[34]

Even after Miles was buried, yet another of Calvin's sons actively sought out the opportunity to join the war effort. In July 1862 Ingram sent his father a telegram while Calvin was visiting family in the Boston area asking if he could join up. "You can't imagine my burning desire to help put down this rebellion," Ingram wrote his father. Two days later, he sent another note: "Indianapolis is turning out her best sons. When I see them going I am ashamed almost."[35]

Ingram's repeated requests opened up for Calvin and many of his sons a larger question: Who would be available and able to work at their father's bank and manage the family farms if too many sons went off to war? "I can be spared better than any in [the] Bank," Ingram argued. "Albert wants to go; but I want him to stay & take care of you. What say you, my dear father? . . . I wish to do duty to my father—my country and my God." Elijah attempted to weigh in on the family controversy: "We are all seething on the volunteer question, music, drums, speeches & all stirring up the patriotism of young America," he wrote his father. "Ingram has caught the fire & almost will go. I tell him *no*—having done all that I can to induce him to wait until he hears from you. Stoughton & I persuaded him to telegraph you."[36]

Torn between the same patriotic urges that were whipping up young men's spirits to join the war and an understandable need to take care of business and family matters at home, Calvin decided that at his advanced age of sixty-four he needed Ingram to stay and help out at home. "He has one brother in the army (Keyes at Cumberland Gap)," Calvin explained. "Billy has been in service & a prisoner for 6 months, his dear brother Miles killed while in the public service & the family have in contributions & early devotion to the first calls done their part & more than their part but not more than the cause deserved." But with old age starting to set in, Calvin felt justified in calling on Ingram for help at the bank and on the farms. "He knows all my business more intimately than anyone else," he wrote. Besides, Ingram suffered from a hernia that would likely disqualify him from military service in any event. So he wrote Ingram that he "could not consent to his going into the war." But Ingram continued to argue for enlistment, insisting that his desire wasn't about selfish manly valor: "It was not for *glory* that I wished to go. This rebellion will end before Christmas and I wished to have a hand in putting it down." Weeks later, Calvin relented. He would give his approval if Ingram could make a suitable arrangement with Calvin's business partner, Thomas Sharpe, to fill his place as a clerk at the bank. Ingram's "burning patriotism" was "noble," Calvin conceded. "I will not restrain him if his convictions are to go." Ingram wrote his father that same day that he hadn't obtained permission to enlist and instead would have to be drafted. "Although it's no disgrace to be drafted, yet the world view it as no credit to a man's character," he observed.[37]

Although he didn't say so in letters to his sons, Calvin clearly felt that what was most needed to win the war was not the fierce patriotism of northern sons like his own, but the use of former slaves as soldiers in the Union Army. Realizing that the conflict was "a bloody war" fought over the evil of slavery, Calvin also became convinced that "we shall be forced to put arms into their [former slaves'] hands." How this would happen, he wasn't sure, but since the war had begun, he now believed that "we can have no success till he [the slave] is provided for his freedom & escape." And the best way to do that was for Congress to authorize the emancipation of the "negros" for service in the Union war effort. The nation would soon, he claimed, "demand employment of the Africans & . . . insist that the negros of rebels be made free even by the proclamation of the President." Calvin felt so strongly about the need for liberation of the slaves and their service in the northern army that without such steps he predicted failure for the Union, mostly as a consequence of moral weakness in dealing with slavery: "I feel that until we say in earnest to the colored man he can go free," Calvin declared, "we shall not have favorable results to our arms. I feel that God indicates to us to let them go or further to open the door for them to flee. We do not hold them but we can show them the way & help them to go out of bondage."[38]

To make matters worse, Calvin had no confidence in the war policy of President Lincoln or his generals. Calvin remained so deeply grieved by the conduct and prospect of the war that his wife grew concerned and critical of him: "My wife called me to see how weak & unmanly was my grief—that it was not [a] Christian nor [a] philosopher that would do thus," Calvin noted. "I have since thought myself wrong & the admonition just."[39]

*   *   *   *   *

Although their uncle Calvin vehemently opposed bondage—as had their own father very early in his life—for Indiana, Betty, and Sidney Fletcher in southwest Virginia, slavery was woven into the very fabric of life. They depended not only on the labor of hundreds of field slaves to work the nearly sixteen thousand acres they owned, scattered over numerous plantations, but on house "servants" to take care of their every need. From Tusculum, Sidney oversaw the bulk of his father's estate on farms throughout Amherst County, producing everything from corn and wheat to clover, oats, and a little tobacco. Eight miles away at Sweet Briar, Indiana managed a few thousand acres that grew similar crops, along with orchards of apples, peaches, plums, cherries, pears, and black and English walnut trees. Fletcher lands also raised cattle, hogs, sheep, and chickens both for their own consumption as well as for the market. In 1859, within a year of losing her father, Betty had married William Hamilton Mosby of Lynchburg and moved away from Sweet Briar, leaving it entirely in the hands of Indiana. During the war, Indiana did her best to manage the plantation, though she did have some help from Sidney, who at forty years old never had an active role in the Confederate effort. Lucian, long since a family pariah as a result of his drunken and ne'er-do-well conduct, wandered about, mostly unemployed and disconnected from his siblings and their families.

The war disrupted life for Indiana and her siblings, especially when northern troops blockaded southern ports and destroyed the railroad to Lynchburg, reducing, among other items, the supply of luxury goods such as coffee and tea, dress fabrics, and metal coins. But the Sweet Briar plantation was never raided during the war, even though conflict did come as close as eight miles away, where skirmishes occurred on the Tye River in Amherst County. The Union Army's General Sheridan and his cavalry fought in some small battles in the southern part of the county, about fifteen miles away. Amid the nearby fighting and devastation of war, Indiana wrote anxious letters to her family and friends in the North, including Calvin, referring to "the great destruction of property in some parts of the state." She was clearly worried, as Calvin noted, that "she may suffer." But for the most part, the world of Indiana and her siblings remained safe from direct contact with the war.[40]

With so much experience in the North as a result of her schooling and numerous trips to New York City, Indiana reached out frequently to her "Yankee" friends and family during the war, eagerly seeking refuge from the conflict. Among those she contacted was Calvin, hoping that a "pass" could be secured for her to visit. But Calvin's unyielding hatred for slavery and the "traitorous" rebels in the South collided with his steadfast loyalty to his beloved Fletcher kin, leaving him uncharacteristically uncertain about what to do.

When Indiana first approached Calvin in April 1863 asking him to procure a pass for her to "come into the Federal lines north," he talked to his brother Stoughton about the matter and decided to postpone any action "for further consideration." "I hope & rather think she is loyal," Calvin wrote. A few days later, he appeared to make a positive decision and instructed Bishop Ames to get a "passport" in Washington for Indiana "to come into our lines from the confederacy." But a clerk in Washington said there were hundreds of applications still on file for passes for travel going both ways and thus was unable to arrange one for Indiana at the time.[41]

Indiana persisted in trying to get out of Virginia, knowing that her brother Sidney would manage her plantations in her absence. A few months later Calvin received a letter from Elizabeth Kirkland, the daughter of the prominent founder of a New York City girls' school Indiana and Betty had attended, who was trying to intercede on Indiana's behalf to obtain a "Federal passport for her to come to the U. states." Again, Calvin inquired through Bishop Ames, but again he failed to get a pass. This time, though, his comments about Indiana (and her family's) politics were more judgmental: "I could not vouch for her loyalty," Calvin noted, "& felt it a delicate matter to act in the affair & let it drop." A few days later, after Indiana asked yet again through Miss Kirkland about getting "a flag of truce letter [and] a Federal permit to go north from Va.," Calvin consulted with his son Elijah but could not bring himself to honor her request.[42]

Complicating matters—and ultimately dooming Indiana's chances—was the possibility that Indiana wasn't just looking to get out of the war-torn South and visit her northern kin; Calvin suspected that she also wanted to get to Vermont and lay claim to the Fletcher ancestral estate, which for two years Calvin had been strenuously laboring to have declared forfeited property by the federal government: "I know not but she comes to claim the estate I think they have forfeited &c.," he wrote. "So I have to write cautiously or my letter may be used to show my approval of the disloyalty of herself & family."[43] Nearly a year later, in the spring of 1864, Indiana tried to explain that neither she nor Sidney were disloyal rebels, an explanation Calvin clearly found unpersuasive: "She gives an account of herself & brother Sidney who, she says, has not entered the army of the rebels but is exempt under a law to carry on the rebellion by *giving* all he raises to the government," Calvin noted. "This is doing more than Service in the field. She expresses a desire to get away from the South, says fortunes are vanishing like the glories of the setting sun."[44] Loyalties were vanishing as well, and though he struggled to honor his allegiance to his Fletcher kin, Calvin simply could not let go of his overriding antagonism toward the slave South and his growing suspicion of all those, including beloved family members, who resided within it.

The suspicion Calvin revealed toward Indiana's presumed divided loyalties grew out of a much larger conspiracy mentality that gripped both North and South during the war. Both rebel and Union sympathizers became immersed in secrecy and were devoted to rooting out hidden pockets of opposing "disloyal" people. "The fears are great here lest a conspiracy will take place by & thro the secession sympathisers," Calvin noted in January 1863. "It is said a counter society is getting up." His biggest worry was that "an assault would be made on the arsenal & secess get the arms." Called Union Clubs, secret Union, pro–Lincoln administration societies were formed in some of the larger towns in Indiana and merged into the Union League that spread across the North during the war. Their main goal was espionage aimed at discovering secessionist sympathizers.[45]

If Calvin was vigilant about rooting out traitors in his midst, Keyes was positively on fire on a battlefield in southern Kentucky. Writing his father from Danville, Kentucky, at 2:30 a.m., Keyes declared: "You will perhaps wonder at my being up writing at this early hour. To explain it, I am on *guard*." He had just read the Indianapolis newspapers, which gave an account of secessionist activity in the city and state legislature that had left him livid:

> It makes me mad, it makes me *boil* when I think that the power of Indiana has thus fallen into the hands of traitors, when I think that *we, the one hundred thousand* Soldiers who are now enduring the hardships of a winter's campaigne . . . [must] put down *traitors,* whip out *treason,* & restore the government . . . I never have heard more *disloyal* sentiments spoken, than have been in the Ind. Legislature. I am *disgusted* with it. They ought to be *hung,* shot down like *dogs.*[46]

Keyes's brother Ingram likewise voiced this same, deep-seated distrust of all things "secesh." While visiting Keyes in Nashville—thanks to a pass received during one of Keyes's brief furloughs—Ingram was struck by the level of "destruction and ruin" the rebels had caused. "Fine mansions deserted and the windows broken out, walls demolished and yards and shrubbry [. . .] destroyed," he observed. "Soldiers were tearing up the floors what two years ago was an elegant parlor—or a valuable library— where everything was luxury and refinement . . . I walked up beautiful avenues and through once beautiful landscapes—and could but think as I saw an old negress making soap *in front of the female seminary* 'How are the mighty fallen.'" Ingram told a story about the two brothers walking into a house to get a drink and finding "three fine looking lasses of the brunette stamp" playing the piano and singing southern songs who "would play nothing gotten up in the North." "In fact," he reported, they "talked *Secesh very certainly.* Denounced the Yankee for *banishing ladies* and sending them beyond the lines . . . You would laugh to see the wilted, faded-bleached Aristocracy of Nashville! Don Quixote in his burlesque on Chivalry can't surpass the reality of these fallen lords."[47]

As much as Calvin wholeheartedly concurred with his sons about the danger of traitorous southern sympathizers, he sometimes found himself distracted by a small civil war going on inside his own household. In

May 1863 his twenty-year-old daughter Lucy's marriage plans with Cyrus Hines became a flash point of anger and disapproval in the Fletcher family. Previously married to Lucy's older sister, Maria, who had died three years earlier, Hines had been courting the younger Lucy for a year, and by May 1863 they planned to be married, despite disapproval from Calvin and several of her brothers. The very idea of Lucy marrying her brother-in-law put her "in bad taste & bad manners & bad faith towards" her father, Calvin noted. Hines was the opposite of the "firm" man Calvin most admired and sought to cultivate in his sons; rather, he saw him "as a man of eccentricities—Dizzy, as to morals & religions, has no clear view of either." Worse yet, Hines refused to repudiate slavery, apparently because "the moral & religious oppose it," Calvin speculated. An undeclared anarchist, Hines therefore believed "the rebellion no great crime & that the South will not be subdued or the rebellion suppressed or negro slavery abolished. His views on all these subjects are opposed to the good, great & loyal. I despise them & feel my daughter who was of age, has made a bad choice." Calvin stopped short of calling Hines "a positively bad man," but averred that his view of moral and religious values as "a sham" rendered him "inert, lazy [but] not positively wicked." And instead of listening to her father's sound advice, Calvin complained, Lucy "began a course of idle dissipation—she danced at Knightstown springs, having left my care & counsel—done as she pleased—snubbed the humble acquaintance & advice of her dear mothers old friends—became unhealthy."[48]

Deepening the divide over Lucy's wedding, especially for Calvin, was the more unnerving reality that ever since Calvin had remarried, Lucy had struggled with her father's authority and constant counsel. Early on, some of her older brothers had advised Lucy to call Keziah "Mrs. Fletcher" rather than "mother," thus poisoning her relationship with her father and stepmother. But despite the visible tension in the family, Lucy and Hines's wedding managed to go off on May 19, with her brother Elijah presiding. But with unhappiness still roiling the family—both over Lucy's marriage to her brother-in-law and over her blatant disregard of Calvin's overt disapproval—young Keyes two days before the wedding felt obliged to step in to bridge the gap between his younger sister and their parents. He advised his father to "talk to her kindly, don't use *harsh* words." And, he insisted, she did have "*some* ground . . . [a] just complaint, but which should have been looked over by a forgiving daughter." But he was mostly upset, as Ingram had been years before over a squabbling family, that this sort of internal fighting was marring life inside the Fletcher household. "A war in my father's house," Keyes declared from an actual battlefield, "I can neither *enlist in,* nor stand by and see carried on."[49]

Later that summer, after a Sunday visit with Lucy and Cyrus, Calvin still couldn't disguise the disdain he felt for his daughter. Calling her "indulged & spoiled," Calvin blamed her disobedient and imprudent life choices on her decision to avoid his and Keziah's "control." Because she presumably found her stepmother unwelcome, Lucy had construed all acts of parental discipline as unfair "acts of tyranny," her father argued. Thus, having "slipt from under a controle that would have made her a different" and doubtless better person, Lucy, in Calvin's highly jaundiced view, was now a bit of a family pariah: his daughter, he claimed, "has no family interests or pride." So Calvin pledged to simply leave her alone: "I can't have any familiarity with her till she feels differently."[50]

Calvin's unhappiness with his "spoiled" newlywed daughter may well have been supplanted by his pride over Billy's emergence as a progressive reformer. Now twenty-six, Dr. William Baldwin Fletcher, as Billy was now officially known, had been practicing medicine for several years in Indianapolis, and in November and December of 1863 he composed three letters addressed to the citizens of the city that were published in the Indianapolis *Daily Journal*. "My dear Indianapolis," Billy wrote, "I have some complaints to make [regarding] . . . some of your errors and disproportions, which are ugly in the sight of your sister cities." Well aware of the "beauties of your broad streets," Billy gently scolded the city for its poor sanitation (allowing its streets "to be used as pig-sties and cow stables"); its meat-packing companies that allow "the offal of five thousand hogs per day to be cast into" the White River, there to "decompose and spread contagion and pestilence"; its horrifying excuse for a "*poor,* poor house" and underfunded institution for the "deaf and blind and insane"; and the desperate need for a good library, better schools, and street lighting. Finally, sounding a great deal like his father, he put forth an appeal for the city to close up its "liquor shops, rum holes and gin mills" on the Sabbath. "Have you forgotten," he implored, "that a whole world acknowledges the sanctity of the Sabbath? If in your kindness of heart you allow men to sell poison and seeds of crime, damnation and death, can't you limit them to six days?"[51]

Not surprisingly, Billy's thoughtful critique of the failings of his native city met with the enthusiastic approval of his father. The evening the first "lecture," as Calvin called it, was published, the local Benevolent Society met and discussed Billy's article with great interest, especially the subjects of furnishing medicine and better treatment for the poor. "The object of all such communications," Calvin wrote, "is to make the readers feel & act. So this is surely well timed & effectual. I am pleased with it."[52] Calvin must have marveled at how this young man had transformed from a volatile runaway teen into a civic-minded professional in just eight short years. And doubtless he imagined Billy as a latter-day version of himself.

More broadly, Billy's concerns for Indianapolis reflected his father's progressive view of what made Indianapolis the quintessential "Western" city. In what was clearly a partly autobiographical claim, Calvin declared that "our best citizens have had a controlling influence over the morals, Religion & enterprise of the city from its early settlement." More so than other cities in the West, Indianapolis, he argued, had avoided the usual "sectarian bitterness" and rallied around "good causes," in large part owing to prudent large investments early on for "churches & ministers of talent." In this statement Calvin was reacting to an article by Oliver P. Morton, editor of the Dayton, Ohio, *Journal,* who had compared the "Buckeyes" of his state who "move along with silent energy" with "the Hoosiers [who] go at things with a perfect rush." "In short," Morton had concluded, "we are more Eastern—they more Western. Perhaps, indeed, they are the best representative in the West of what is recognized as 'western character.'"[53]

Dr. William (Billy) Fletcher

A key part of that "Western character" was a fierce dedication to individual liberties, which, in Calvin's view, meant an abiding antagonism to slavery. As yet another indication of his abolitionist commitment, Calvin, believing he was answering "the devout wishes & prayers of thousands of pious & patriotic persons," was elected in September 1863 to the Indianapolis Freemen's Aid Society. The Society brought together his three greatest progressive impulses: racial equality, moral uplift, and education. Founded in 1861 by the American Missionary Society—itself a group mostly backed by Congregational, Presbyterian, and Methodist churches in the North—the Freemen's Aid Society organized and provided teachers from the North to help educate freedmen and their children in the South. One can sense that Calvin regretted that his war "duty" seemed so much smaller than what his soldier son Keyes was performing. "It seems the Country calls Keyes to the war & most of the able & efficient men," Calvin observed. "It seems to be my duty to devote my whole time to my own affairs save the benevolence to the Freedmen & the care of the poor."[54]

Despite the carnage and his own stress over the ongoing war, Calvin clung to this driving hope in the end of slavery. The promise of this mission was especially apparent to him during an important trip he made to Washington. In January 1864, Calvin traveled to the capital through a local connection, J. Dufrees, to visit the White House and see the president. Mostly critical of Lincoln's handling of the war, Calvin had been deeply upset the previous summer by the Battle of Gettysburg, which demonstrated that the war had now invaded the North. "The administration is justly charged, I think, with imbecility," he noted. "Poor Lincoln . . . God alone can direct & it may be this imbecility & inefficiency is to show the present [and] future that God alone [has] done the work with very weak instruments."[55]

Despite his doubts about "poor Lincoln," Calvin was eager to meet the president. On January 19, after a cabinet meeting adjourned, Calvin had his moment with Lincoln. "He seemed plain & kind," Calvin commented after their "short interview." A few days later, on his way home, he reflected on the significance of the meeting: "I went to Washington under a former & old running prophecy or presentiment that I should & there find that Capital represented by free state or anti Slavery men . . . I feel thankful to God. He has thus permitted me to see the excellency of his power & wisdom in destroying, I trust & pray, Slavery as part of the human family—which has so long been a reproach to us as a nation & people." By the spring, Calvin believed the tide of war was turning in favor of the Union forces. "In his good time," Calvin declared, "I believe that God will relieve us from this gigantic rebellion & the poor Negro will be a freeman."[56]

At home, Calvin, who a year earlier had retired from the banking world, kept himself busy putting freed "contraband" ex-slaves to work on his farm. In the summer he supervised an average of twenty hands working over three hundred acres of hay and one hundred acres of oats and wheat. Most of those fieldworkers were runaways who had left their Kentucky masters. "They were good hands," Calvin noted, "but required direction as any others," although they were willing "to acquire [a] good name for work more so than so many emigrants from the states they came from, with a white skin." Calvin paid the men about $2 a day. On one occasion two of his "contraband" boys did not show up for work, so he went looking for them. "I got in a bad humor & scolded, showed anger—foolishly showed a bad temper," he confessed. He pledged to himself to "not speak for a half day" after any similar angry outbursts. "I feel I am a ruined man unless I reform."[57]

Such "fretfulness," as he often called it, was a recurring pattern in Calvin's life. And while he lamented its frequent appearance, he especially worried about its painful impact on his relationships at home, in particular with his wife—his first wife. He frequently contrasted his own impatience and bad temper with the more controlled, pious temperament that he had witnessed and remembered in his beloved Sarah. On the tenth anniversary of her death, Calvin spent time reading over the "incidents of the death of my dear wife" and "brought the scenes up & made them vivid before my eyes." In Sarah, he recalled "a pure & perfect woman." "Oh, that . . . my fretful & chaferings of life had not been made unpleasant & interrupted as I fear they did, her pious life," he worried. His "present dear wife," he was quick to point out, was just as "pure & excellent [a] being."[58]

Cooley Fletcher, another major source of Calvin's "fretfulness," found a way, finally, to brighten, rather than darken, his father's mood. In January 1865 Cooley gave a speech in London before the British Royal Geographical Society on the growth of cotton in Brazil that was quoted—with considerable praise—in the Cincinnati *Gazette* and the Indianapolis *Daily Journal*. "These are flattering notices," Calvin observed, clearly proud that Cooley had reached "so eminent [a] position. He has had a mixed cup

& had he a faint heart he would have long since succumbed to a pressure that would have killed most any other man. I deeply sympathize with him in the trials he has endured with such firmness & resolution." Of course, what "pressure" and "trials" Cooley had endured, from his father's perspective, were financial ones imposed on him by "an unworthy wife who [has] done much to depress & ruin [Cooley]."[59] Calvin continued to hold on to bitter feelings not only about Cooley's shrewish wife but also about his eldest son's weaknesses and "pecuniary" dependence. Cooley's accomplishments as a writer and missionary, however, helped mend some broken emotional fences between father and son.

❦ • • • ❦

Early on the morning of April 10, 1865, the Fletcher family was awakened by the sound of cannon "discharges"—three of them. "I heard the reverberation of the cannon," Calvin noted, "being somewhere near the court house square." As more "discharges" were heard, Calvin turned to his wife and told her "it announced the Surrender of Lees army." The newspaper boy arrived at the house at 5:00 a.m. "singing." Calvin asked the boy what the cannon fire was all about and was told Lee had surrendered. "Glory to God in the highest!" Calvin exclaimed. "May this event hasten the total downfall of the rebellion . . . & clear the way for equal rights among men, liberty to our nation including black & white (for the poor Southern white man has suffered & been ignorantly wronged as much as the blacks)."[60]

Calvin's joyful sense of deliverance, though, soon turned vengeful. Three days after getting the uplifting news about Lee's surrender at Appomattox, Calvin's mind turned to his brother Timothy in Lynchburg, Virginia, and his ongoing—and traitorous—designs on the family estate in Ludlow. "Uncle Tim," he wrote, "who has been with rebels the last 4 years will now escape or rather go by permission to Vt." So Calvin made a note to write Vermont governor Ryland T. Fletcher, a distant relative, that "if this brother & my brother Elijah's children go there to Ludlow, Vt.

& claim their lands—if proved to have been loyal during this contest, let them have them, not otherwise." Anyone like his Lynchburg relatives, he argued, who had been under four years of "Rebeldom," carried a special burden "to prove their loyalty."[61]

Before anyone had time to truly digest the meaning of the Union victory, some shattering news arrived. On April 15, as Calvin and his family were sitting down to breakfast, "Elijah came, pale & in trouble of countenance & announced the assassination of President Lincoln . . . last night at Washington." It was, Calvin noted, "one of the most appalling announcement[s] except the announcement of the sudden death of my poor son Miles in 1862 that has ever been made to me." Bells tolled all over Indianapolis, and "citizens ran to & fro in wild & sad confusion," Calvin reported. "Such a shock can't be described."[62]

The reaction in Indianapolis portrayed a community in shock, anger, and mourning over their dead president. Most local "secessionists" were quick to show outrage at the assassination, but some southern sympathizers, upon expressing "joy at the foul deed . . . were at once taken by the mob or by infuriated citizens." Almost every house was draped with "insignias of moaning . . . a day when more true hearts were afflicted than any day since the Crucifixion of our Savior." Calvin attended Roberts Chapel to hear a sermon from the otherwise-peaceful Reverend John Miller, who shouted from the pulpit that "had any one justified the act that day, he would have shot him, had he a pistol in his hands." "To this declaration, the congregation gave loud applause," Calvin reported. Calvin accompanied the governor and his close circle to a ceremony outside the statehouse, at which some four thousand soldiers and an estimated ten to fifteen thousand citizens, "all solemn," waited respectfully as the soldiers marched by in symbolic respect for Lincoln. On April 30, Lincoln's funeral train arrived at the Indianapolis depot at 7:00 a.m. The coffin was carried to the statehouse, where it was opened for public viewing. According to one newspaper, sidewalks and streets were packed with people "jealously holding on, frequently through great personal discomfort, to every inch of distance gained" to pay their final respects. A few weeks later, Calvin and

Keziah visited the statehouse to see the funeral badges and drapery from Lincoln's funeral, which proved to be a moving experience for them. It was, Calvin remembered, "one of the finest scenes of the kind I expect that was ever arranged . . . I am glad the commonest people—the freedmen, the negros have participated in the funeral services of the nation."[63]

Lincoln's assassination only underscored that the fighting may have ended but the wounds of disloyalty festered in the aftermath of such a bloody and troubling civil war. Like many in the North, Calvin believed that "the subjugation of the rebels should first be complete" before any attempt should be made to fully reconcile with the South. "There is a growing disposition," he observed, "that Traitors should be punished." Such beliefs complicated Calvin's relationship with his Virginia relatives. In November 1865 he wrote his niece Indiana that he would send her $3,665, funds from her father's stock in the Indiana Branch Bank. When Indiana notified Calvin in December that she hadn't yet received the funds, Calvin wrote in his diary a telling confession about family versus national loyalty: "I sent it against my Judgment."[64]

🜲 • • 🜲

In December 1865 a series of worrisome "presentiments" began to haunt Calvin Fletcher. Even for a man keenly alert to matters of Providence or premonitions, Calvin could not dismiss the persistent feelings of foreboding. A few days before Christmas, Keyes came to Calvin and asked him if he wanted to go with him to the Dogwood Farm to conclude some business, but, suffering from a "sleepy" spell, Calvin declined. So Keyes took off in his buggy with his warhorse, Rosa, and headed for the farm. Moments later, the horse struck some trees and broke the shaft of the buggy, throwing Keyes from the carriage. Keyes hurt his head badly—Calvin at first feared he had cracked his skull—but was able to go on with the day. "Had I have gone," Calvin observed, "I feel it would have been a serious injury or death to me. Thus God has again Providentially saved my life." A month later, he reported that his wife had experienced "an incontrollable presentiment that something is going to happen that will bring anguish upon her. It may, she says, originate in physical debility." That same day Calvin recalled an anecdote from his father's life about dealing with worrisome, haunting dreams. Jesse Fletcher had told Calvin a story when he was a young boy about "a certain King who dreamed that something would occur, destructive or injurious to himself or family." He then sent for the wisest man in the kingdom to help him understand the dream. The wise man's answer was that "virtue triumphed over all presages—all he had to do was to live & act strictly, virtuous, just & upright & it would be well with himself, family & Kingdome."[65] This was Calvin's life credo as well: live virtuously, and all will be well.

On his birthday, February 4, Calvin turned sixty-eight, and in his annual account he was able to report a life of good character and generally robust physical shape: "In very good health, weigh about 182 . . . I ride horseback as well as when 30 without much fatigue, but can't walk so well." His sons Ingram and Elijah came by after breakfast to celebrate. For gifts, Elijah, like Ingram and Albert, gave him new books on subjects ranging from physical geography to commentaries on the gospels and the laws of England. A week later, Calvin and Keziah treated themselves to a lecture by writer/philosopher Ralph Waldo Emerson at the Indianapolis Masonic Hall, "a Eulogy on good manners."[66]

On March 30, 1866, Calvin rode his mare Kitty downtown. When he returned home around 1:00 p.m., he tried to turn into the gate as it opened from the street. But the saddle on Kitty, who was "fat & round," suddenly shifted to the left, and Calvin found himself hanging off her left side, which scared her. The horse began running along the hedgerow, and Calvin's leg struck the ground hard, his right foot hanging in the stirrup as the frightened horse continued to drag him along until the saddle finally slipped off under the mare's legs, with Kitty kicking him, "saddle & all," onto the ground. "I sprang to my feet badly hurt and hallowed" for relief, Calvin reported. Some neighbors came and brought him into their house. He wasn't badly bruised on his body, but elsewhere the damage was clear to see: "the small bone on the right leg" protruded some two to three inches outside his ankle joint. His own son Billy was sent for, and he splinted Calvin's "somewhat painful" leg.[67]

A few days later his leg remained sore, but he still made arrangements to go supervise work on his farm. With his leg "painful & swollen," Calvin still felt strong enough to move about on his own. But "while fixing for bed," he wrote, "I strained the leg while attempting to bathe & I fear wrenched the broken bone from the place it had been fixed. It gave some pain." Nonetheless, in the following days, he got a new saddle and again got on his horse, as it was "the only independent way I can travel as I have to pass all over my farm often. Most persons tell me I am too old to ride horseback." Somewhat energized, he even talked about a possible "excursion" to New Orleans with Keziah. Indeed, Calvin seemed to be back to his old self, getting into an angry encounter with the paperboy for "wadding up my papers," leading to yet another moment of self-flagellation about his problematic temper. For the next week, he continued to ride his horse to the farm and to town.[68]

But soon his leg became infected, and, in a day without antibiotics, there was little to be done. He remained confined at home for the next two weeks. On May 26, 1866, he lay on a sofa on the main floor of the house while his youngest child, twenty-year-old Albert, soon to become a banker like his father, stayed nearby and tried to comfort him. According to Albert, Calvin was in a peaceful mood that day and asked him to play the piano and sing "Flow Gently Sweet Afton" and "Bonnie Doon," two of his favorite songs from the Scottish poet Robert Burns. Calvin remarked that his beloved first wife, Sarah, "sang these most sweetly and better than anyone he had ever heard." She especially loved "Flow Gently Sweet Afton":

> Flow gently sweet Afton among thy green braes
> Flow gently I'll sing thee a song in thy praise
> My Mary's asleep by thy murmuring stream
> Flow gently sweet Afton, disturb not her dream

Upon finishing the song, Albert remembered, Calvin asked him to turn the sofa around "so that I can look on the face of my dear wife. And I turned the sofa around, and he gazed and gazed on the portrait of Mother [Sarah] and myself" on the wall that now faced him.[69] Perhaps, as Albert believed, Calvin felt Sarah's "loving spirit hovering near." Later that afternoon, Calvin Fletcher died at the age of sixty-eight.

Calvin was remembered in newspaper accounts and resolutions throughout Indianapolis as well as in Cincinnati, where he had conducted a lot of business. Following his death, the bankers of Indianapolis met to pass resolutions honoring him. Among many other traits, they praised his "vigilant and generous attention to every call of benevolence . . . and his admirable success in securing the happiness and promoting the culture of a large family." He was appropriately remembered for his educational zeal. As the Indianapolis *Daily Journal* observed, "Mr. Fletcher, in particular, was anxious to have a perfect school system by which every child in the city should have at least a good English education."[70]

Calvin's funeral was held, as he had requested, in his own home on North Pennsylvania Street, with the pastors of the Roberts Park Methodist Episcopal Church officiating. The funeral cortege out to Crown Hill Cemetery stretched for nearly a mile. Among those present were "a large number of colored people whose friend he [Fletcher] had always been, and who now testified their deep affection and veneration for him."[71]

As one eulogist noted, "there were no lazy bones about him." The son of a hardscrabble New England farmer, raised with strict Congregationalist principles of self-reliance and moral uplift, Calvin Fletcher was an indefatigable seeker—always looking forward, strenuously laboring for self-improvement and wider social reform. As he said early on, "I feel a thirst for improvement." But what sometimes accompanied such personal vigilance was a demanding, fault-finding temperament, ever restless, never truly joyful or content. There was always a field to plow, a misbehaving son to correct, an inefficient school to reform, an enslaved people to liberate. Such a man might not have been popular or easygoing, but he was a man to be reckoned with. The quintessential "Western" man, he looked west, like much of the young America of his generation, to find his future.

While he (mostly) shunned the limelight of public life, Calvin left a powerful legacy in Indianapolis. His pivotal role in Indiana's history is reflected in the state capitol building, where his marble bust is on display. An amateur historian himself, Calvin was a member of the New England Historical and Genealogical Society and one of the original members of the Indiana Historical Society, founded in 1830. Perhaps his most enduring legacy, though, are the five thousand-plus pages of his diary that his family donated to the Indiana Historical Society in 1920, which offer unrivaled insights into life in the antebellum Midwest.

His more enduring legacy, though, was entirely personal: like his father, he raised a large family of sons and daughters, with even larger expectations for *their* futures—especially when it came to schooling. As one local paper noted, "that he set the highest valuation upon education is shown by the pains taken to have his own family thoroughly educated."[72]

All of his children bore the earmark of a strong educational experience—they became writers, teachers, doctors, bankers, and progressive farmers—but oddly enough, the most lasting Fletcher commitment to education lay outside Calvin's immediate family. Little did he know that it was in the life and legacy of Indiana Fletcher that Calvin's zeal for a well-lived life through education would find its fullest expression.

Eight

LEGACIES

The death of a prominent, wealthy patriarch usually prompts either an enhanced commitment to his legacy or, released from his control and supervision, a purposeful decision to go in new directions. In the case of Calvin Fletcher, both tendencies were at play after his death in the spring of 1866. Those descendants who found comfort in his wealth and purpose in his progressive values carried on the Fletcher tradition by staying in Indianapolis and continuing his legacy of benevolence and civic-mindedness. Nearly as many Fletcher offspring, though, whatever they thought of their vigilant, demanding father, moved away from their home and, like many of their fellow Americans, crafted individual destinies (both successful and tragic in outcome) that, save the very act of striking out on their own, bore only the faintest connection to Calvin Fletcher.

Perhaps not surprisingly, the Fletcher least caught up in Calvin's world was his second wife of ten years, Keziah. After Calvin's death, she made a rather hasty decision to leave Indianapolis. Keziah sold the family home on Pennsylvania Street that she had inherited to Calvin's business partner, Joseph K. Sharpe, and returned to her own roots in the Boston area. Surrounded by her New England relatives, Keziah spent the rest of her life in

Boston, where she died in 1899. She left behind a middling estate worth about $23,000, reflecting a far more modest life than the one she had shared with Calvin.[1] There is no evidence that Keziah remained in any sort of regular contact with Calvin's children after her departure from Indianapolis.

Cooley Fletcher, who had already carved out his own unique path—much to the discomfort of his captious father—simply continued his highly independent life as a writer and missionary. Living mostly in Rio de Janeiro and ministering to the sailor population there, Cooley remained influential in Brazil and Portugal, serving from 1869 to 1873 as the U.S. consul at Oporto, Portugal. In the early 1870s he divorced his first wife, Henriette Malan—a decision his father doubtless cheered from the grave—and in 1875 married an Englishwoman, Frederica Jane Smith, with whom he lived mostly in Naples, Italy, where he also served as a missionary while writing articles for American newspapers. Cooley finally returned to America permanently in 1890, when he moved to Los Angeles to serve as a pastor in a Presbyterian church. Always a man with his own vision, Cooley spent the last six years of his life as president of the Los Angeles School of Art and Design. He died in 1901.[2]

Solidly devoted to his father's legacy, Calvin Jr. took a leading role, as his father would have done, in helping fund the building of the Indianapolis-Vincennes Railroad, which was completed in 1869. From the profits he made in the nursery business and from fruit farms in neighboring counties, Calvin Jr. in the early 1870s built a large mansion in Owen County, Indiana, that he called Ludlow Hall in honor of the ancestral Fletcher home he had frequently visited. Calvin Jr.'s penchant for spending more than he saved led him to join many other Indianans in the 1870s in buying up and subdividing property in Southern California in present-day Pasadena. But as his father had prophetically noted a decade before, Calvin Jr. was "adventurous, indiscreet, begins many things, finishes none ... will live a *helter*-skelter life & mostly probably will die insolvent & in bad repute." Calvin Jr. in fact fell victim to the Panic of 1873. With his California investments destroyed, he returned to Indianapolis, where he lived, very modestly, until his death in 1903.[3]

Ingram became a partner in the Fletcher & Sharpe Bank, but, like his brother Calvin Jr., was nearly destroyed by a financial crisis, in his case, the bank failure of 1884. Burdened with overvalued real estate, Ingram was forced to sell what he could, and he and his family left Indianapolis in the mid-1880s, moving to Orlando, Florida, where his wife's parents lived. After working in real estate and insurance, Ingram operated a bookstore and then near the end of his career was appointed postmaster of Orlando by President Benjamin Harrison in 1891.[4]

The Reverend Elijah T. Fletcher, Calvin's second son, like his older brother Cooley was a gifted writer and deeply religious, but his father clearly saw him as a disappointment. A few years before he died, Calvin had looked with sympathy on Elijah, noting that he was "unwell & sickly—gives me comfort & sympathy but physically can only aid me in writing & copying." Elijah's failing health prompted him to resign his last post as minister of the New Albany Methodist Church and return in May 1862 to Indianapolis, where he filled in for local ministers and conducted occasional weddings and funerals. Often in debt, Elijah, like Cooley, had a literary bent and wrote book reviews. In 1864 he became assistant editor of the Indianapolis *Daily Journal*. After Calvin's death, Elijah served as executor of his father's estate, but his ongoing health problems reduced his ambitions, and he was essentially an invalid during his final years. In 1877 he died at age fifty-two.[5]

Least appreciated by the patriarch because of their relative youth during Calvin's lifetime were his youngest children, Albert and Lucy. Lucy led a life completely devoted to family, much of it seemingly determined by circumstances rather than by her own unique decisions. When she married Cyrus Hines, the widower of her deceased older sister Maria, she simply took over her sister's childrearing responsibilities; she and Cyrus were themselves childless. Never willing to accept Keziah as her "mother," Lucy struggled to get along with Calvin in the wake of his remarriage, and so she focused her life on Cyrus, who became a prominent lawyer and judge. Lucy connected with her brother Albert toward the end of her life in Farmington, Connecticut, where he and his family had moved around the turn

of the century. Albert, like Ingram, became a partner in the Fletcher &
Sharpe Bank, solidifying the connection when he married the daughter
of Thomas Sharpe, the bank's chairman. He made a good living at the
bank, which allowed him to build an elegant Italianate Renaissance home
on North Pennsylvania Street. After the 1884 bank failure, Albert sold his
house but remained in Indianapolis, where he worked as a traveling agent
for the Pneumatic Company until 1890. Like his brother Calvin Jr., he
made risky investments in real estate in California in the early twentieth
century that didn't pan out, and he eventually moved to Farmington. Like
Lucy, he died in 1918.[6]

Among the more devoted—and thus more esteemed—of Calvin's sons
were Stoughton and Keyes. They stayed in Indianapolis and pursued careers and values that Calvin would have applauded. Stoughton, always
viewed approvingly by his father for his "prudent maturity," was elected
president of the Indianapolis Gas Company in 1878 and ten years later
took over as head of the Atlas Engine Works. He remained involved in

Brothers James Cooley and Stoughton Fletcher

charitable work, becoming the first president of the Indiana Reformatory for Women and Girls. Keyes managed farms—always an honorable profession to Calvin—and by the early 1870s had begun his own tile- and brick-manufacturing business. Widely viewed as one of the city's "most charitable men," Keyes founded the Flower Mission in 1876, which provided food, clothing, and bedding to Indianapolis's poor. Toward the end of his life, he ran a training school for nurses. He died in Indianapolis in 1897.[7]

Calvin's most prominent descendant was Allen M. Fletcher, who served as governor of Vermont from 1912 to 1915. The son of Calvin's youngest brother Stoughton (who remained the most devoted to their mother and to the mission of keeping the family mansion intact), Allen grew up in Indianapolis and like his father became a successful banker and businessman.

Perhaps no son more fully expressed Calvin Fletcher's perspective and legacy than Billy—the very son who modeled his own episode of family leave-taking directly after his father's departure from Ludlow at the very same age. Billy, whose Civil War prison experience served as a shaping influence on his character and career, also remained in Indianapolis. In 1868, he helped to organize the Indiana Medical College, where he served on the faculty for six years. He traveled throughout Western Europe in 1875 studying hospitals in London, Paris, Dublin, and Glasgow and returned to become a professor of nervous diseases at the city's newly established Central College for Physicians and Surgeons. In 1883 he was appointed superintendent of the Indiana Central Hospital for the Insane, where he abolished physical restraints on patients, inaugurated new therapies, and introduced female doctors to work with female patients. An ardent advocate for temperance, Dr. Fletcher published articles and books on more progressive treatments for insanity, the ill effects of alcohol, and the history of cholera. He died in 1907.[8]

❦　•　•　❧

Calvin Fletcher trudged into the pioneer world of central Ohio in 1817 a bedraggled, penniless, but determined teenager. Nearly fifty years later he died as one of Indianapolis's wealthiest and most prominent citizens. Calvin's departure from his ancestral home in Ludlow, Vermont—a cautionary tale he loved to repeat and recall for his own good and for the betterment of whomever else would take it to heart—taught him all he needed to know about what mattered most in life: self-reliance, firmness of purpose, a commitment to being useful, an eye and heart for the common good, a strong religious sensibility, and an allegiance to moral uplift. Despite his many heartaches and "fretful" moments, one suspects Calvin Fletcher succeeded more than most fathers in nourishing these qualities in his children. And those qualities happened to match what nineteenth-century middle-class Americans most valued: hard work, independence, self-improvement, and civic-mindedness.

The world Calvin and his Fletcher kin witnessed and to which they made critical contributions in the century following the American Revolution saw enormous change. Over three generations, a slow-moving, mostly rural culture that relied on horseback travel transformed into a far more efficient, interconnected, and fast-moving world thanks to canals, turnpikes, steamboats, railroads, and the telegraph. A series of equally transformative wars—two conflicts over imperial issues with England, a struggle for land and expansion rights against both Indian nations (the Blackhawk War) and Mexico, and the heartrending Civil War with its rancorous racial divide that placed loyalty to family and country in deep and dangerous jeopardy—all tested the nation and its families in difficult and sometimes disturbing ways. Beneath all the contention, though, a progressive culture emerged that sought to bring reform and civic-minded improvements to the nation—ranging from abolition and the introduction of common schools to the temperance movement and a revolution in transportation.

In confronting all these changes, Calvin, like nearly all the Fletchers, placed great stress on the power and necessity of education. And, as much as he achieved in educating himself and his children, the family's abiding concern for learning found perhaps its fullest expression beyond its New England origins and Midwestern branches in the life and work of Elijah Fletcher's Virginia-raised daughter, Indiana. Calvin may have been troubled about Indiana's "loyalty" to the Union—a misplaced anxiety, as it turned out—but he would have been deeply moved by the choices she made to safeguard and advance educational experiences not only for her own child but also for subsequent generations.

Like Calvin, Indiana did not devote herself to any sort of formal program of schooling or educational goal. She led a privileged life as one of two daughters of a very well-to-do slaveholding planter. Elijah placed her in exclusive, prominent finishing schools for girls, but her desire to be something more than an accomplished, agreeable companion to some southern gentleman only added to her allure. She returned in 1846 from a grand tour across Europe as a teenager with advanced ideas about culture, art, and music, and the experiences and values she had gained abroad stuck with her. Her frequent trips north, especially to New York City, before the war interrupted movement between the nation's two sections, brought her into contact with all manner of cosmopolitan men and women.

One of those acquaintances was James Henry Williams, a tall, red-headed Irishman who graduated from New York's General Theological Seminary in 1858 and then served for six years as a pastor of Zion Episcopal Church in Dobbs Ferry, New York. Almost immediately, it seemed, Reverend Williams formed a close bond with Indiana, so much so that shortly after the war ended in August 1865 he showed up on her doorstep proposing marriage. They did not waste time: a few weeks later, at 10:00 a.m. on August 23, they got married at St. Paul's Episcopal Church in Lynchburg. By noon they had caught the only train leaving that day back to New York City. Because of the extraordinary wealth that Indiana brought to the marriage, Williams gave up his work with the church, instead joining her in the business of running apartment hotels in New York City. Although Williams still gave an occasional sermon in Virginia (he was apparently an effective preacher), he surrendered his ministerial life. After his death, Indiana conceded to a friend, "He didn't have to work as we didn't need the money, but I am afraid that I ruined an excellent preacher."[9]

As a business couple, James and Indiana prospered, allowing them to cultivate a life filled with music, art, travel, and the collection of fine objects.

Indiana Fletcher's Sweet Briar home

James was drawn to unique clocks, pictures, fine silver, and bronzes, while Indiana filled their home at Sweet Briar with high-end carpets, furniture, china, and silver.

But the Williams's most precious possession was their daughter, Maria Georgiana (Daisy), born September 10, 1867. Doted on by both her parents, Daisy came to love her summers spent on the Sweet Briar plantation, no doubt because the rest of the time she spent in New York, living in rented rooms in various hotels, eating out at restaurants, or having meals delivered to the family. In contrast to the impermanent atmosphere of her New York life, Sweet Briar's bucolic plantation world—complete with servants (who had previously worked as slaves before the war) and thousands of acres in which to roam around, often on her favorite pony, Bounce—gave her a more palpable sense of home. Her diary and letters refer lovingly to "my house, my garden, my room, my trees." Indiana made certain that her daughter would become a cultured young lady and early on introduced her to opera and taught her piano and the harp. The harp was indeed a special instrument, purchased in London in 1845 during Indiana's European

Daisy Williams

travels. By age fourteen, Daisy was studying languages, music, algebra, literature, geography, sewing, and drawing, and was given elaborate music lessons at the New York Conservatory.

Alas, a cloud of doom hung over young Daisy, who was always a fragile child: she apparently inherited from her father a devastating genetic defect that destroyed her lungs. Called antitrypsin deficiency, this disease involves excessive abnormal deposits of protein in the liver, leading to an emphysema-like condition that is often fatal. On January 22, 1884, at the age of sixteen, Daisy died. To say that Daisy's death devastated her parents, especially her mother, is an understatement. Indiana suffered a nervous breakdown at the loss. She left everything in Daisy's room exactly as it had been before she died—the piano was locked, the harp was covered, her clothes remained in her closet, and fresh sheets were placed on her bed. Indiana instructed the servants to bring Daisy's breakfast to her graveside on Sweet Briar's Monument Hill each morning, where, according to one servant, they "had to stay for one half hour." Also required was that Daisy's pony, Bounce, be brought to the gravesite ready to ride, with Daisy's riding outfit lying across the saddle. For six months after her daughter's death, Indiana made daily vigils to the grave and would read aloud any mail Daisy had received. Some of the family servants and close friends worried openly that Indiana "wouldn't come 'round to herself."[10]

Indiana did recover, and in the summer of 1884 she finally returned to New York and rejoined James in running the family business. Over the next five years, it was her husband's turn to encounter serious health problems. Suffering from cirrhosis of the liver, James's health declined steadily, and on April 25, 1889, at the age of fifty-six, he died. He was buried next to Daisy on Monument Hill. The next year Indiana buried her younger sister, Elizabeth, also on Monument Hill. Betty's final years had been unpleasant as a result of the struggle she had faced with her "fortune hunter" husband, William Hamilton Mosby. He had systematically run through most of her assets by the time Betty died in 1890. So Indiana provided a bit of familial revenge on William: her sister's gravestone deliberately left out the name "Mosby" and any reference to "wife," referring to her simply as "Elizabeth Fletcher," "sister," and "daughter."

Indiana's other remaining sibling, her brother Sidney, stayed at the Tusculum plantation. Despite being a prominent, well-to-do plantation owner and physician, Sidney was the only child of Elijah who never married. But, like Lucian, he did apparently have a mate. Federal census records in 1880 and Sidney's will suggest that Harriet Edwards, a twenty-four-year-old mulatto woman, lived in the same home with Sidney. In 1883 Sidney deeded seventy acres of land to Harriet and her two sons. The land gift, along with the living arrangements and local rumors, point to Harriet as Sidney's common-law wife. When Sidney died in 1898 he was buried in the Crawford family cemetery, but none of the Edwards can be found there.[11]

After her husband's death, in her sixties and mostly alone—other than her house servants and a few close friends—Indiana decided to sell off her properties in New York. With the proceeds, she made mostly smart and profitable investments in bonds and railroads, banks and gas companies. By the late 1880s she had amassed huge parcels of land in Virginia and West Virginia. In Amherst County alone, she collected rent on twenty-three different farms. In an era when there was no federal income tax, Indiana Fletcher Williams was able to build quite a fortune.

All of this meant that she faced prospects that were simultaneously hopeful and threatening. The threatening element came from those family and friends who were anxious to lay claim to Indiana's considerable estate. Here her chief annoyance came in the form of her despised and troubled brother Lucian and his numerous children (more than ten) born to him through his various wives, one an escaped slave, another a white "mountain" woman. Lucian made several threats to his sister's life if she didn't offer him his fair share of the estate from which his father had deliberately excluded him. He and his children brought several suits against the estate, claiming that Indiana's property was properly theirs because the bulk of her assets were initially acquired by their grandfather, Elijah Fletcher. But since six out of the seven children that Lucian had were born out of wedlock, Indiana refused to recognize these nieces and nephews as true members of the family. Once Daisy died in 1884, an itinerant minister convinced Lucian that by marrying the mother of his children, he would be making them legitimate heirs, which would allow for a successful attack on Indiana's will as the genuine next of kin.[12]

Lucian had long since become a family and local pariah with a significant criminal record. During the 1901 court hearings over the estate, the retired sheriff described Lucian as "the worst outlaw in the history of the county," with a criminal history that escalated from alcohol abuse, disturbing the peace, and blackmail to armed assault, child abuse, and murder. Lucian had been acquitted of the murder charge, but, given his ongoing pattern of personal failures and criminal conduct, he faced an unforgiving family that publicly and privately shamed him. Lucian died in 1895, and his remains were not allowed in the Fletcher/Williams cemetery on Monument Hill. Rather, he was buried in an inconspicuous far corner of his mother's Crawford family cemetery. His small, plain gravestone reads simply "Born, 1824" and "Died, 1895." In death, then, as in life, Lucian was ostracized by the Fletcher family. But his children pressed on in their demands for a part of Indiana's estate, arguing that their aunt was mentally unbalanced and that thus her will was invalid.[13]

To be fair, the legal case against Indiana was not without merit. The lawyers for Lucian and his children claimed she had developed an "insane aversion" to her nieces and nephews, refusing, as she did, to recognize or have any contact with them, and even instructing her servants to keep them away at all costs. But, given her brother's dangerous background and known intentions, she perhaps wisely did not allow Lucian to enter her house at Sweet Briar. She even took the precaution of placing angled iron, backed with heavy boards, inside the doors that led into the yard to prevent Lucian from breaking into the house. Still, her well-known, quasi-hoarding habits regarding all her collectibles, plus her emotional breakdown and subsequent behavior over the loss of Daisy, certainly suggest some emotional imbalance.

But Indiana was a formidable and independent woman, and she came well prepared for the assault on her estate, engaging some of the most expert inheritance lawyers in New York. They were determined to eliminate any loopholes and protect her will against self-interested parties. As she told her Amherst County friend Elizabeth Payne, she was afraid "there are those who would try to destroy my will." After considerable care and consultation, Indiana signed her will in New York on April 22, 1899.[14]

That will, besides protecting the large estate she owned—valued at approximately $800,000—also reflected an extremely hopeful, even visionary, side of Indiana Fletcher Williams. After the death of Daisy, she began thinking about a way to remember her, to honor her, and to nourish the lives of girls and young women (like Daisy) for generations to come. What she chose to do reflected a long-standing principle that stretched back to her grandfather Jesse Sr. and most of his children, especially her

Indiana Fletcher

uncle Calvin and her own father, Elijah: the absolute necessity of a good education.[15]

Indiana's will contained a powerful bequest and commitment: she gave $700,000 (or roughly $14 million in today's currency) to establish a girls' and women's college. She bequeathed her entire Sweet Briar plantation, along with some other adjacent tracts of land, together totaling about three thousand acres, and directed her trustees to set up a corporation called the "Sweet Briar Institute" for the express purpose "of establishing and maintaining . . . a school or seminary for the education of white girls and young women." The school was to be run by a board of seven directors with a "general scope and object . . . to impart to its students such education in sound learning, and such physical, moral and religious training as shall in the judgment of the directors best fit them to be useful members of society." No part of the Sweet Briar Institute bequest was at any time to be sold or alienated but was to "be kept inviolate as an endowment fund" to be used strictly for supporting and maintaining the school. Moreover, Indiana requested that the new school "establish free scholarships, affording tuition and maintenance for a limited number of deserving students." Indiana made clear that Sweet Briar College, as it would soon be called, originated from her and her late husband's own desires and as a way to establish "a perpetual memorial of our deceased daughter, Daisy Williams."[16]

The creation of Sweet Briar College—born out of a mother's sadness in honoring her daughter's untimely death, as well as the unique faith, for that era, in the power of educating young women—offers a revealing window into the Fletcher family's journey across nineteenth-century America. By returning to the family's origins and guiding principles and looking forward to the implications and consequences of personal choices, both small and large, we can see the thread of a purposeful legacy. But there were countervailing impulses and biases that shaped that legacy as well. While an impressive tribute to the value of education, the college, with its explicit restriction that it was established only for "white girls," also laid bare the ongoing racism in America, even among progressive individuals like

Sweet Briar College

Indiana Fletcher Williams. She was, after all, the product of an enlightened Vermont-bred schoolteacher-turned-southern-slaveholder. Had she grown up with all the same privileges she enjoyed, but under the parental eye of Calvin Fletcher in Indianapolis, her perspective on race might have been different.

What she left behind was on one level a very successful liberal arts college for young white women in rural Virginia. But Sweet Briar also contributed, perhaps unwittingly, to the ongoing controversy over race. Just as Indiana's father changed his perspective on race once he moved to Virginia and met and married Maria Crawford, Sweet Briar College too would find reason to change its position on this very subject some sixty-three years after its founding. With the passage of the Civil Rights Act of 1964, the college awakened to a new understanding of who could attend the school and what the school's original mission truly meant. Amid the turmoil of 1960s civil rights activism, the college attempted to reinterpret the will of its founder—getting around the language about the school serving the "education of white girls and young women." In a petition to the Amherst County Circuit Court, the school's board argued that this restrictive regulation "perpetuates particular local conditions of time and place which have so changed that the major emphasis in the foundation of the College can no longer be realized by adhering to that condition." But Judge C. G. Quesenbery of the Amherst County Circuit Court and Amherst County Commonwealth's attorney William M. McClenny rejected the petition, claiming that accepting African American students at Sweet Briar in effect meant breaking the will of the founder. "The will of Mrs. Williams," Quesenbery argued, "is not ambiguous and therefore needs no further interpretation." Changing the school's charter, he said, by erasing the word "white" was improper, as it would "destroy the entire purpose of the will."

But Sweet Briar College's bill of complaint in August 1964 argued that if it couldn't remove the restrictions imposed by Indiana's will, the school couldn't achieve its founder's main goal—to "impart to its students such education in sound learning . . . as shall in the judgement of the directors best fit them to be useful members of society." Sweet Briar College president Anne Gary Pannell insisted that it was necessary to reinterpret the founder's will in light of new realities of race relations and the changing social conditions of a new era.

The college's attempt to fulfill the desegregation goals of the civil rights movement disturbed its neighbors in southwest Virginia. An editorial in the Lynchburg paper, entitled "A Matter of Honor," criticized Sweet Briar College's effort to integrate, calling for the resignation of all the college's senior officers and board trustees. The Commonwealth's attorney McClenny tried to dismiss the college's motion, calling the suit "frivolous," since Sweet Briar "did not come into court with clean hands or good faith." By that, he meant that the college was simply interested in getting its hands on federal financial assistance (which required compliance with anti-discrimination policy), rather than truly supporting the struggle for civil rights. Sweet Briar pushed back, claiming that the college sought the change because it "was morally right." Moreover, the school argued, it was not intending to break the will of Indiana Fletcher Williams, but was simply "reinterpreting it."[17] The faculty believed that the founder's intent and the college's original spirit would be damaged if the college failed to evolve along with the contemporary shift in values. Besides, as Sweet Briar's initial bill of complaint noted, the will's racial restrictions were in effect required by highly outdated Virginia legal statutes from the nineteenth century that demanded that educational institutions be only for white or only for black students—not for both. Racially integrated schools were never imagined as an option. Thus, the founder was left with no choice but to pick one race in order for her educational trust to be valid in Virginia.

On April 25, 1966, Sweet Briar College took its case to the U.S. District Court for the Western District of Virginia and got a temporary restraining order from Judge Thomas J. Michie—preventing any further racial restrictions from the attorney general of Virginia or the Commonwealth's Attorney for Amherst County regarding the college. Under this injunction, the Sweet Briar College board was able to admit students "unrestricted as to race, creed or color." That fall semester, on August 31, 1966, Sweet Briar admitted its first African American student, Marshalyn Yeargin. Yeargin was eighteen but had already completed two years at a black women's school, Bennett College, in Greensboro, North Carolina, and was transferring. She wanted a school that would offer her a stronger science background to better prepare her to become a doctor. Yeargin's great-uncle had earned a doctorate from the University of Chicago in 1935 and had served as president of Morehouse College; her parents were college educated and worked as school administrators and teachers. So Yeargin arrived at Sweet Briar well prepared to take on the challenge of being the first African American student in the college's sixty-five-year history. Although she faced a generally wary response from her white classmates—she was given a single room in the dorms because no one wanted to room with her—Yeargin clearly profited from her time at Sweet Briar. Despite her unique status in an otherwise all-white girls' school, she encountered a faculty that encouraged her to excel and made little reference to her racial makeup. The faculty, she said, "never gave me the feeling that I was different. They treated me like all the other students . . .

At Sweet Briar, I was being asked to take learning to the next level . . . and never encountered any ugly behavior towards me." In 1968, she completed her premed studies at Sweet Briar with great success and then became the first African American woman to enroll in Emory University's School of Medicine, earning her M.D. in 1972. She went on to work at the Centers for Disease Control and Prevention in Atlanta, where she is chief of the developmental disabilities branch.[18] While Indiana's expectations for Sweet Briar did not include educating African American students, she would doubtless have admired Yeargin's fierce love of learning and relentless drive to succeed.

❧ • • • ❧

Sweet Briar's successfully evolving mission continued to honor its founder's spirit in its vision for educating young women. But a half century later yet another challenge to the school emerged, producing a near-fatal coda to Indiana's educational vision. In March 2015, Sweet Briar College president James F. Jones suddenly announced that the college would be closing by August. Citing "insurmountable financial challenges," administrators told a stunned and tearful faculty and student body that the college, with its dwindling $95 million endowment and declining student demand, could simply not survive in an increasingly volatile educational market. With single-sex colleges on the decline (there were 230 women's colleges in the United States in 1965 compared to a little more than 40 in 2015) and enrollments sliding, Sweet Briar's seven hundred students no longer supported the college's needs. "This is a sad day for the entire Sweet Briar College community," Paul G. Rice, the board chairman, noted in a prepared statement.[19]

The news about the school's closing spread quickly, and attention quickly focused on the specific intent of Indiana Fletcher Williams in bequeathing her land for the foundation of the school. Excerpts from Indiana's will appeared all over the country as commentators on and critics of the Sweet Briar administration tried to determine if the various options for the school—going co-ed or committing to closing and selling off all the property—would be an act of support for or betrayal of the founder's vision. Because Indiana's will stipulated that none of the land associated with the creation of the college "shall at any time be sold or alienated" by the governing board, the bequest was termed a "restricted gift." Modifying Indiana's will and original intent would be necessary, legal critics claimed, in order to close and sell the school. And few believed that such a fundamental modification would pass legal muster. In response to a series of passionate petitions and lawsuits from faculty and angry alumnae, the Virginia Supreme Court in June 2015 ruled that the decision to close Sweet Briar had been ill-considered and premature. Days later a last-minute mediation between the school's board members and passionate supporters of Sweet Briar led to a settlement agreement to reopen the college. Invoking the clear-headed intent of its founder, the supporters of Sweet Briar fought a valiant fight that ended in victory, one that only confirmed the enduring vision of Indiana Fletcher.[20]

❧ • • ❧

As these pages have argued, a fierce commitment to learning fueled much of the Fletcher journey. That journey began with Jesse's leadership in the small village of Ludlow, Vermont, setting up a school where the town's children—provided they supplied their own firewood—could at least learn to read and write and do some basic math. Beyond that, only the most careful saving and sacrifice allowed for additional schooling—and usually only for the eldest children in a family, as in the case of Elijah. Fittingly, the Fletcher home and land in Ludlow were eventually converted into an educational enterprise: a nonprofit foundation called Fletcher Farm, which was created in the early twentieth century for the express purpose of life-long education. Today the remaining buildings from the "old mansion" have been renovated into an artists' studio and a pottery shop. The entire farm now hosts music camps, teacher conferences, and religious conventions, as well as arts and crafts programs for adults and children. Among its

many notable trustees have been the New England writers Dorothy Can-
field Fisher and Robert Frost.

Perhaps because he was so painfully aware of how *un*schooled he was,
Calvin Fletcher became the most vocal and relentless advocate for learning
in the entire Fletcher clan. And he saw education in the broadest sense—
not only as a means for acquiring a profession (such as his own legal and
banking career), but also as a necessary background for developing perspective and becoming a truly civic-minded person who could thoughtfully
participate in public life, even critiquing its flaws and trying to reform it.
As evidenced by all their energies spent on the common school movement
and temperance, as well as on their advocacy for abolition and internal
improvements, most of the Calvin Fletcher family used their educational
achievements in order to remake their world into what they believed would
be a better place. Indiana Fletcher, following her father's generous and
wise guidance, did the same in the context of female education. Like most
middle-class Americans today, then, the Fletchers invested huge emotional
capital in the conviction that education—rather than sheer effort or wealth
or family privilege—is pivotal to the success of an individual and the larger
world.

Propelling the Fletchers' unswerving devotion to education, of course,
was something even more quintessentially American: the deeply felt need
to cultivate personal ambition and use it to advance oneself. Once considered a character trait fraught with dangerously selfish and secular impulses,
ambition by the early nineteenth century had evolved into a powerful and
necessary motivating personal quality believed to produce success and
high levels of achievement. The Fletchers cultivated ambition with near-
reckless abandon. Almost every choice that Elijah and Calvin—and, just as
obviously, their own children—made grew out of an often-unexpressed but
clearly evident premise: that the decisions they made would improve their
lives, advance their careers, and produce more individual (and familial)
happiness. And while the Fletchers certainly didn't have a monopoly on
ambition, they were acutely aware of it and exceedingly good at making it
work in their lives. Finally, we should remember that all this concern for

being bold and seizing opportunity came at a time when there was virtually no social safety net in case of failure—unemployment insurance, Social Security, welfare, and medical insurance lay far in the future. When men and women in the nineteenth century became unemployed, suffered severe illness, made bad marriages, or simply lost their way, there were no soft landings. There was only the family and kin network to absorb—temporarily and only to a modest degree—the pain, suffering, and embarrassment of failure. As the Fletcher family's story reveals, while the family could serve as a safe haven in times of trouble, the emotional stress on everyone could be long-lasting.

All of this led to the many sleepless, "fretful" nights that gripped Calvin—and no doubt Sarah and Keziah, Elijah and Maria—as he lay awake wondering, as many of us today do, whether his careful admonitions and elaborate educational plans (not to mention emotional expectations) for his children would produce a Billy or a Lucian or someone altogether different and worrisome. The Fletchers remind us that the American dream is a full-throated adventure, which, like Elijah, we can observe with detached interest, or, like Calvin, we can follow with worry and hope.

Fletcher Family Genealogy

JESSE FLETCHER FAMILY

Jesse Fletcher (1762–1831) and Lucy Keyes (1763–1846) were married at Westford, Massachusetts, in 1782.

Children

Charlotte	b. 1782	d. 1795
Stephen	b. 1784	d. 1790
Michael	b. 1785	d. 1859
Fanny	b. 1786	d. 1872
Jesse	b. 1787	d. 1848
Elijah	b. 1789	d. 1858
Timothy	b. 1791	d. 1870
Lucy	b. 1792	d. 1888
Stephen II	b. 1794	d. 1818
Laura	b. 1796	d. 1844
Calvin	b. 1798	d. 1866
Miles	b. 1799	d. ?
Dexter	b. 1801	d. 1803
Louisa	b. 1804	d. 1836
Stoughton	b. 1808	d. 1882

ELIJAH FLETCHER FAMILY

Elijah Fletcher (1789–1858) married Maria Antoinette Crawford (1792–1853) on April 15, 1813, in Tusculum, Amherst County, Virginia.

Children

Sidney	b. 1821	d. 1898
Lucian	b. 1824	d. 1895
Laura	b. 1825	d. 1826
Indiana	b. 1828	d. 1900
Twin, male	b. 1828	d. 1828
Elizabeth	b. 1831	d. 1890

CALVIN FLETCHER FAMILY

Calvin Fletcher (1798–1866) married Sarah Hill (1801–1854) on May 1, 1821, in Urbana, Ohio.

Children

James Cooley	b. 1823	d. 1901
Elijah	b. 1824	d. 1877
Calvin, Jr.	b. 1826	d. 1903
Miles	b. 1828	d. 1862
Stoughton	b. 1831	d. 1895
Maria	b. 1833	d. 1860
Ingram	b. 1835	d. 1903
William	b. 1837	d. 1907
Stephen Keyes	b. 1840	d. 1897
Lucy	b. 1842	d. 1918
Albert	b. 1846	d. 1918

Acknowledgments

The origin of this book came from my wife and fellow historian, Lorri Glover, who years ago pointed out that someone needed to write a book about Elijah Fletcher, the young antislavery New Englander who moved to Virginia in 1810 to become a schoolteacher, only to turn into a major slave-holding planter. Elijah's history is a great fish-out-of-water story that plays a prominent role in these pages, but it didn't seem quite large enough for a book. But then I encountered Calvin Fletcher, Elijah's younger brother, whose massive diary spans nearly fifty years and almost five thousand pages. Soon a provocative individual story evolved into a family saga.

Along the way to uncovering the Fletcher family story, my own journey has been made easier and more useful thanks to a number of good people who know the Fletchers extremely well themselves. At the J.V. Fletcher Library in Westford, Massachusetts, Ginny Moore deserves thanks for her helpful local history insights into the family. Many thanks also to Layne Herschel, chairman of the board of the Fletcher Farm School for the Arts and Crafts in Ludlow, Vermont, who graciously walked the grounds with me and answered my questions—right where Jesse and Lucy and their children first began their odyssey. Likewise, Jill Tofferi, director of the Fletcher Memorial Library in Ludlow, led me to some little-known Fletcher materials. The hardworking research assistants at the Indiana Historical Society patiently guided me to the most useful portions of the

Fletcher Family Papers. And at a once embattled but now triumphant Sweet Briar College—which has successfully waged a valiant struggle to stay open despite an administration in the spring of 2015 that prematurely gave up on the remarkable commitment of the school's founder, Indiana Fletcher Williams—I want to thank Lisa Johnston, Director of Libraries, and Karol Ann Lawson, Director of the Sweet Briar Museum, for all their sound advice and knowledge regarding the "southern" Fletchers. Finally, thanks to my physician brother, Dr. Steven Smith, for wise counsel on how to assess various ailments and treatments in nineteenth-century medicine.

I am also happy to acknowledge the shrewd and faithful work of my agent, Geri Thoma of Writer's House, in finding a good home for this book. At St. Martin's, my editor, Elisabeth Dyssegaard, has been encouraging and helpful at every stage—a dream editor for any writer. I also want to thank Sarah Vogelsong for her thorough and insightful copyediting, and Donna Cherry for effectively guiding me through the production of the book.

This book is dedicated to my parents, Emerson Smith and Marjorie Megivern, who early on showed me the adventure of life and the love of learning.

Notes

INTRODUCTION

1. Indianapolis *Daily Journal,* December 28, 1858.
2. Gayle Thornbrough, ed., *The Diary of Calvin Fletcher* (Indianapolis: Indiana History Society, 1978), 6:279–280 (hereafter *Fletcher Diary*).

CHAPTER ONE: BEGINNINGS

1. See Edward H. Fletcher, comp., *Fletcher Genealogy: An Account of the Descendants of Robert Fletcher, of Concord, Massachusetts* (Privately printed, 1871), 9, 72–73; D. P. Lacroix, comp., *Entries for Westford Men Found in Massachusetts Soldiers and Sailors of the Revolutionary War* (Westford, MA: J.V. Fletcher Library, January 2004), 22, 107–08.
2. Joseph N. Harris, *The History of Ludlow, Vermont* (Charlestown, NH: Black River History Society Publishers, 1949), 15.
3. *Fletcher Diary,* 1:xix. See also Martha von Briesen, ed., *The Letters of Elijah Fletcher* (Charlottesville: University of Virginia Press, 1965), xv (hereafter *Letters of Elijah Fletcher*).
4. Harris, *History of Ludlow,* 69–70.
5. *Fletcher Diary,* 1:xix.
6. On Lucy's character and traits, see Fanny Fletcher, "Founder's Day Speech" (Sweet Briar College, October 16, 1961), Fletcher Memorial Library, Ludlow, Vermont.
7. Harris, *History of Ludlow,* 46.
8. Ibid., 59.
9. Ibid., 16, 78, 82, 85, 87.
10. *Fletcher Diary,* 1:xix–xx.
11. *Letters of Elijah Fletcher,* xvi.
12. Elijah Fletcher to Jesse Fletcher, April 20, 1810, *Letters of Elijah Fletcher,* 4. Jesse Fletcher's letters to his children have not survived.
13. Elijah Fletcher to Jesse Fletcher, August 4, 1810, *Letters of Elijah Fletcher,* 7–8.
14. Elijah Fletcher to Jesse Fletcher, April 20, 1810, *Letters of Elijah Fletcher,* 4–5.
15. Elijah Fletcher to Jesse Fletcher Jr., July 6, 1810, *Letters of Elijah Fletcher,* 5.
16. Elijah Fletcher to Jesse Fletcher Jr., August 29, 1810, *Letters of Elijah Fletcher,* 11–12.
17. Elijah Fletcher to Jesse Fletcher, July 17, 1810, *Letters of Elijah Fletcher,* 6.
18. Elijah Fletcher to Jesse Fletcher Jr., August 29, 1810, *Letters of Elijah Fletcher,* 12–13.
19. Elijah Fletcher to Jesse Fletcher, August 4, 1810, *Letters of Elijah Fletcher,* 7.
20. Ibid., 8.
21. Ibid., 8.
22. Elijah Fletcher to Jesse Fletcher Jr., August 29, 1810, *Letters of Elijah Fletcher,* 14–15.

23. Ibid., 14.

24. Elijah Fletcher to Jesse Fletcher Jr., December 7, 1810, *Letters of Elijah Fletcher,* 23–24.

25. Elijah Fletcher to Jesse Fletcher, January 11, 1811, *Letters of Elijah Fletcher,* 25–26.

26. Quoted in Lorri Glover, *Southern Sons: Becoming Men in the New Nation* (Baltimore: Johns Hopkins University Press, 2007), 85.

27. Elijah Fletcher to Jesse Fletcher, March 1811, *Letters of Elijah Fletcher,* 32.

28. Elijah Fletcher to Jesse Fletcher, May 24, 1811, *Letters of Elijah Fletcher,* 36. See also Annette Gordon-Reed, *Thomas Jefferson and Sally Hemings: An American Controversy* (Charlottesville: University of Virginia Press, 1997).

29. Elijah Fletcher to Jesse Fletcher, March 1811, *Letters of Elijah Fletcher,* 32.

30. Elijah Fletcher to Laura Fletcher, August 16, 1812, *Letters of Elijah Fletcher,* 61.

31. Elijah Fletcher to Jesse Fletcher, November 6, 1812, *Letters of Elijah Fletcher,* 65.

32. Elijah Fletcher to Jesse Fletcher, June 20, 1813, *Letters of Elijah Fletcher,* 73.

33. Elijah Fletcher to Jesse Fletcher, February 17, 1813, *Letters of Elijah Fletcher,* 72. For more on how well-to-do southern parents carefully policed outsiders marrying into their families, see Glover, *Southern Sons,* chapter 5.

34. Elijah Fletcher to Jesse Fletcher, June 20, 1813, *Letters of Elijah Fletcher,* 74.

35. Elijah Fletcher to Jesse Fletcher, May 2, 1814, *Letters of Elijah Fletcher,* 80.

36. Elijah Fletcher to Jesse Fletcher, April 24, 1812, *Letters of Elijah Fletcher,* 42.

37. Elijah Fletcher to Jesse Fletcher, February 22, 1811, *Letters of Elijah Fletcher,* 29.

38. Elijah Fletcher to Jesse Fletcher, December 23, 1811, *Letters of Elijah Fletcher,* 48.

39. Elijah Fletcher to Jesse Fletcher, February 7, 1813, *Letters of Elijah Fletcher,* 71. See also Elijah's letters to his father on February 22, 1811, and March 1811, *Letters of Elijah Fletcher,* 30, 32.

40. Elijah Fletcher to Jesse Fletcher, May 2, 1814, *Letters of Elijah Fletcher,* 79.

41. Elijah Fletcher to Jesse Fletcher, January 11, 1811, *Letters of Elijah Fletcher,* 28.

42. Elijah Fletcher to Jesse Fletcher, October 1, 1810, *Letters of Elijah Fletcher,* 16.

43. See Mary Kelley, *Learning to Stand and Speak: Women, Education, and Public Life in America's Republic* (Chapel Hill: University of North Carolina Press, 2008).

44. Elijah Fletcher to Jesse Fletcher, January 11, 1811, *Letters of Elijah Fletcher,* 25. See also J. M. Opal, *Beyond the Farm: National Ambitions in Rural New England* (Philadelphia: University of Pennsylvania Press, 2011).

45. Elijah Fletcher to Jesse Fletcher, September 5, 1813, *Letters of Elijah Fletcher,* 78.

46. Elijah Fletcher to Jesse Fletcher, June 9, 1811, *Letters of Elijah Fletcher,* 38.

47. Elijah Fletcher to Jesse Fletcher, July 4, 1812, *Letters of Elijah Fletcher,* 56.

48. Elijah Fletcher to Jesse Fletcher, July 2, 1814, *Letters of Elijah Fletcher,* 82.

49. Elijah Fletcher to Laura Fletcher, August 16, 1812, *Letters of Elijah Fletcher,* 61.

50. Elijah Fletcher to Jesse Fletcher, December 4, 1812, *Letters of Elijah Fletcher,* 69.

51. Elijah Fletcher to Jesse Fletcher, January 11, 1811, *Letters of Elijah Fletcher,* 27–28.

52. Elijah Fletcher to Jesse Fletcher, September 6, 1813, *Letters of Elijah Fletcher,* 78.

53. Elijah Fletcher to Jesse Fletcher, July 2, 1814, *Letters of Elijah Fletcher,* 82.

54. Elijah Fletcher to Jesse Fletcher, July 4, 1815, *Letters of Elijah Fletcher,* 84.

55. Ibid.

56. Elijah Fletcher to Jesse Fletcher, August 31, 1815, *Letters of Elijah Fletcher,* 84.

CHAPTER TWO: HEADING WEST

1. *Fletcher Diary,* 1:xxii.

2. See Joseph F. Kett, *Rites of Passage: Adolescence in America, 1790 to the Present* (New York: Basic Books, 1977).

3. *Fletcher Diary,* 1:xxi.

4. Ibid.

5. Ibid., 1:xxi–xxii.
6. Ibid. On the War of 1812, see Alan Taylor, *The Civil War of 1812: American Citizens, British Subjects, Irish Rebels, and Indian Allies* (New York: Knopf, 2010).
7. *Fletcher Diary,* 1:xxii–xxiii.
8. Ibid., 1:xxiii–xxiv.
9. Calvin Fletcher to his parents, April 10, 1817, *Fletcher Diary,* 1:3.
10. Calvin Fletcher to his parents, June 27, 1817, *Fletcher Diary,* 1:4. This was Samuel Fletcher of Westford, Massachusetts, a church deacon, but not a true uncle.
11. Calvin Fletcher to his parents, June 27, 1817, *Fletcher Diary,* 1:4–5.
12. Ibid., 1:5.
13. Ibid., 1:5–6.
14. Letter of Recommendation (signed by Stephen Steward) for Calvin Fletcher, May 21, 1817, Fletcher Papers, Indiana Historical Society, Indianapolis, Indiana.
15. Elijah Fletcher to Jesse Fletcher Sr., July 24, 1817, *Letters of Elijah Fletcher,* 86.
16. Calvin Fletcher to his parents, June 27, 1817, *Fletcher Diary,* 1:9.
17. Ibid.
18. Calvin Fletcher to his parents, June 27, 1817, *Fletcher Diary,* 1:4.
19. Calvin Fletcher to Jesse Sr., January 24, 1818, *Fletcher Diary,* 1:10–11.
20. Calvin Fletcher to Jesse Sr., July 25, 1818, *Fletcher Diary,* 1:11–12.
21. Calvin Fletcher to Jesse, Sr., January 24, 1818, *Fletcher Diary,* 1: 11.
22. Calvin Fletcher to Jesse Sr., November 21, 1818, *Fletcher Diary,* 1:13. For more on how education was thought to make boys into men in the early Republic, see Glover, *Southern Sons;* Stephen M. Frank, *Life with Father: Parenthood and Masculinity in the Nineteenth-Century American North* (Baltimore: Johns Hopkins University Press, 1998).
23. Calvin Fletcher to Stephen Fletcher, January 13, 1818, *Fletcher Diary,* 1:9–10.
24. Calvin Fletcher to Jesse Sr., July 25, 1818, *Fletcher Diary,* 1:11.
25. Calvin Fletcher to Jesse Sr., November 21, 1818, *Fletcher Diary,* 1:12–13. See also Elliott J. Gorn, "'Gouge and Bite, Pull Hair and Scratch': The Social Significance of Fighting in the Southern Backcountry," *American Historical Review* 90 (February 1985): 18–43.
26. Calvin Fletcher to Jesse Sr., June 18, 1819, *Fletcher Diary,* 1:14.
27. Ibid., 14–15.
28. Elijah Fletcher to Jesse Sr., June 11, 1820, *Letters of Elijah Fletcher,* 89–90.
29. Ibid.
30. Ibid.
31. Elijah Fletcher to Jesse Sr., August 31, 1820, *Letters of Elijah Fletcher,* 91.
32. November 30, 1820, *Fletcher Diary,* 1:16.
33. December 5, 1820, *Fletcher Diary,* 1:18–19.
34. December 6, 1820, *Fletcher Diary,* 1:19.
35. Ibid.
36. Ibid.
37. December 10, 1820, *Fletcher Diary,* 1:20.
38. December 17, 1820, *Fletcher Diary,* 1:21.
39. December 21, 1820, *Fletcher Diary,* 1:21–22.
40. December 25, 1820, *Fletcher Diary,* 1:22.
41. December 30, 1820; January 1, 1821, *Fletcher Diary,* 1:22.
42. February 4, 1821, *Fletcher Diary,* 1:23–24.
43. Sarah Hill Fletcher to Louisa Fletcher, June 20, 1821, *Fletcher Diary,* 1:39–40.
44. February 4, 1821, *Fletcher Diary,* 1:24.
45. Ibid.
46. March 2, 1821, *Fletcher Diary,* 1:26. See also Anya Jabour, *Marriage in the Early Republic: Elizabeth and William Wirt and the Companionate Ideal* (Baltimore: Johns Hopkins University Press, 2002).
47. March 28, 1821, *Fletcher Diary,* 1:27.

48. April 1, 1821, *Fletcher Diary,* 1:28.
49. April 30, 1821, *Fletcher Diary,* 1:30.
50. Ibid.
51. May 1–May 8, 1821, *Fletcher Diary,* 1:30–31.
52. May 12, 1821, *Fletcher Diary,* 1:31.
53. May 17, 1821, *Fletcher Diary,* 1:32.
54. May 19, 1821, *Fletcher Diary,* 1:32–33.
55. May 26, 1821, *Fletcher Diary,* 1:33.
56. May 29, 1821, *Fletcher Diary,* 1:34.
57. Ibid.
58. Ibid.
59. July 12, 1821, *Fletcher Diary,* 1:36.
60. Sarah Hill Fletcher to her father, October 2, 1821, *Fletcher Diary,* 1:41.
61. Sarah Hill Fletcher to her father, October 2, 1821; Sarah Hill Fletcher to Miss Maria Britten, October 15, 1821, *Fletcher Diary,* 1:41–42.
62. Sarah Hill Fletcher to Miss Maria Britten, October 15, 1821, *Fletcher Diary,* 1:42.
63. Andrew R. L. Cayton, *Frontier Indiana* (Bloomington: Indiana University Press, 1996), 271, 275. See also Malcolm J. Rohrbough, *The Trans-Appalachian Frontier: People, Societies, and Institutions, 1775–1850* (New York: Oxford University Press, 1978).
64. Sarah Hill Fletcher to her father, October 2, 1821, *Fletcher Diary,* 1:41.

CHAPTER THREE: SETTLING IN

1. November 8, 1821, *Fletcher Diary,* 1:81–82.
2. December 31, 1821, *Fletcher Diary,* 1:86.
3. Calvin Fletcher to Michael Fletcher, February 23, 1823, *Fletcher Diary,* 1:89; Simon Yandes, "Recollections of Calvin Fletcher as a Lawyer," Fletcher Family Papers, Indiana Historical Society, Indianapolis, Indiana.
4. Calvin Fletcher to Michael Fletcher, February 23, 1823, *Fletcher Diary,* 1:89.
5. March 1, 1822, *Fletcher Diary,* 1:54.
6. November 1, 1821, November 5, 1821, November 16, 1821, and November 17, 1821, *Fletcher Diary,* 1:43–44.
7. See May 31–June 15, 1822, *Fletcher Diary,* 1:63–64.
8. November 25, 1821, *Fletcher Diary,* 1:44.
9. January 29, 1822, *Fletcher Diary,* 1:51.
10. April 12, 1822, *Fletcher Diary,* 1:58.
11. March 12, 1823, December 16, 1821, and December 21, 1821, *Fletcher Diary,* 1:71, 46, 48.
12. February 14, 1822, *Fletcher Diary,* 1:53.
13. Malinda Hill to Sarah Fletcher, June 1, 1824, Fletcher Family Papers, Indiana Historical Society, Indianapolis, Indiana.
14. December 12, 1823, *Fletcher Diary,* 1:73. See Jabour, *Marriage in the Early Republic.*
15. April 15, 1823, *Fletcher Diary,* 1:72.
16. Calvin Fletcher to Michael Fletcher, February 23, 1823, *Fletcher Diary,* 1:90, 92.
17. Quoted May 5, 1823, *Fletcher Diary,* 1:95fn.
18. *Letters of Elijah Fletcher,* 286.
19. November 30, 1823, *Fletcher Diary,* 1:98.
20. July 31, 1824, *Fletcher Diary,* 1:122.
21. May 19, 1824, *Fletcher Diary,* 1:104.
22. May 19, 1824, May 20, 1824, and May 21, 1824, *Fletcher Diary,* 1:104–105.
23. May 22, 1824, *Fletcher Diary,* 1:106.
24. May 24, 1824, *Fletcher Diary,* 1:107, 109.
25. Ibid., 109.
26. May 27, 1824, *Fletcher Diary,* 1:110–111.

27. June 6, 1824, *Fletcher Diary*, 1:117.

28. June 7, 1824, and June 8, 1824, *Fletcher Diary*, 1:117–118.

29. Peter L. Bernstein, *Wedding of the Waters: The Erie Canal and the Making of a Great Nation* (New York: W. W. Norton, 2005).

30. June 8, 1824, and July 3, 1824, *Fletcher Diary*, 1:118–119, 122.

31. July 4, 1824, *Fletcher Diary*, 1:122.

32. July 5, 1824, and July 11, 1824, *Fletcher Diary*, 1:123–124.

33. July 11, 1824, *Fletcher Diary*, 1:124.

34. July 12, 1824, and July 14, 1824, *Fletcher Diary*, 1:124–125.

35. July 20, 1824, *Fletcher Diary*, 1:126.

36. July 25, 1824, and August 21, 1824, *Fletcher Diary*, 1:125, 128.

37. Sarah Fletcher to sisters, December 8, 1824, *Fletcher Diary*, 1:131.

38. Calvin recalled his absence years later: see August 21, 1838, *Fletcher Diary*, 2:27; August 21, 1824, *Fletcher Diary*, 1:132, 134.

39. Sarah Fletcher to sisters, December 8, 1824, *Fletcher Diary*, 1:132, 134.

40. Elijah Fletcher to Jesse Fletcher, November 14, 1824, *Letters of Elijah Fletcher*, 92.

41. Elijah Fletcher to Jesse Fletcher, July 23, 1825, *Letters of Elijah Fletcher*, 96.

42. Lynn Rainville, "African-American History at the Sweet Briar Plantation," *Sweet Briar College Alumnae Magazine*, Spring/Summer 2004, 7.

43. Elijah Fletcher to Jesse Fletcher, July 23, 1825, *Letters of Elijah Fletcher*, 96, 98. See Jeffrey L. Pasley, *"The Tyranny of Printers": Newspaper Politics in the Early American Republic* (Charlottesville: University of Virginia Press, 2001).

44. *Gazette* (Indianapolis), March 28 and June 6, 1826.

45. Elijah Fletcher to Calvin Fletcher, September 8, 1827, *Letters of Elijah Fletcher*, 147–148.

46. Elijah Fletcher to Calvin Fletcher, August 10, 1828, *Letters of Elijah Fletcher*, 102.

47. Calvin Fletcher to Jesse Fletcher, January 17, 1828, *Fletcher Diary*, 1:148.

48. Calvin Fletcher to Jesse Fletcher, January 27, 1828, *Fletcher Diary*, 1:148–149.

49. Calvin Fletcher to Elijah Fletcher, September 8, 1827, *Fletcher Diary*, 1:146.

50. Elijah Fletcher to Calvin Fletcher, May 25, 1829, *Letters of Elijah Fletcher*, 105. On the rise of Jackson and the pivotal importance of the 1828 election, see Lynn Hudson Parsons, *The Birth of Modern Politics: Andrew Jackson, John Quincy Adams, and the Election of 1828* (New York: Oxford University Press, 2009).

51. Elijah Fletcher to Calvin Fletcher, August 3, 1828, *Letters of Elijah Fletcher*, 101.

52. Elijah Fletcher to Calvin Fletcher, November 10, 1828, *Letters of Elijah Fletcher*, 104.

53. Elijah Fletcher to Jesse Fletcher, November 7, 1825, *Letters of Elijah Fletcher*, 98.

54. Elijah Fletcher to Jesse Fletcher, April 3, 1826, *Letters of Elijah Fletcher*, 99.

55. Elijah Fletcher to Calvin Fletcher, August 3, 1828, *Letters of Elijah Fletcher*, 101.

56. Dr. Kenneth A. Scudder to Calvin Fletcher, October 12, 1826, *Fletcher Diary*, 1:141. On infant mortality in the central Illinois community of Sugar Creek in this era, see John Mack Faragher, *Sugar Creek: Life in the Illinois Prairie* (New Haven, CT: Yale University Press, 1986).

57. *Fletcher Diary*, 1: 141–142n.20.

58. January 8, 1829, and January 11, 1829, *Fletcher Diary*, 1:156–157.

59. Elijah Fletcher to Calvin Fletcher, August 10, 1828, *Letters of Elijah Fletcher*, 102.

60. Elijah Fletcher to Jesse Fletcher, November 10, 1828, *Letters of Elijah Fletcher*, 104.

61. January 1, 1829, *Fletcher Diary*, 1:150.

62. Ibid., 150–151.

63. Ibid., 152.

64. On the Second Great Awakening, see Christine Leigh Heyrman, *Southern Cross: The Beginnings of the Bible Belt* (New York: Knopf, 1997); and Nathan O. Hatch, *The Democratization of American Christianity* (New Haven, CT: Yale University Press, 1989).

65. January 26, 1829, and February 22, 1829, *Fletcher Diary*, 1:160, 164.

66. January 31, 1829, *Fletcher Diary*, 1:161.

67. February 22, 1829, May 1, 1829, and May 4, 1829, *Fletcher Diary,* 1:164–166.
68. Elijah Fletcher to Jesse Fletcher, May 25, 1829, *Letters of Elijah Fletcher,* 105.
69. Elijah Fletcher to Jesse Fletcher, March 21, 1830, *Letters of Elijah Fletcher,* 113.
70. Elijah Fletcher to Jesse Fletcher, August 2, 1829, *Letters of Elijah Fletcher,* 106.
71. Elijah Fletcher to Jesse Fletcher, September 5, 1830, *Letters of Elijah Fletcher,* 113.
72. Elijah Fletcher to Jesse Fletcher, August 2, 1829, *Letters of Elijah Fletcher,* 106.
73. Elijah Fletcher to Stoughton Fletcher, November 1, 1829, *Letters of Elijah Fletcher,* 108.
74. December 25, 1829, *Fletcher Diary,* 1:167.
75. Ibid., 1:167–168.
76. December 26, 1829, *Fletcher Diary,* 1:168; John H. B. Nowland, *Early Reminiscences of Indianapolis* (Indianapolis: Sentinel Book and Job Printing House, 1870), 186–187. See also Fergus M. Bordewich, *Bound for Canaan: The Epic Story of the Underground Railroad, America's First Civil Rights Movement* (New York: Amistad, 2005).
77. December 25, 1829, January 1, 1830, and February 4, 1830, *Fletcher Diary,* 1:166, 169, 170.
78. Sarah Hill Fletcher, "Journal of a Visit to Ohio, June 8–29, 1830," *Fletcher Diary,* 1:171.
79. Calvin Fletcher to Jesse Fletcher, August 16, 1830, *Fletcher Diary,* 1:172–173.
80. Ibid., 1:173–174.
81. Elijah Fletcher, "Recollections of My Mother," in Fletcher Family Papers, Indiana Historical Society, Indianapolis, Indiana.
82. Calvin Fletcher to Jesse Fletcher, August 16, 1830, *Fletcher Diary,* 1:173–174.
83. Ibid.
84. Elijah Fletcher to Calvin Fletcher, March 29, 1831, *Letters of Elijah Fletcher,* 122.

CHAPTER FOUR: "THE BEST FORTUNE WE CAN GIVE OUR CHILDREN"

1. Elijah Fletcher to Calvin Fletcher, August 20, 1831, *Letters of Elijah Fletcher,* 125.
2. Ibid., 124.
3. Ibid.
4. Ibid., 124–125.
5. Elijah Fletcher to Calvin Fletcher, December 12, 1831, *Letters of Elijah Fletcher,* 127.
6. Calvin Fletcher to Lucy Keyes, January 1, 1832, *Fletcher Diary,* 1:179–80.
7. Patrick J. Jung, *The Black Hawk War of 1832* (Norman: University of Oklahoma Press, 2007).
8. Calvin Fletcher to Lucy Keyes, June 10, 1832, *Fletcher Diary,* 1:181–182.
9. Ibid., 183–184.
10. Elijah Fletcher to Calvin Fletcher, April 11, 1833, *Letters of Elijah Fletcher,* 133.
11. See Daniel D. Pratt to Dr. William B. Fletcher, October 6, 1876, Fletcher Family Papers, Indiana Historical Society, Indianapolis.
12. April 25, 1835, *Fletcher Diary,* 1:250.
13. August 10, 1835, and October 15, 1835, *Fletcher Diary,* 1:271–272, 279.
14. January 12, 1836, *Fletcher Diary,* 1:299.
15. December 5, 1835, January 1, 1836, and March 3, 1836, *Fletcher Diary,* 1: 287, 296–297, 317.
16. See Jessica M. Lepler, *The Many Panics of 1837: People, Politics and the Creation of a Transatlantic Financial Crisis* (Cambridge: Cambridge University Press, 2013).
17. Elijah Fletcher to Calvin Fletcher, April 15, 1837, and May 3, 1837, *Letters of Elijah Fletcher,* 146–147.
18. January 16, 1837, June 11, 1836, and September 19, 1836, *Fletcher Diary,* 1:402, 354, 377.
19. Calvin Fletcher to Nicholas McCarty, June 13, 1836, *Fletcher Diary,* 1:355–356.
20. Elijah Fletcher to Calvin Fletcher, February 16, 1835, and March 7, 1836, *Letters of Elijah Fletcher,* 136–137, 139.
21. June 13, 1836, *Fletcher Diary,* 1:355–356.
22. *Indiana Democrat* (Indianapolis), May 31, 1837.
23. May 20, 1837, *Fletcher Diary,* 1:431.
24. March 29, 1837, April 16, 1836, and September 21, 1836, *Fletcher Diary,* 1:419, 331, 378.

25. May 20, 1837, *Fletcher Diary,* 1:431.

26. Elijah Fletcher to Calvin Fletcher, March 29, 1831, *Letters of Elijah Fletcher,* 123.

27. August 18, 1837, and June 22, 1835, *Fletcher Diary,* 453–454, 258.

28. Elijah Fletcher to Calvin Fletcher, March 29, 1831, *Letters of Elijah Fletcher,* 122.

29. See Lorri Glover, *Southern Sons: Becoming Men in the New Nation* (Baltimore: Johns Hopkins University Press, 2007).

30. Elijah Fletcher to Calvin Fletcher, March 29, 1831, November 2, 1836, February 4, 1838, and April 8, 1838, *Letters of Elijah Fletcher,* 123, 144, 156, 157.

31. Elijah Fletcher to Calvin Fletcher, November 27, 1837, *Letters of Elijah Fletcher,* 154. On raising sons in the early Republic South, see Daniel Blake Smith, *Inside the Great House: Planter Families in Eighteenth-Century Chesapeake Society* (Ithaca, NY: Cornell University Press, 1980); Glover, *Southern Sons.*

32. Sidney Fletcher to Calvin Fletcher, June 1837, *Letters of Elijah Fletcher,* 148–149.

33. Sidney Fletcher to Calvin Fletcher, August 28, 1838, *Letters of Elijah Fletcher,* 159.

34. Elijah Fletcher to Calvin Fletcher, January 14, 1839, *Letters of Elijah Fletcher,* 160.

35. Elijah Fletcher to Calvin Fletcher, October 16, 1839, *Letters of Elijah Fletcher,* 163. See Bertram Wyatt-Brown, *Southern Honor: Ethics and Behavior in the Old South* (New York: Oxford University Press, 1982).

36. Elijah Fletcher to Indiana Fletcher, October 16, 1841, *Letters of Elijah Fletcher,* 172.

37. Maria Fletcher to Calvin Fletcher, December 4, 1841, *Letters of Elijah Fletcher,* 175.

38. Elijah Fletcher, "Memories of My Mother," Fletcher Family Papers.

39. Calvin Fletcher to Lucy Keyes, June 1, 1834, in *Fletcher Diary,* 1:224–225.

40. Sarah Fletcher to Calvin Fletcher, January 11–12, 1838, *Fletcher Diary,* 1:476–477.

41. July 7, 1838, *Fletcher Diary,* 2:7–8.

42. January 1, 1836, *Fletcher Diary,* 1:196.

43. February 12, 1833, *Fletcher Diary,* 1:200.

44. January 20, 1839, *Fletcher Diary,* 2:53; April 3, 1836, *Fletcher Diary,* 1:328; September 16, 1838, and October 21, 1838, *Fletcher Diary,* 2:38, 43; February 26, 1837, *Fletcher Diary,* 1:412.

45. January 2, 1837, January 7, 1837, and October 19, 1837, *Fletcher Diary,* 1:400–401, 461–462.

46. August 21, 1838, *Fletcher Diary,* 2:27.

47. January 23, 1840, and March 23, 1839, *Fletcher Diary,* 2:141, 76–77.

48. March 2, 1840, *Fletcher Diary,* 2:155–156.

49. April 5, 1840, *Fletcher Diary,* 2:171.

50. Simon Yandes to Calvin Fletcher, June 1, 1839, *Fletcher Diary,* 2:95–96.

51. Gideon Soule to Calvin Fletcher, March 3, 1840, *Fletcher Diary,* 2:161–2.

52. July 4, 1840, July 16, 1840, and July 5, 1840, *Fletcher Diary,* 2:198–199, 204, 199.

53. September 1, 1840, September 8, 1840, September 28, 1840, and January 17, 1841, *Fletcher Diary,* 2:225, 227, 235–236, 272.

54. April 14, 1841, May 29, 1841, and July 3, 1841, *Fletcher Diary,* 2:307, 328, 337.

55. October 18, 1841, *Fletcher Diary,* 2:362.

56. Elijah Fletcher to Calvin Fletcher, November 26, 1841, *Letters of Elijah Fletcher,* 174.

57. December 8, 1841, *Fletcher Diary,* 2:366.

58. December 13, 1841, and April 13, 1842, *Fletcher Diary,* 2:369, 402–403.

59. September 9, 1842, September 11, 1842, and September 25, 1842, *Fletcher Diary,* 2:436, 439.

60. See Kett, *Rites of Passage,* 5–55.

61. Walter C. Brunson, *The History of Brown University, 1746–1914* (Providence: Brown University Press, 1914), 206, 211, 229–232.

62. Elijah Fletcher to Calvin and Sarah Fletcher, November 13, 1842, *Fletcher Diary,* 2:452; Elijah Fletcher to Calvin Fletcher, October 21, 1842, *Fletcher Diary,* 2: 448.

63. Elijah Fletcher to Calvin Fletcher, December 13, 1842, *Fletcher Diary,* 2:456.

64. June 6, 1843, *Fletcher Diary,* 2:503.

65. January 7, 1844, *Fletcher Diary,* 3:8, 12; Calvin Fletcher to Cooley, January 28, 1844, *Fletcher Diary,* 3:12.

66. July 2, 1843, *Fletcher Diary,* 2:508.

67. Elijah Fletcher to Calvin Fletcher, June 29, 1843, and July 25, 1843, *Fletcher Diary,* 2:509-510.

68. Elijah Fletcher to Calvin Fletcher, January 16, 1841, *Letters of Elijah Fletcher,* 167.

69. Sidney Fletcher to Calvin Fletcher, February 15, 1842, *Letters of Elijah Fletcher,* 180-181.

70. Ibid; Elijah Fletcher to Calvin Fletcher, June 19, 1843, *Fletcher Diary,* 2:506.

71. Elijah Fletcher to Calvin Fletcher, April 27, 1841, *Letters of Elijah Fletcher,* 168; Elijah Fletcher to Calvin Fletcher, March 13, 1842, *Letters of Elijah Fletcher,* 181.

72. On boarding schools for girls in this era, see Mary Kelley, *Learning to Stand and Speak: Women, Education, and Public Life in America's Republic* (Chapel Hill: University of North Carolina Press, 2008).

73. Elijah Fletcher to Calvin Fletcher, January 10, 1843, and June 12, 1843, *Letters of Elijah Fletcher,* 185-186.

74. Elijah Fletcher to Calvin Fletcher, March 13, 1842, *Letters of Elijah Fletcher,* 181; Elijah Fletcher to Calvin Fletcher, September 1, 1844, *Letters of Elijah Fletcher,* 192.

75. Elijah Fletcher to Calvin Fletcher, February 7, 1845, *Letters of Elijah Fletcher,* 194; Elijah Fletcher to Calvin Fletcher, June 2, 1845, *Letters of Elijah Fletcher,* 196.

76. Elijah Fletcher to Calvin Fletcher, June 2, 1845, *Letters of Elijah Fletcher,* 196.

77. Ibid.

CHAPTER FIVE: PUBLIC LIFE

1. Elijah Fletcher to Calvin Fletcher, October 6, 1844, *Letters of Elijah Fletcher,* 192-195.

2. Indiana Fletcher to Elijah Fletcher, October 19, 1845, Indiana Fletcher Williams Papers, Sweet Briar College. This letter was also published in the February 5, 1846, edition of the *Virginian.*

3. Elijah Fletcher to Calvin Fletcher, August 22, 1846, *Letters of Elijah Fletcher,* 201.

4. Elijah Fletcher to Sidney, Indiana, and Betty Fletcher, August 22, 1846, *Letters of Elijah Fletcher,* 201-202.

5. Ibid.

6. Elijah Fletcher to Calvin Fletcher, May 9, 1847, *Letters of Elijah Fletcher,* 207.

7. Elijah Fletcher to Calvin Fletcher, October 24, 1847, *Letters of Elijah Fletcher,* 211.

8. Elijah Fletcher to Calvin Fletcher, April 18, 1851, *Letters of Elijah Fletcher,* 228; Elijah Fletcher to Calvin Fletcher, November 7, 1852, *Letters of Elijah Fletcher,* 238. See also Ann Marshall Whitley, "Indiana Fletcher Williams of Sweet Briar" (unpublished booklet, Sweet Briar College Library, Sweet Briar, Virginia), 17-18.

9. February 4, 1844, *Fletcher Diary,* 3:16.

10. February 26, 1844, *Fletcher Diary,* 3:23-24.

11. April 22, 1844, *Fletcher Diary,* 3:35.

12. See Eric Burin, *Slavery and the Peculiar Institution: A History of the American Colonization Society* (Gainesville: University Press of Florida, 2005).

13. October 28, 1844, and October 31, 1844, *Fletcher Diary,* 3:83, 85.

14. November 4-6, 1844, *Fletcher Diary,* 3:86-88.

15. November 13, 1844, and November 16, 1844, *Fletcher Diary,* 3:90-92.

16. January 31, 1845, and March 4, 1845, *Fletcher Diary,* 3:115, 124.

17. May 22, 1845, and May 25, 1845, *Fletcher Diary,* 3:143-145.

18. Timothy Fletcher to Elijah Fletcher, September 1, 1844, *Letters of Elijah Fletcher,* 188, 191; March 23, 1846, *Fletcher Diary,* 3:243.

19. Elijah Fletcher to Calvin Fletcher, April 26, 1846, *Letters of Elijah Fletcher,* 197.

20. Elijah Fletcher to Calvin Fletcher, August 22, 1846, *Letters of Elijah Fletcher,* 202.

21. May 24, 1846, *Fletcher Diary,* 3:259; Jane Shaffer Elsmere, *Henry Ward Beecher: The Indiana Years, 1837-1847* (Indianapolis: Indiana Historical Society, 1973), 264-266.

22. May 15, 1846, *Fletcher Diary*, 3:257; Anders Stephanson, *Manifest Destiny: American Expansionism and the Empire of Right* (New York: Hill & Wang, 1995).

23. May 25, 1846, *Fletcher Diary*, 3:262.

24. July 9, 1846, *Fletcher Diary*, 3:279; Elijah Fletcher, "Recollections of My Mother."

25. June 26, 1846, *Fletcher Diary*, 3:281; Fletcher, "Recollections of My Mother."

26. July 2, 1846, July 31, 1846, October 16, 1846, and October 26, 1846, *Fletcher Diary*, 3:273, 283, 310, 315.

27. Stephen A. Carney, *Desperate Stand: The Battle of Buena Vista* (Washington, D.C.: U.S. Army Center for Military History, 2012).

28. March 23, 1847, *Fletcher Diary*, 3:361; Elijah Fletcher to Calvin Fletcher, May 31, 1847, and July 18, 1847, *Letters of Elijah Fletcher*, 209–10.

29. May 31, 1847, June 26, 1847, and July 26, 1847, *Fletcher Diary*, 3:385, 392, 397; Fletcher, "Recollections of My Mother."

30. Calvin Fletcher Jr. to Calvin Fletcher, August 10, 1846, *Fletcher Diary*, 3:287.

31. August 23, 1846, *Fletcher Diary*, 3:292.

32. Miles Fletcher to Calvin Fletcher, September 1, 1846, *Fletcher Diary*, 3:295; August 27, 1846, *Fletcher Diary*, 3:293.

33. August 12, 1848, and January 21, 1849, *Fletcher Diary*, 4:61, 91.

34. Calvin Fletcher, "Address to the Temperance Society at Noblesville, Indiana, June 20, 1845," *Fletcher Diary*, 3:156.

35. Ibid., 153–154.

36. November 13, 1846, *Fletcher Diary*, 3:320; Calvin Fletcher Jr. to Calvin Fletcher, November 23, 1846, *Fletcher Diary*, 3:321.

37. Calvin Fletcher Jr. and Miles Fletcher to Calvin Fletcher, December 10, 1846, *Fletcher Diary*, 3. 321, n.119.

38. November 30, 1846, and December 21, 1846, *Fletcher Diary*, 3: 322, 325, 332.

39. April 6, 1847, *Fletcher Diary*, 3:365.

40. Elijah Fletcher to Calvin Fletcher, April 9, 1854, *Letters of Elijah Fletcher*, 247–248; September 23, 1855, *Fletcher Diary*, 5:457.

41. Elijah Fletcher to Calvin Fletcher, September 5, 1855, and December 5, 1855, *Letters of Elijah Fletcher*, 254, 257.

42. *Indiana State Journal* (Indianapolis), June 12, 1848.

43. See James H. Madison, *The Indiana Way: A State History* (Bloomington: Indiana University Press, 1986), 94.

44. *Indiana State Journal* (Indianapolis), February 9, 1847. On the common school movement, see Carl E. Kaestle, *Pillars of the Republic: Common Schools and American Society, 1780–1860* (New York: Hill & Wang, 1983).

45. May 14, 1847, and June 7, 1847, *Fletcher Diary*, 3:376, 389.

46. Samuel Merrill to Rev. David Merrill, July 1, 1847, Samuel Merrill Papers, Indiana Historical Society, Indianapolis, Indiana.

47. June 9, 1854, *Fletcher Diary*, 5:232.

48. August 4, 1848, *Fletcher Diary*, 4:59.

49. John Kingsbury to Calvin Fletcher, June 19, 1849, *Fletcher Diary*, 4:113; Cooley Fletcher to Calvin Fletcher, July 11, 1849, *Fletcher Diary*, 4:117.

50. Miles Fletcher to Calvin Fletcher, September 11, 1847, *Fletcher Diary*, 3:413.

51. Calvin Fletcher Jr. to Calvin Fletcher, September 28, 1847, *Fletcher Diary*, 3:412–413, 415. Calvin's comment to his sons is quoted in Calvin, Jr.'s letter to him.

52. Miles Fletcher to Calvin Fletcher, September 28, 1847, *Fletcher Diary*, 3:413.

53. On the gold rush, see H. W. Brands, *The Age of Gold: The California Gold Rush and the New American Dream* (New York: Anchor Books, 2003).

54. December 25, 1848, *Fletcher Diary*, 4:84.

55. Elijah Fletcher to Calvin Fletcher, June 1, 1849, *Letters of Elijah Fletcher*, 217; June 11, 1849, *Fletcher Diary*, 4:112.

56. Elijah Fletcher to Calvin Fletcher, January 21, 1850, and August 20, 1850, *Letters of Elijah Fletcher*, 223, 225.

57. Elijah Fletcher to Calvin Fletcher, August 20, 1851, and November 10, 1851, *Letters of Elijah Fletcher*, 231.

58. Elijah Fletcher to Calvin Fletcher, June 3, 1850, and April 10, 1848, *Letters of Elijah Fletcher*, 224, 213.

59. Elijah Fletcher to Calvin Fletcher, November 4, 1848, and June 1, 1849, *Letters of Elijah Fletcher*, 216–217.

60. Elijah Fletcher to Calvin Fletcher, August 4, 1852, *Letters of Elijah Fletcher*, 237. On the tragedy of the *Henry Clay*, see Kris A. Hansen, *Death Passage on the Hudson: The Wreck of the Henry Clay* (New York: Purple Mountain Press, 2004).

61. Sarah Fletcher to Stoughton and Billy Fletcher, July 10, 1853, *Fletcher Diary*, 5:98.

62. Timothy Fletcher to Richardson Fletcher, October 10, 1853, *Letters of Elijah Fletcher*, 244; Elijah Fletcher to Calvin Fletcher, December 2, 1853, *Letters of Elijah Fletcher*, 245. See also Whitley, "Indiana Fletcher Williams of Sweet Briar," 20.

63. July 31–August 6, 1854, *Fletcher Diary*, 5:258.

64. That is the conclusion of my medical advisor, Dr. Steven Smith, who has studied the sources involving the case of Sarah Fletcher, as well as the illness and death of others detailed in this book. Steven Smith to author, e-mail correspondence, April 28, 2015.

65. September 22, 1854, September 24, 1854, and September 26, 1854, *Fletcher Diary*, 5:261–263.

66. September 26, 1854, *Fletcher Diary*, 5:263; Albert Fletcher, "Memories of My Mother," Fletcher Family Papers, Indiana Historical Society, Indianapolis, Indiana.

67. September 26, 1854, and September 27, 1854, *Fletcher Diary*, 5:263–265.

68. Albert Fletcher, "Memories of My Mother"; September 28, 1854, *Fletcher Diary*, 5:266–267.

69. Fletcher, "Memories of My Mother."

CHAPTER SIX: CALAMITIES

1. Elijah Fletcher to Calvin Fletcher, October 30, 1854, *Letters of Elijah Fletcher*, 250.

2. February 4, 1854, *Fletcher Diary*, 5:173.

3. Miles Fletcher to Calvin Fletcher, August 26, 1854, *Fletcher Diary*, 5:272.

4. James Cooley Fletcher to Calvin Fletcher, July 6, 1854, *Fletcher Diary*, 5:272.

5. October 7, 1854, *Fletcher Diary*, 5:271.

6. November 1, 1854, and November 2, 1854, *Fletcher Diary*, 5:293, 295.

7. November 1, 1854, November 3, 1854, November 7, 1854, November 20, 1854, November 30, 1854, October 29, 1854, and October 30, 1854, *Fletcher Diary*, 5:293, 295, 297, 306, 310, 292–293.

8. December 2, 1854, *Fletcher Diary*, 5:313.

9. December 11, 1854, *Fletcher Diary*, 5:316–317.

10. December 1, 1854, *Fletcher Diary*, 5:312.

11. December 17, 1854, and February 4, 1855, *Fletcher Diary*, 5:318, 353.

12. February 9, 1855, *Fletcher Diary*, 5:357.

13. March 5, 1855, March 18, 1855, April 5, 1855, April 20, 1855, and April 25, 1855, *Fletcher Diary*, 5:374, 376, 381, 390, 395, 397.

14. May 30, 1855, *Fletcher Diary*, 5:410; Elijah Fletcher to Calvin Fletcher, June 16, 1855, Fletcher Family Papers, Indiana Historical Society, Indianapolis, Indiana; Miles Fletcher to Calvin Fletcher, June 20, 1855, Fletcher Family Papers, Indiana Historical Society, Indianapolis, Indiana; April 24, 1855, *Fletcher Diary*, 5:397.

15. July 15, 1855, and July 17, 1855, *Fletcher Diary*, 5:428, 430; X. B. Sanders to Calvin Fletcher, November 2, 1855, Fletcher Family Papers, Indiana Historical Society, Indianapolis, Indiana. "His character alone," Sanders noted, "added to the length of time he has deserted his wife, would entitle her to a divorce in any court in the Union."

16. November 4, 1855, and November 9, 1855, *Fletcher Diary,* 5:474.

17. November 9, 1855, *Fletcher Diary,* 5:475–476; Elijah Fletcher to Calvin Fletcher, November 27, 1855, *Letters of Elijah Fletcher,* 255.

18. May 19, 1854, and November 20, 1855, *Fletcher Diary,* 5:221, 477–478.

19. June 30, 1853, *Fletcher Diary,* 5:87.

20. January 1, 1856, and January 10, 1856, *Fletcher Diary,* 5:485, 489.

21. Ingram Fletcher to "Dear Mother," January 19, 1856, Fletcher Family Papers, Indiana Historical Society, Indianapolis, Indiana.

22. January 21, 1856, *Fletcher Diary,* 5:493.

23. February 4, 1846, *Fletcher Diary,* 5:496.

24. March 8, 1856, *Fletcher Diary,* 5:500.

25. Ibid.

26. February 4, 1856, March 8, 1856, and March 29, 1856, *Fletcher Diary,* 5:496, 500–503, 509–510.

27. April 20, 1856, and March 17, 1856, *Fletcher Diary,* 5:510, 504.

28. July 29, 1856, *Fletcher Diary,* 5: 556.

29. Ingram Fletcher to Calvin Fletcher, October 27, 1856, Fletcher Family Papers, Indiana Historical Society, Indianapolis, Indiana.

30. November 17, 1856, and June 4, 1856, *Fletcher Diary,* 5:600, 528.

31. Elijah Fletcher to Calvin Fletcher, February 12, 1856, Fletcher Family Papers, Indiana Historical Society, Indianapolis, Indiana; Elijah Fletcher to Calvin Fletcher, November 30, 1856, *Letters of Elijah Fletcher,* 263.

32. September 28, 1856, *Fletcher Diary,* 5:574.

33. Elijah Fletcher to Calvin Fletcher, July 28, 1856, *Letters of Elijah Fletcher,* 262; Elijah Fletcher to Calvin Fletcher, November 30, 1856, *Letters of Elijah Fletcher,* 264.

34. June 5, 1856, *Fletcher Diary,* 5:529.

35. July 15, 1856, *Fletcher Diary,* 5:546.

36. October 8, 1856, and October 9, 1856, *Fletcher Diary,* 5:578.

37. October 11, 1856, October 12, 1856, October 14, 1856, and October 15, 1856, *Fletcher Diary,* 5:579–582.

38. Elijah Fletcher to Calvin Fletcher, September 30, 1856, *Letters of Elijah Fletcher,* 262.

39. Elijah Fletcher to Calvin Fletcher, November 30, 1856, February 5, 1857, and May 2, 1857, *Letters of Elijah Fletcher,* 264–265.

40. Elijah Fletcher to Calvin Fletcher, May 27, 1857, *Letters of Elijah Fletcher,* 266.

41. Elijah Fletcher to Calvin Fletcher, September 13, 1857, *Letters of Elijah Fletcher,* 267.

42. Elijah Fletcher to Calvin Fletcher, November 12, 1857, *Letters of Elijah Fletcher,* 267–268.

43. January 1, 1858, and February 4, 1858, *Fletcher Diary,* 6:159, 181; Cooley to Calvin Fletcher, February 1, 1858, Fletcher Family Papers, Indiana Historical Society, Indianapolis, Indiana.

44. Indiana Fletcher to Calvin Fletcher, February 18, 1858, *Letters of Elijah Fletcher,* 271.

45. See Dr. Steven Smith to author, e-mail correspondence, April 28, 2015.

46. Indiana Fletcher to Calvin Fletcher, February 18, 1858, *Letters of Elijah Fletcher,* 272.

47. February 18, 1858, *Fletcher Diary,* 6:195.

48. February 19, 1858, February 21, 1858, and February 24, 1858, *Fletcher Diary,* 6:196, 198.

49. March 5, 1858, February 28, 1858, March 13, 1858, and March 4, 1858, *Fletcher Diary,* 6:203, 199, 205.

50. Sidney Fletcher to Calvin Fletcher, March 13, 1858, *Letters of Elijah Fletcher,* 205; Amherst County (Virginia) Will Book, XIV, 527–528.

51. July 11, 1858, *Fletcher Diary,* 6:239.

52. November 25, 1858, November 26, 1858, December 10, 1858, and December 11, 1858, *Fletcher Diary,* 6:267, 272.

53. January 9, 1858, January 10, 1859, and June 22, 1860, *Fletcher Diary,* 6:292, 570.

54. December 27, 1858, *Fletcher Diary,* 6: 279-280.

55. January 1, 1859, *Fletcher Diary,* 6:286–287.

56. Ibid., 288; April 29, 1860, *Fletcher Diary,* 6:533–534.

57. July 6, 1858, and August 17, 1858, *Fletcher Diary,* 6:236, 250. See also John Steele Gordon, *A Thread Across the Ocean: The Heroic Story of the Transatlantic Cable* (New York: Walker & Company, 2002).

58. October 18, 1859, November 4, 1859, December 2, 1859, October 19, 1859, and November 1, 1859, *Fletcher Diary,* 6:425–426, 434, 452, 427, 432.

59. Dr. Steven Smith to author, e-mail correspondence, April 28, 2015.

60. May 3, 1860, and May 4, 1860, *Fletcher Diary,* 6:538–540.

61. May 5, 1860, *Fletcher Diary,* 6:540.

62. October 29, 1860, and October 30, 1860, *Fletcher Diary,* 6:620–622.

63. December 7, 1860, December 15, 1860, and December 20, 1860, *Fletcher Diary,* 6:643, 650, 653.

64. December 30–31, 1860, *Fletcher Diary,* 6:661–662.

CHAPTER SEVEN: WAR AND LOYALTY

1. January 14, 1861, *Fletcher Diary,* 7:16.

2. January 14, 1861, January 22, 1861, and January 24, 1861, *Fletcher Diary,* 7:16, 23, 24.

3. February 11, 1861, February 21, 1861, and February 26, 1861, *Fletcher Diary,* 7:43, 51, 55; *Daily Journal* (Indianapolis), February 11, 13, 1861.

4. April 1, 1862, *Fletcher Diary,* 7:77.

5. April 13, 1861, April 14, 1861, and April 16, 1861, *Fletcher Diary,* 7:87–88, 90, 92; *Daily State Sentinel* (Indianapolis), April 13, 1861; *Indiana State Guard,* April 13, 1861.

6. April 13, 1861, and April 17, 1861, *Fletcher Diary,* 7:87, 93.

7. Stephen Keyes Fletcher to Calvin Fletcher, April 14, 1861, Fletcher Family Papers, Indiana Historical Society, Indianapolis, Indiana; April 18, 1861, and April 24, 1861, *Fletcher Diary,* 7:94, 103.

8. April 26, 1861, *Fletcher Diary,* 7:104.

9. Elijah Fletcher to Calvin Fletcher, April 16, 1861, Fletcher Family Papers, Indiana Historical Society, Indianapolis, Indiana; April 26, 1861, *Fletcher Diary,* 7:104.

10. April 27, 1861, *Fletcher Diary,* 7:105.

11. April 27, 1861, April 28, 1861, and May 2, 1861, *Fletcher Diary,* 7:105–109.

12. Perry McCandless, ed., "The Civil War Journal of William B. Fletcher," *Indiana Magazine of History* 57 (1960): 53–54.

13. April 19, 1861, *Fletcher Diary,* 7:95; William B. Fletcher to Calvin Fletcher, June 7, 1861, Fletcher Family Papers, Indiana Historical Society, Indianapolis, Indiana; July 1, 6, 1861, *Fletcher Diary,* 7:139, 144; Colonel Thomas Crittenden to Miles Fletcher, July 6, 1861, quoted in *Fletcher Diary,* 7:144.

14. William B. Fletcher to Calvin Fletcher, July 16, 1861, *Fletcher Diary,* 7:151–152.

15. August 13, 1861, August 14, 1861, and August 15, 1861, *Fletcher Diary,* 7:169–170; Elijah Fletcher to Calvin Fletcher, August 15, 1861, *Fletcher Diary,* 7:172.

16. August 23, 1861, and August 30, 1861, *Fletcher Diary,* 7:176–177, 181.

17. September 26, 1861, and October 2, 1861, *Fletcher Diary,* 7:198, 200–201.

18. October 10, 1861, *Fletcher Diary,* 7:208. See also McCandless, "Civil War Journal," 143.

19. October 10, 1861, and October 11, 1861, *Fletcher Diary,* 7:208–209.

20. October 31, 1861, and November 7, 1861, *Fletcher Diary,* 7:220, 227; McCandless, "Civil War Journal," 143.

21. November 11, 1861, and November 21, 1861, *Fletcher Diary,* 7:231–232, 239; *Daily Journal* (Indianapolis), November 21, 1861.

22. William B. Fletcher to Calvin Fletcher, December 28, 1861, *Fletcher Diary,* 7:274–275. Ely's comments were printed in the *Daily Journal* (Indianapolis), January 3, 1862.

23. January 4, 1862, *Fletcher Diary,* 7:286.

24. January 10, 1862, *Fletcher Diary,* 7:294.

25. January 28, 1862, February 2, 1862, February 4, 1862, and February 7–9, 1862, *Fletcher Diary*, 7:317, 324, 326, 331–332; *Daily State Sentinel* (Indianapolis), February 8, 1862.

26. February 10, 1862, *Fletcher Diary*, 7:333; Elijah Fletcher to Calvin Fletcher, February 12, 1862, *Fletcher Diary*, 7:339.

27. "Speech of the Hon. J. A. Wright of Indiana . . . delivered in the Senate of the United States," April 30, 1862 (Washington, D.C.: Congressional Globe Office, 1862), copy in Indiana State Library, Indianapolis. See also June 10, 1862, *Fletcher Diary*, 7:388.

28. Patricia M. L. Lucie, "Confiscation: Constitutional Crosssroads," *Civil War History* 23 (1977): 307–321.

29. March 6, 1862, *Fletcher Diary*, 7:368.

30. May 10, 1862, and May 11, 1862, *Fletcher Diary*, 7:422–423.

31. May 11, 1862, *Fletcher Diary*, 7:423, 425–426.

32. Ibid., 426.

33. Ibid., 427. The engineer of the special train carrying Governor Morton and Miles was later charged with "gross recklessness" in going 23 miles per hour through town instead of slowing down. See *Daily Journal* (Indianapolis), May 21, 1862.

34. Stephen Keyes Fletcher to Calvin Fletcher, May 16, 1862, *Fletcher Diary*, 7:430.

35. Ingram Fletcher to Calvin Fletcher, July 12, 1862, and July 14, 1862, Fletcher Family Papers, Indiana Historical Society, Indianapolis, Indiana.

36. Ingram Fletcher to Calvin Fletcher, July 14, 1862, Fletcher Family Papers, Indiana Historical Society, Indianapolis, Indiana; Elijah Fletcher to Calvin Fletcher, July 15, 1862, Fletcher Family Papers, Indiana Historical Society, Indianapolis, Indiana.

37. July 16, 1862, and July 19, 1862, *Fletcher Diary*, 7:471, 474–475; Ingram Fletcher to Calvin Fletcher, July 23, 1862, Fletcher Family Papers, Indiana Historical Society, Indianapolis, Indiana; May 15, 1862, *Fletcher Diary*, 7:501.

38. January 5, 1862, July 29, 1862, and August 1, 1862, *Fletcher Diary*, 7:289, 484, 488.

39. September 8, 1862, and September 9, 1862, *Fletcher Diary*, 7:523, 526.

40. August 13, 1861, *Fletcher Diary*, 7:176. For background information on Sidney, Indiana, and Elizabeth during the war, see Whitley, "Indiana Fletcher Williams," 21.

41. April 17, 1863, and May 12, 1863, *Fletcher Diary*, 8:113, 136; Calvin Fletcher to Bishop Ames, April 20, 1863, Fletcher Family Papers, Indiana Historical Society, Indianapolis, Indiana.

42. August 1, 1863, and August 3, 1863, *Fletcher Diary*, 8:188, 190.

43. Ibid.

44. April 26, 1864, *Fletcher Diary*, 8:383.

45. January 2, 1863, January 3, 1863, and January 11, 1863, *Fletcher Diary*, 8:6, 8, 16. See also Gilbert R. Tredway, *Democratic Opposition to the Lincoln Administration in Indiana* (Indianapolis: Indiana Historical Bureau, 1973), 122–123.

46. Stephen Keyes Fletcher to Calvin Fletcher, January 11, 1863, *Fletcher Diary*, 8:17–19.

47. Ingram Fletcher to Calvin Fletcher, April 30, 1863, *Fletcher Diary*, 8:125.

48. May 9, 1863, and May 4, 1863, *Fletcher Diary*, 8:141–142, 129.

49. Stephen Keyes Fletcher to Calvin Fletcher, May 17, 1863, Fletcher Family Papers, Indiana Historical Society, Indianapolis, Indiana.

50. August 2, 1863, *Fletcher Diary*, 8:190.

51. Dr. William B. Fletcher to the Citizens of Indianapolis, November 23, 1863, and December 26, 1863, *Fletcher Diary*, 8:257, 291.

52. November 27, 1863, *Fletcher Diary*, 8:262.

53. March 4, 1864, *Fletcher Diary*, 8:346; *Daily Journal* (Indianapolis) reprint of *Dayton Journal* article from February 23, 1864.

54. September 3, 1863, and February 4, 1864, *Fletcher Diary*, 8:199, 338.

55. June 25, 1863, *Fletcher Diary*, 8:164.

56. January 19, 1864, January 23, 1864, and May 2, 1864, *Fletcher Diary*, 8:319–320, 387.

57. July 26, 1864, and May 20, 1864, *Fletcher Diary*, 8:433, 399.

58. October 1, 1864, *Fletcher Diary*, 8:441.

59. January 6, 1865, *Fletcher Diary,* 9:8.
60. April 10, 1865, *Fletcher Diary,* 9:64.
61. April 13, 1865, *Fletcher Diary,* 9:66.
62. April 15, 1865, *Fletcher Diary,* 9:68. On the nation's reaction to Lincoln's death, see Martha Hodes, *Mourning Lincoln* (New Haven, CT: Yale University Press, 2015).
63. April 15, 1865, April 16, 1865, April 30, 1865, and May 2, 1865, *Fletcher Diary,* 9:68, 71, 73, 82, 84; *Daily Journal* (Indianapolis), April 30, 1865.
64. May 4, 1865, November 8, 1865, and December 27, 1865, *Fletcher Diary,* 9:84–85, 156, 184. See also *Fletcher Diary,* 3:40; Martha Lou Lemmon Stohlman, *The Story of Sweet Briar College* (Lynchburg: Alumnae Association of Sweet Briar College, 1956).
65. December 21, 1865, and January 17, 1866, *Fletcher Diary,* 9:179, 203.
66. February 4, 1866, and February 13, 1866, *Fletcher Diary,* 9:211, 220.
67. March 30, 1866, *Fletcher Diary,* 9:245.
68. April 6, 1866, May 1, 1866, May 2, 1866, and May 4, 1866, *Fletcher Diary,* 9:247, 250–252.
69. Albert Fletcher, "Memories of My Mother." That Calvin's death resulted most likely from septic shock involving his leg fracture is the conclusion of Dr. Steven Smith. Steven Smith to author, e-mail correspondence, April 28, 2015.
70. *Daily Journal* (Indianapolis), May 28, 1866; *Daily Herald* (Indianapolis), May 30, 1866; Jacob Piatt Dunn, *Greater Indianapolis: The History, the Industries, the Institutions, and the People of a City of Homes* (New York: Nabu Press, 2010), 2:647.
71. Ibid.
72. *Daily Journal* (Indianapolis), May 28, 1866; November 30, 1823, *Fletcher Diary,* 1:98.

CHAPTER EIGHT: LEGACIES

1. *Fletcher Diary,* 9: 265.
2. Ibid., 266–267.
3. January 17, 1863, *Fletcher Diary,* 8:24.
4. *Fletcher Diary,* 9: 270.
5. Ibid., 9:267; January 17, 1863, *Fletcher Diary,* 8: 25.
6. *Fletcher Diary,* 9: 274–275.
7. January 17, 1863, *Fletcher Diary,* 8:25; ibid., 9: 270.
8. Ibid., 9:271.
9. Ann Marshall Whitley, "Indiana Fletcher Williams of Sweet Briar" (unpublished pamphlet, Sweet Briar College), 28.
10. Ibid., 32.
11. See Lynn Rainville, "Social Memory and Plantation Burial Ground: A Virginian Example," *African Diaspora Archeology Network Newsletter* (March 2008), 10–11.
12. Whitley, "Indiana Fletcher Williams," 2.
13. Rainville, "Social Memory," 11.
14. Whitley, "Indiana Fletcher Williams," 2.
15. Elijah Fletcher to Calvin Fletcher, March 13, 1842, *Letters of Elijah Fletcher,* 181.
16. Will of Indiana Fletcher Williams, Amherst County Court, November 23, 1900.
17. "Plea Made to Dismiss Suit by Sweet Briar," *Washington Post,* December 30, 1965; "Sweet Briar Can't Mix, Says Quesenbery," *Lynchburg News,* June 5, 1965.
18. "Sweet Briar Finally Reaches Finish Line," *Washington Post,* May 30, 1967.
19. "Sweet Briar to Close Because of Financial Challenges," *Washington Post,* March 3, 2015.
20. Among the vast national coverage of the dramatic closing of Sweet Briar College, see Sheryl Gay Stolberg, "Anger and Activism Greet Plan to Shut Sweet Briar College," *New York Times,* March 22, 2015; Abigail Jones, "The End of Sweet Briar College and the Problem with Women's Colleges," *Newsweek,* April 29, 2015; William G. Bowen and Judith Shapiro, "The Sad Saga of Sweet Briar College," *Richmond Times-Dispatch,* May 2, 2015; and Steve Szkotak, "Sweet Briar College Stays Open," *U.S. News & World Report,* June 20, 2015.

Index

abolitionism
    Calvin Fletcher and, 131–32, 135, 221, 250
    John Brown and, 187
    reform and, 143–44, 236
    Whig Party and, 131–32
Adams, John Quincy, 73–74
alcohol
    see temperance
American and Foreign Christian Union, 160
Ames, Ed, 196
Ames Institute, 206
Amherst County, Virginia, 21, 72, 184–85, 214, 241–42, 246–47
Amherst, Jeffrey, 6
antislavery
    Abraham Lincoln and, 189–90
    Calvin Fletcher and, 43, 130–31, 135–36, 139–40, 155, 177–78, 194
    churches and, 133, 135–36
    Elijah Fletcher and, 15, 25
    Free Soil Party and, 139–40
    J.M. Ray and, 133
    Jesse Fletcher Sr. and, 17
    John Brown and, 187
    Kansas Territory and, 155, 177
    Martin Van Buren and, 139
    see also abolitionism; slavery
Asbury University, 160

Barnard, Henry, 18
Battle of Buena Vista, 138
Battle of Camp Wildcat, 203
Battle of Gettysburg, 222
Beecher, Catherine, 145
Beecher, Henry Ward, 135, 187
Bennett College, 247

Birney, James, 131–32
Bishop Ames, 194, 196, 208, 215
Bishop, Austin, 65
Blackhawk War, 92, 236
Blake, James, 65–66
"bleeding Kansas," 176–77
Bobbs, Dr., 209
Britten, Maria, 54, 61
Brooks, Preston, 176
Brown, John, 187–88
Brown University, 115–17, 132, 141, 147, 168
Buchanan, James, 177, 187
Bunker Hill, 5, 117–18
Burhans, K.E., 107–8
Burns, Robert, 228

Calhoun, John C., 125
Central College for Physicians and Surgeons, 235
Charlottesville, Virginia, 18
Civil Rights Act of 1964, 245
civil rights movement, 245–46
Civil War, 194–230, 235
Clay, Henry, 131–32, 145
Coburn, John, 211
College of William and Mary, 120–21
colonization, 128, 131
Confiscation Bill, 207–8
Conner, William, 65–66
Cooley, James, 39, 42–43, 48
Crawford, Maria Antoinette, 19–21, 71–72, 76, 88, 97, 102, 104, 127–28, 151, 154, 157, 245
Crawford, William Sidney, 19, 27, 150
Crittenden, Thomas T., 193, 199
Crown Hill Cemetery, 229

Crumbaugh, Dorio, 85
Cumberland Gap, 203, 211–12

Democratic Party, 132, 177
desegregation, 246
Dogwood Farm, 226
Dufrees, J., 222
Durham, James H., 201

Emory University, 248
Erie Canal, 67–68
ethnography, 13, 66

Flagler, Gilbert, 36
Fletcher & Sharpe Bank, 233–34
Fletcher, Albert, 155–56, 160–61, 169, 180,
    186, 205, 208–9, 212, 227–29, 233–34
Fletcher, Betty, 99, 102, 104, 119–20, 126, 129,
    151, 178, 180, 183–84, 207, 213–15, 240
Fletcher, Calvin
    abolitionism and, 131–32, 135, 221, 250
    birth of son Elijah, 71
    Elijah Fletcher and, 29–31, 36–37, 42–43,
        68–69, 73–78, 82–83, 95–96
    ethnography and, 66
    family, 104–5, 107–23
    family genealogy, 254
    Ingram Fletcher and, 180, 190, 196, 199,
        211–21, 227
    Jesse Fletcher Sr. and, 34, 63, 69, 87–88,
        227
    Kentucky and, 61, 216, 223
    Panic of 1837 and, 95–97
    slavery and, 43, 50, 84–85, 130–31, 133–40,
        143, 157, 190, 193–95, 208, 213–16, 218,
        221–23
Fletcher, Charlotte, 7
Fletcher, Elijah
    business ventures, 72–75
    Calvin Fletcher and, 29–31, 36–37, 42–43,
        68–69, 73–78, 82–83, 95–96
    early life, 7–10
    education and, 22–23
    ethnography and, 66
    family and, 71–72, 98–102
    family genealogy, 254
    generosity, 21
    Jesse Fletcher Sr. and, 20–23, 25–27, 43,
        73, 83–84
    marriage, 19–21
    move to Virginia, 10–16
    ordination, 5
    as plantation owner, 23–28

Panic of 1837 and, 95–97
    politics, 75–76
    public life and, 125–29, 152, 154
    religion and, 82
    slavery and, 12–13, 15–19, 21, 24–25, 28,
        43, 72, 75, 83–84, 99–101, 184
    Stoughton Fletcher and, 88–91, 93
    Sweet Briar Estate and, 150–51, 183
Fletcher, Elizabeth, 181, 196, 240
Fletcher, Fanny, 27, 70
Fletcher, Indiana
    birth, 76
    Elijah Fletcher and, 76, 83
    slavery and, 237–38, 241, 245
    Sweet Briar College and, 247–49
    Sweet Briar Estate and, 184, 214, 238, 242,
        244
Fletcher, Ingram
    antislavery and, 177
    Billy Fletcher and, 206
    Calvin Fletcher and, 180, 190, 196, 199,
        211–21, 227
    career, 186, 233–34
    childhood, 108
    Keyes Fletcher and, 202–3
    Keziah and, 170
    Miles Fletcher and, 211
    move from home, 172–74
    Native Americans and, 180–81
    secession and, 217
Fletcher, James Cooley, 63, 77–78, 86–87,
    100–1, 104–5, 107–10, 112–18, 130, 132,
    139, 141, 146, 151, 156, 159–61, 163,
    170–72, 181, 186, 211, 223–24, 232–33
Fletcher, Jesse Jr., 12, 15–16, 29–31
Fletcher, Jesse Sr.
    antislavery views, 17, 25
    Calvin Fletcher and, 34, 63, 69, 87–88, 227
    death, 88–89
    early life, 5–7
    Elijah Fletcher and, 20–23, 25–27, 43, 73
    family, 7–10, 76
    genealogy, 253
    illness, 83
    Indiana Fletcher Williams and, 242
    legacy, 89–91, 242
    religion and, 87–88
Fletcher, Keziah (Calvin's second wife), 2,
    145, 164–70, 182–83, 185–88, 218–19,
    226–28, 231–33, 251
Fletcher, Laura (Jesse's daughter), 19, 26, 68
Fletcher, Laura (Elijah's daughter), 76
Fletcher, Louisa, 47, 61, 68

Fletcher, Lucian, 71, 76, 78, 82–83, 99–102,
    104, 118, 120–22, 125, 149–50, 157,
    175–76, 182–85, 214, 240–42, 251
Fletcher, Lucy, 20, 23, 29, 31, 68, 106, 160,
    169, 180, 186, 195–96, 205, 218–19,
    233–34
Fletcher, Lucy Keyes, 6–9, 69, 90, 134
Fletcher, Maria, 106, 146, 160, 166, 168–70,
    180, 183, 186, 188–89, 218, 233, 238
Fletcher, Michael, 31, 34, 43, 58, 63, 68, 105
Fletcher, Miles (Calvin's son), 77–78, 104, 108,
    111, 137–39, 141–42, 147–48, 160–61,
    163, 166, 168, 174, 180, 186, 189–90,
    198, 201–2, 204–5, 208–11, 225
Fletcher, Miles (Jesse's son), 31, 68
Fletcher, Sarah (Calvin's first wife), 38, 40,
    42, 45–55, 58–64, 70–71, 77–78, 85–88,
    91–92, 98, 105–109, 139, 152–157, 159,
    164, 172, 223, 228–229
Fletcher, Sidney, 71–72, 76, 82–83, 99–102,
    104, 118–20, 126, 128, 135, 149–51, 154,
    181–84, 196, 213–16, 240
Fletcher, Stephen, 7–8, 23, 30–31, 40
Fletcher, Stephen Keyes, 139, 160, 169, 177,
    180, 183, 186, 189–90, 193–96, 202–3,
    206, 208, 211–12, 216–19, 222, 226,
    234–35
Fletcher, Stoughton, 7, 70, 83–84, 88, 90, 93,
    104–5, 108, 130, 153, 159, 166, 173, 175,
    186, 199, 202, 205, 207, 212, 215, 234–35
Fletcher, Timothy, 5, 8, 31, 43, 63, 83, 114,
    134, 143, 179–80, 196, 207–8, 224
Fletcher, William Baldwin (Billy), 139,
    153, 160–63, 177, 186, 190, 193, 195,
    198–208, 212, 219–21, 228, 235, 251
Flower Mission, 235
Fort Defiance, 66
Fort Leavenworth, 137
Fort Meigs, 66
Fort Monroe, Virginia, 205
Fort Sumter, 194–96
Fort Wayne, Indiana, 65–66, 93
Fox, Charles James, 122
Free Soil Party, 139
Freeman's Aid Society, 221–22
Fremont, John C., 177
French and Indian War, 6

Garland, David, 18
Gentry, Reuben, 137–38
Gwynne, James, 50
Gwynne, Llewellyn, 51
Gwynne, Thomas, 41–42, 45, 51–52

Hamlin, Hannibal, 194
Harpers Ferry, Virginia, 187–88
Harrison, Alfred, 117, 168
Harrison, Benjamin, 233
Hemings, Sally 18–19
Henry Clay (steamboat), 152
Hill, James, 78–79
Hill, Joseph, 38, 46, 50
Hill, Malinda, 62
Hill, Sarah
    see Fletcher, Sarah
Hill, Susan, 166
Holliday, William, 105

Indiana Branch Bank, 226
Indiana Medical College, 235
Indiana Reformatory for Women and Girls, 235
Indianapolis Freeman's Aid Society, 221
Indianapolis Gas Company, 234
Indian tribes
    see Native Americans

Jackson, Andrew, 74–75, 95
Jefferson, Thomas, 18
Jones, James F., 248

Kent, Frances, 104
Kentucky
    Calvin Fletcher and, 61, 216, 223
    Civil War and, 202–3, 216
    Indiana and, 54, 59
    secession, 197
    slavery and, 130–31
    Virginia and, 40
Keyes, Stephen, 139, 160, 169, 177, 180, 183,
    186, 189–90, 193–96, 202–3, 206, 208,
    211–12, 216–20, 222, 226, 234–35
King, France Rufus, 125
Kingsbury, John, 146
Kirkland, Elizabeth, 215

Laurel Hill, 199
Lee, Robert E., 202, 224
Liberty Party, 131
Lincoln, Abraham, 189–90, 194, 207, 213,
    216, 222, 225–26
Lister, Keziah
    see Fletcher, Keziah
Lynchburg, Virginia, 19, 35, 42–43, 72, 82,
    127–28, 138, 142–43, 150–51, 154, 178,
    181, 183–84, 196, 214, 224–25, 246

Malan, Henrietta, 171, 232

Manifest Destiny, 136, 174
Mason, George, 15
Mason, Thomas, 15–18
"Matter of Honor" (editorial), 246
McCarty, Nicholas, 94–96
McClenny, William M., 246
McCord, Sam, 51–52
Messer, Asa, 116
Mexican War, 136
Mexico, 2, 22, 132, 135–38, 149, 236
Michie, Thomas J., 247
Middlebury College, 10, 23, 31
Miller, John, 225
Milroy, Robert, 201
Monument Hill, 240, 242
Morehouse College, 247
Morton, Oliver P., 197, 208–9, 220
Mosby, William Hamilton, 184, 196, 214, 240
Moulson, John, 36

National Intelligencer (newspaper), 180
Native Americans, 65–66, 92–93, 128, 180–81, 236
New Albany, Indiana, 197, 233
New York College of Physicians, 190
Noble, General, 209
Noblesville, Indiana, 77, 140

Panic of 1837, 95–96
Pannell, Anne Gary, 246
Patten, John, 27, 34–36
Payne, Elizabeth, 242
Phillips Exeter preparatory school, 101, 112–14, 116
Polk, James K., 131–33, 136
Potawatomi tribe, 93
Princeton Theological College, 171

Quakers, 17, 36–37, 82, 131, 183
Queen Victoria, 187
Quesenbery, C.G., 246

Ray, James M., 64–66, 75, 79, 81, 133, 170
Ray, Johnny, 170, 177
Republican Party, 177, 189, 194
Rice, Paul G., 248
Rives, William Cabell, 125
Russell, Alexander, 61

Sauk tribe, 92
Scott, Charles, 118
Scudder, Kenneth, 77

secession, 189–90, 193–97, 201–2, 208, 216–17, 225
Seminole Indians, 128
Sewell, William, 84
Sheridan, Philip, 214
Slade, William, 145
slavery
    Calvin Fletcher and, 43, 50, 84–85, 130–31, 133–40, 143, 157, 190, 193–95, 208, 213–16, 218, 221–23
    Civil War and, 189, 195, 213–16
    Elijah Fletcher and, 12–13, 15–19, 21, 24–25, 28, 43, 72, 75, 83–84, 99–101, 184
    expansion into territories, 135–36, 155, 176
    Free Soil Party and, 139–40
    Indiana Fletcher and, 237–38, 241, 245
    Jesse Fletcher Sr. and, 17
    John Brown and, 187–88
    Kansas and, 155, 176–77
    Nebraska and, 176
    popular sovereignty, 177
    Sidney Fletcher and, 125, 128
    South and, 21, 24–25, 42, 189–90, 206–7
    Texas and, 135–36
    see also abolitionism; antislavery
Sons of Temperance, 142
Soule, Gideon, 112
Steward, Stephen, 36
Sumner, Charles, 176
Sweet Briar College
    civil rights and, 245–46
    creation of, 244
    Indiana Fletcher's will and, 247–49
    integration and, 245–47
    mission, 248–49
Sweet Briar estate
    Elijah Fletcher and, 150–51, 183
    Indiana Fletcher and, 184, 214, 238, 242, 244
    Keyes Fletcher and, 196
    Marshalyn Yeargin and, 247–48
    Monument Hill, 135, 240
    purchase, 88
    redesign, 128–29

taxes, 6, 13, 73, 144, 146, 167, 171, 241
Taylor, Zachary, 136–38
temperance, 125, 140–43, 157, 235–36, 250
Temperance Society, 140
Texas, 130–36, 164, 167, 190
Tusculum, 20, 150, 154, 214, 240

Tye River, 214
Tyler, John, 118

Underground Railroad, 131
University of Chicago, 247
University of Vermont, 10, 12, 31

Van Buren, Martin, 139
Virginian, The (newspaper), 73,
   126

Wabash Canal, 94
War of 1812, 31, 38, 66, 92, 140
Wayland, Francis, 115–16
Webster, Daniel, 118
Whig Party, 73, 75, 131–32, 167

White River Canal, 94
Williams, Daisy, 238–42, 244
Williams, Indiana Fletcher
   see Fletcher, Indiana
Williams, James Henry, 237–38
Williams, Roger, 116
Woodlawn house, 168, 199
Woodworth, Samuel D., 65
Wright, John, 207

Yale University, 18, 99–101, 118, 120–21
Yandes, Simon, 58, 112
Yeargin, Marshalyn, 247–48

Zion Episcopal Church, 237
Zouaves, 193–94, 196